RAISING KIDS WITH HIDDEN DISABILITIES

of related interest

Autistic Logistics, Second Edition
A Parent's Guide to Tackling Bedtime, Toilet Training, Meltdowns, Hitting, and Other Everyday Challenges
Kate Wilde
ISBN 978 1 78775 749 3
eISBN 978 1 78775 750 9

The Parents' Guide to ADHD Medicines
Professor Peter Hill
ISBN 978 1 78775 568 0
eISBN 978 1 78775 569 7

Connecting and Communicating with Your Autistic Child
A Toolkit of Activities to Encourage Emotional Regulation and Social Development
Act for Autism
ISBN 978 1 78775 550 5
eISBN 978 1 78775 551 2

A Parent's Guide to Autism Diagnosis
What to Expect and How to Support Your Child
Dr Sophia Mooncey and Adele Devine
ISBN 978 1 78775 424 9
eISBN 978 1 78775 425 6

Helping Your Child with PDA Live a Happier Life
Alice Running
ISBN 978 1 78775 485 0
eISBN 978 1 78775 486 7

RAISING KIDS WITH HIDDEN DISABILITIES

Getting It

NAOMI SIMMONS

Jessica Kingsley Publishers
London and Philadelphia

First published in Great Britain in 2022 by Jessica Kingsley Publishers
An imprint of Hodder & Stoughton Ltd
An Hachette Company

1

Front cover image source: iStockphoto® and Shutterstock®.

Disclaimer: The information contained in this book is not intended to replace the services of trained medical professionals or to be a substitute for medical advice. The treatments and therapies described in this book may not be suitable for everyone to follow. You are advised to consult a doctor on any matters relating to your and your children's health, and in particular on any matters that may require diagnosis or medical attention.

A CIP catalogue record for this title is available from the
British Library and the Library of Congress

ISBN 978 1 83997 155 6
eISBN 978 1 83997 156 3

Printed and bound in Great Britain by TJ Books Limited

Jessica Kingsley Publishers' policy is to use papers that are natural, renewable and recyclable products and made from wood grown in sustainable forests. The logging and manufacturing processes are expected to conform to the environmental regulations of the country of origin.

Jessica Kingsley Publishers
Carmelite House
50 Victoria Embankment
London EC4Y 0DZ

www.jkp.com

To William, for taking my hand and making anything feel possible.

CONTENTS

PART 1: UNDERSTANDING OUR CHILD

PART 2: RESPONDING TO OUR CHILD

ACKNOWLEDGEMENTS

This book is a result of the help, inspiration and support of hundreds of families living with hidden disabilities over a period of many years. My deepest gratitude to you, for being my teachers, my support network and for encouraging me on those many days when I was doubting myself.

A particular thank you to my wonderful circle of readers for your time and effort in commenting on the various drafts of this book. Your wisdom, support and suggestions have been invaluable and helped me to find the confidence to complete this project. I would particularly like to mention Sue Dickson for going beyond anything I could have hoped for from a reader. The same applies to Susan Raes – I don't think I could have done this without you. A big thank you also to Shara Cohen, Sarah Beskine, Dani Zur, Sarah James, Jane Hudson and Clare Goldfinch.

I am also indebted to my clinical advisors for sharing their ideas, encouragement and suggested amendments. A deep thanks to Dr Patricia Rios, Consultant Clinical Psychologist and Dr Georgie Siggers, Consultant Neurodevelopmental Paediatrician.

To the organisations and parent forums that got me through the many years when I was struggling, in particular the Balanced Mind Parent Network (www.dbsalliance.org). Thank you.

It has been my great fortune to have the support of a wonderful editorial team at Jessica Kingsley Publishers, with particular mention to Lisa Clark and everyone there who shared ideas, suggestions and insights.

My biggest acknowledgement is obviously to my family, for helping me, challenging me and being the reason for everything I do.

And to my canine family for making sure I exercise every day and have a constant supply of unconditional love, wagging tails and licked noses. Thank you to Ruby the large münsterländer and Sooty the flat-coated retriever (now sadly departed).

INTRODUCTION

When one of my children was 11, we were faced with diagnoses of a range of hidden disabilities, including Asperger's, OCD and bipolar disorder. Another of my children also had difficulties which I suspected were undiagnosed hidden disabilities. Before, during and after this time I was pretty clueless about what to do and how to cope. Life was tough and frightening on every level and this affected us all.

Happily, I came out the other side of this with brilliant and thriving kids as well as a huge amount of accumulated knowledge and insights. I wrote this book to share this knowledge with you in the hope that you will not have to make the same mistakes that I made. I hope that some of this will be helpful to you in your own journey of parenting a child with a hidden disability.

So, do you have a child with a hidden disability such as autism spectrum, ADHD, Asperger's, bipolar, clinical anxiety or depression? Maybe you just know in your bones that something needs looking at.

Before I go further, just a quick note about the very word 'disability'. It's a tricky word that can bring up strong feelings and mean different things to different people. In this book I am using the *legal* meaning of disability, which is about our child's *needs* and *rights*. This is different from whether or not our child *identifies* as being disabled. It is perfectly possible to recognise disability needs and at the same time not identify personally as having a disability. I, for example, do not really think of myself as disabled although I have a number of hidden disabilities that affect my life.

How we can use the legal definition of disability to help us is looked at in some detail in the first chapter.

Raising kids with hidden disabilities is not a fringe or niche area of parenting. At least 10 per cent of children have hidden disabilities, according to the US government.[1] When we add to this all those with unidentified difficulties, we can see that we are dealing with a lot of kids and a lot of confused and overwhelmed parents.

Sadly, there is still a stigma about hidden disabilities and our loved ones may be burdened by shame about who they are. This stigma and shame can make it really hard to talk openly about hidden disabilities and our children's legitimate needs. It is not surprising that so many of our loved ones deal with this by doing what they can to hide and disguise who they are and what their needs may be.

I believe that recognising our needs, championing our rights and standing proud about who we are is the best way to challenge stigma.

Maybe you have a diagnosis or are trying to get one. You may be unsure whether or not to have your child diagnosed. Maybe you are not happy with the diagnosis you have or have disagreements in your family about whether or not your child has a hidden disability.

Your daughter may be having dramatic meltdowns or may be cut off from you and the world in shutdown. She may be refusing to go to school or have crippling depression and anxiety. Maybe your son's defiant behaviour goes beyond what is 'normal'. He may be self-harming, refusing to eat, lying or stealing from you.

Your son's teacher may be telling you that he is absolutely fine at school, but every bone in your body is telling you that he is suffering and struggling there.

Maybe you have tried every parenting technique out there to correct difficult behaviour and nothing has worked. In fact, it might actually be making things worse.

This may be even more confusing if we have other children who are responding well to our discipline and parenting techniques. If it works on our other children, maybe we are not such terrible parents after all? The frustration that our child is not responding like their siblings can even make us resent them, making us feel even more guilty.

I was in this situation for many years and went through just about every challenge out there, both with my children and other people's reactions to us. This included clashes with the 'authorities' and other so-called 'experts'. I looked everywhere for advice and tried absolutely everything.

Everyone and their dog had an opinion about what I should be doing, and what I was apparently doing wrong.

Every time my child had a meltdown, I felt like I was personally failing as a parent.

The more I tried to follow the advice I was given, the worse things got. I felt judged and like a total failure. I felt that I was letting myself and my children down.

The lightbulb moment came when I realised that the reason nothing was working was that the parenting advice was designed for children *without* hidden disabilities, often known as 'neurotypical' children. Most of the people giving me the advice had never walked in my shoes and didn't really know or understand my children or me. This applied to many professionals and 'experts' too, who in my experience are unlikely to have children with hidden disabilities themselves.

I was being urged to treat what I now understand to be the *symptoms* of their hidden disabilities as if they were *bad* behaviour to be corrected.

I was as guilty of this as anyone else. I was trying to bring my children up in a similar way to how I was brought up, thinking about what had worked or hadn't worked for me. I needed to learn to parent the child I actually had, not the child I had been.

Treating my children's symptoms as 'bad behaviour' may have made them feel even more judged and misunderstood. This would naturally fuel their anger and anxiety even more, resulting in the symptoms getting stronger and more dramatic. It was almost as if each child's body, through these symptoms, was screaming at me to listen, to try to understand, to help rather than to punish.

To properly support my children, I needed to learn to understand what their behaviour was trying to communicate to me. I had to learn to *decode* it.

Doing this meant putting judgement of 'right and wrong' to one side, as well as decisions on how to react to behaviours until I was sure that I had 'got it' and had learned to understand my child's code.

If we go into a history examination and do not understand a question, we have little chance of being able to answer it correctly. In the same way, until we can understand what is happening with our children, what they are feeling and why they are reacting the way they are, we cannot possibly see how best to respond to their behaviour.

As soon as we are able to 'get it', the right way to react becomes much clearer and more obvious.

How do we know what is behaviour to be corrected and what are symptoms of the hidden disabilities? Will understanding our child mean that they 'get away with' bad behaviour?

These are questions that I and many parents of hidden disabilities are grappling with.

Along with the biggies: Is there hope? Will my child be OK? Will I be able to cope and if so, how?

Like many of us, I was also terrified about the effect of parenting a child with hidden disabilities on my relationships with family and other people. How can we support siblings and keep our parenting fair and consistent under these circumstances? How can we get family members and our partners on board? And how can we respond when they and professionals do not want to listen to us?

And when it came to treatment options, or how to get treatments or whether to get treatments, I was totally overwhelmed. There were so many contradictory points of view and I needed guidance on how to look at this question in a way that felt comfortable for me.

When I looked for help, the books out there were mainly written by doctors about an individual condition, with little or no guidance on how to deal with this on a day-to-day basis at home.

To confuse things further, many of our children have *multiple* conditions. Although estimates vary, some research suggests that as many as 95 per cent of kids with an autism spectrum diagnosis may also have three other hidden disabilities. Seventy-five per cent have five or more. The most common additional diagnoses were ADHD (attention deficit hyperactivity disorder) and OCD (obsessive compulsive disorder).[2]

This is another reason why we need to learn skills to parent children with *any* hidden disability, rather than getting too bogged down in any specific one.

When I went online to look for support through parent forums, I mainly found the opposite, endless stories of despair and anguish. There was little in the way of the hope and guidance that I was seeking.

That horrible feeling of fear and lack of hope for the future fuelled me to take on this project. This is the book that I craved to find during those dark and frightening years. Judging by the number of people calling out for help with these questions on the forums, I was far from alone.

As well as learning from my own many mistakes, I also learned by hunting down and listening to the real experts, people who 'get it' because they are living it day to day.

I looked for ideas from parents whose kids were thriving, productive and happy in their own skins, whose homes were peaceful and full of love and compassion. Mixing with successful parents of kids with hidden disabilities gave me so much hope that everything would work out OK and I was inspired by their examples.

Probably the people I learned the most from were young adults with hidden disabilities themselves who were happy to share memories and tips about what really helped and supported them during their childhoods. These are the real experts.

And of course, I learned from my own children, whose advice and insights were invaluable, and who offered ongoing support and their blessing for this project.

The more I was able to 'decode' my children's behaviour, the more listened to they felt and the more we were able to trust and really know each other.

Learning how to decode my children had another amazing gift, it helped them to learn how to decode *their own* behaviour. This helped them to understand their own needs better and what they needed to do to meet them.

Learning how to understand and accept themselves is in my opinion one of the most important thing we can offer our children as they grow into adulthood.

Like us, they may also consider every meltdown or symptom of their hidden disability to be evidence of their failure. Their shame can be so overwhelming that it can stop them from learning about their own needs and how best to meet them. Shame can prevent them from taking responsibility for their behaviour and for managing their symptoms. Just like us they need to replace judgement with understanding.

Our children are dealing with monumental challenges and so are we. To help our kids, we also need to understand *ourselves* better and what we are expecting from both ourselves and our children.

When we are able to do this, parenting our kids with hidden disabilities opens up a journey of personal development not only for them, but for us and our whole families.

This book is about how best we can understand and respond to our children with hidden disabilities. I have also written a companion book called *How to Cope When Your Child Has a Hidden Disability: Self-Care for Parents,* which is about understanding what we as parents are going through when parenting a child with hidden disabilities, and how we can best respond to our own needs, frustrations and anguish. We know that parents of children with hidden disabilities have similar levels of stress hormones to combat soldiers. We have combat stress! This has serious consequences both for us and for our family's mental health.

So, while this book is about dealing with our *child, How to Cope When Your Child Has a Hidden Disability: Self-Care for Parents* is about dealing with *ourselves* and it may be useful to read both books to break the cycle of hopelessness and despair that so many of us are living.

NAVIGATING THE BOOK

This book is divided into two parts.

The first part is about understanding our child. This includes understanding what hidden disabilities are and what makes them different both from visible disabilities and from mental illnesses. I review the pros and cons of seeking a diagnosis and whether we should consider our child as being 'different' rather than as having a disability.

There are then suggestions on ways to decode our children's

behaviours and understand what is happening when they go into meltdowns and shutdowns.

High levels of stress hormones can affect other areas of our child's behaviour that we may not have realised were related to their hidden disabilities. As we learn to decode what we are seeing, it may be clear that a number of their behaviours and states of mind are in fact symptoms of their hidden disability and need to be treated as such. Knowing how to identify this gives us some tools to help answer the question, 'Is this bad behaviour, or is it a symptom of my child's hidden disability?'

The second part of the book is about how we can respond to this understanding. Once we 'get it', we need to be clear about what we need to do. There is no 'one-size-fits-all' answer to this, so this part aims to share some tools and experiences to help you to make your own decisions.

It starts with practical suggestions on how to manage the extremes of meltdowns, rages and shutdowns along with ideas on how to help your child deal with the overwhelming anxiety and stress that can so affect their behaviour.

There are then three chapters containing strategies and ideas to help our child be calm, happy and engaged with life.

Although the book is relevant for children with hidden disabilities of all ages, I have included a chapter on some of the specific concerns we have when we are parenting teenagers and young adults. We may be worried about whether they will cooperate with their treatments, how they will manage college, relationships and getting and holding on to a job.

This is followed by a chapter on supporting the siblings of our children with hidden disabilities, along with the challenge of fairly parenting children whose needs may clash. How can we be fair? How can we support all of our children's welfare and mental health, when one child takes most of our attention due to their hidden disabilities?

There are then three chapters on treatments, by which I mean attempts to relieve symptoms of the hidden disability that are causing suffering to our child. This is very different to talk of 'cures', which are both inappropriate and not possible for disabilities.

As parents, how do we decide on treatments? Should we be treating our child at all? What are the pros and cons of each approach? As well as looking closely at these questions, these chapters take a look at the range of drug and non-drug treatments that may be available and may help our child.

'GETTING' THE TERMS USED

How we choose to deal with the challenge of parenting a child with a hidden disability is highly personal. Every child is different and so is every parent. No-one knows your child or his or her needs better than you and we need to remember not to disregard the power of our intuition. This book is designed to offer some tools to help to guide you. It is not dogma or a 'magic pill'. Please take what resonates and what in your gut 'makes sense' and disregard anything that doesn't. We can all only ever do the best we can as parents and our best has to be good enough.

Throughout this book, for ease of language, I use the words *he* and *she* randomly without implying anything about a particular gender. Similarly, when I talk about *parents* of children with hidden disabilities, it is equally relevant to other people who love and care for our children, such as grandparents, guardians or other carers.

The names of the different hidden disabilities can be incredibly confusing. There are so many initials and terms, such as ASD, PDA, OCD, ADHD, ADD. Sometimes different terms are used for the *same* condition, for example ASD, HFA and Asperger's.[3]

To benefit from this book it is not necessary to know or understand all these different terms and I certainly cannot keep up with them all.

If this is not confusing enough, the 'official' diagnosis names are often changed and there is also often a difference between the words that doctors use and the ones used by families and people with hidden disabilities themselves. Sometimes people judge us if they think we are using the 'wrong' word, which makes talking about our children's needs even more fraught and stressful.

This book is about parenting children with *any* hidden disability or any number of different diagnoses. This includes the many who have undiagnosed difficulties, which means that we may suspect that our child has a hidden disability but do not know which. It also includes children who have a number of apparently overlapping or even clashing diagnoses. This can be particularly confusing until we learn the skills to decode our child, regardless of their specific diagnosis or combo of conditions.

Where I do refer to a particular hidden disability, I use the name most commonly understood by most families at the time of writing. Where I quote a person with a hidden disability, I use the diagnosis word of their choice. This word may be different from the word used in the medical literature.

As an example, the condition Asperger's has been renamed by the medical profession as level one autism spectrum disorder. Despite this, many people prefer to continue to use the word Asperger's and I have yet to come across anyone choosing to use the latest medical term in daily life. Another example of this is ADD (attention deficit disorder), which the medical profession has now reallocated to subsections of ADHD. This can be confusing in everyday speech and many people prefer to stick to the term ADD, which people may understand better.

While on the subject of language, some people, especially adults on the autism spectrum, identify themselves as 'neurodivergent'. They use this term to point out that their brain may work in a rather unconventional way, which although different to many people, is equally valid and normal.

For the avoidance of any doubt, I am not implying by writing this book that everyone who is neurodivergent necessarily has a hidden disability. Many do not meet the legal definition of disability described in the next chapter. I consider myself to be in this category in that I am neurodivergent but do not have a legally defined hidden disability.

However, this book is written for parents of children who *do* meet these criteria and therefore *do* have hidden disabilities.

THERE IS HOPE

Raising a child with a hidden disability is terrifying on so many levels and for so many reasons. As we worry about the future, it is important to remember that no matter how bleak things may look at this moment, things can and often do change very quickly for our children.

This happens when our children 'get' themselves and fully understand and embrace their strengths and gifts along with their very real challenges and additional needs. For them to 'get' themselves, we firstly need to 'get' them and then support them on this journey.

This can be about school or career achievement but need not be. For my children it was.

I despaired for one of mine, who seemed unable to learn to read and write or pick up the skills I knew would be needed in life. Schools labelled my child as low ability and poo-poohed my suspicions of a hidden disability. This child is now an insightful adult who has just graduated with first class honours from one of the top universities in the world. Yesterday I proudly listened to an interview on national radio in connection with an award-winning film my child had written and directed.

I had to fight to keep another of my children out of institutional care and my child was pretty much shut down from life for much of childhood. Unable to get their difficulties recognised, the school refused to allow my child to sit the GCSE maths exam, a basic-level qualification needed for most post-16 education in the UK. The school was confusing my child's hidden disability symptoms with a lack of ability. I am proud to report that my now thriving adult child is about to commence a PhD in applied mathematics.

Other children find different paths to fulfilment. They do not need to have a university education or a career to have a successful life. They may have a part-time job that works with their needs and use their free time to follow their passions.

Ultimately our hope is that our children find self-acceptance and a lifestyle that works for them and that they are happy in their own skin. This is a hope that we can all reasonably aspire to regardless of our child's abilities, potential and challenges.

I hope this book helps you to find some clarity and hope in your own journey towards the light.

Part 1

UNDERSTANDING OUR CHILD

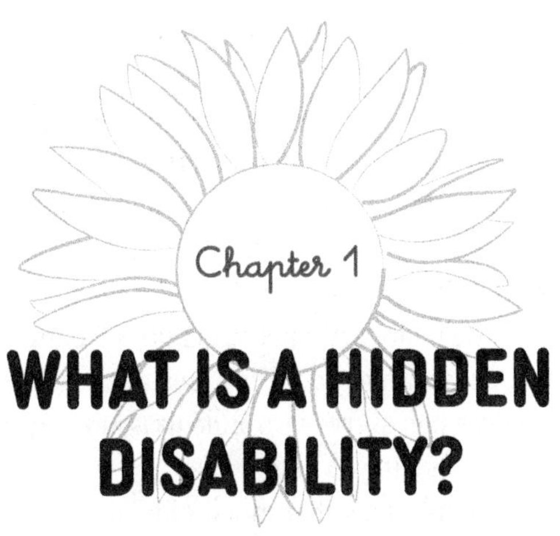

Chapter 1

WHAT IS A HIDDEN DISABILITY?

WHAT DO WE MEAN BY HIDDEN DISABILITY?

Hidden disabilities are hugely confusing for many people, probably for most people. Even well-meaning teachers, doctors and family members may not appreciate the difference between a mental illness and a psychiatric disability. They may not know the difference between examination nerves and anxiety-induced shutdown. How can they distinguish between a tantrum and a meltdown, a naughty child and a sick child?

People may have some vague understanding that autistic kids have problems with eye contact, that ADHD kids won't keep still and that bipolar kids have mood swings. That's probably as much as I knew before I had my own kids with hidden disabilities. Many people believe that only boys have autism spectrum disabilities and would be clueless about how to identify and respond to it in a girl.

We may even have heard people saying that these conditions didn't 'exist' in the past and that these problems were simply dealt with by strict rules and tough love. Some even now continue to insist that hidden disabilities do not exist. Without an understanding of the problem, many insist that strong discipline is the answer, regardless of whether or not this works or helps.

Dealing with so much lack of understanding is a very large part of our job when parenting kids with hidden disabilities. The ignorance is especially hard to deal with when it comes from people who are supposed to be supporting us, like teachers, family and friends. This can extend to some professionals and so-called 'experts' as well.

But if we are really honest with ourselves, how much do *we* really understand our child? We may not share the judgey views we hear every day, but do we really 'get' what our child is feeling and why they might be reacting the way they do? How good are we at *really* listening to them, especially when everyone around us is judging our child, and often watching and judging us too?

For me, although I knew that much of what other people were saying about my child was wrong, I was still confused about what was actually right.

I felt like I was in a little boat on a stormy ocean. I knew it would be wrong to head into the storm but was unsure which other direction would save us.

When we feel directionless in our parenting, we can be unsure what to say to people who we know are telling us things that are untrue or just downright wrong. More importantly, when our child is showing strong symptoms or behaviours, we may know what we don't want to do, but may be more unclear about what we should do.

This is why the first step in navigating parenting a child with a hidden disability is to get really clear about what we are talking about. We need to start with the term 'hidden disability' and be as clear as we can be about what we mean by it. Just about everything comes from this.

Most of the confusion, both in ourselves and in other people, comes from different understandings of what we mean by hidden disability. Getting clarity on this doesn't just help us and other people involved with our child. It also helps our children to understand themselves, something that is essential if they are going to achieve their potential in life and be happy in their own skin.

There are two parts of this to look at, what we mean by 'disability' and what we mean by 'hidden'.

DISABILITY

It is probably best to start with the word 'disability'. According to UK law:

> You're disabled under the Equality Act 2010 if you have a physical or mental impairment that has a 'substantial' and 'long-term' negative effect on your ability to do normal daily activities.[1]

Notice that the definition is not about a particular condition or diagnosis, it is simply about impairment. This means that *any* condition can be a disability if it causes an impairment that is substantial and long term. The definition also does not distinguish between disabilities we can see and those that are hidden.

Moreover:

> An impairment doesn't have to be a diagnosed medical condition. If you're suffering from stress, you might have mental impairments – like difficulty concentrating – as well as physical impairments such as extreme tiredness and difficulty sleeping. It still has to have a substantial and long-term adverse effect on your ability to carry out day-to-day activities.[2]

Regardless of what we may think about the word 'disability', most would agree that many of our children are likely to fit cleanly within this definition. If our children are having *ongoing challenges that cause a substantial impact on day-to-day life*, they are disabled according to the law.

Most countries use very similar definitions, and you will need to check the law where you live. For example, in the United States, the equivalent law is the Americans with Disabilities Act 1990. It defines disability as 'a physical or mental impairment that substantially limits a major life activity'.[3]

We may not like the word 'disability' and consider it negative. We may worry that it is a judgemental label. We may worry that the word implies that our child is 'flawed' in some way. We may choose to use other more positive words to describe our child's challenges, strengths and weaknesses.

However, whatever word we use or don't use in day-to-day life, the reality is that according to the law and the medical world, our child is a disabled child.

Without this recognition, it is very hard to access support for our child. Medical and school support as well as welfare benefits for our families are usually considered to be 'disability services'.

No matter how positive we are about our child, we also need to fully recognise that they have a disability that causes a substantial and long-term negative effect on their ability to do normal daily activities. Without fully recognising the severity of what they are dealing with, we cannot hope to work out a parenting strategy to support them.

In most countries, the law on disability applies equally to physical and mental difficulties.

- A child who has meltdowns in crowded places is as disabled as a child who uses a wheelchair.
- A child whose anxiety causes them to shut down has as much of a communication disability as a child with a mouth deformity.
- A child who cannot get out of bed due to depression is as disabled as a child who cannot get out of bed due to spinal injury.
- A child who hits out due to fear is as disabled as an epileptic child who hits out during a seizure.
- During a meltdown or shutdown, our child may be as unable to hear as a child who is deaf.

I am not saying that our children's disabilities are any more or less severe than those of a child in a wheelchair, simply that they are equally within the definition of disability and equally in need of recognition and attention.

The Equality Act imposes a legal duty on schools and workplaces to make 'reasonable adjustments' to the needs of people with disabilities. This is equally the case whether the disability is visible or hidden.[4] When we understand our children's rights under disability law, we are in a much stronger position to advocate for them and get them the support they need.

Although the term 'reasonable adjustments' is used in UK law, the word 'accommodations' is more common in the United States. It is worth checking the exact wording of the law in your country so that you can quote it where necessary.

When we can really appreciate that our child has a disability, it becomes clear that they have the same entitlement to reasonable adjustments as children whose disabilities are more obvious to see.

Just as it is a reasonable adjustment for a child using a wheelchair to need ramps to get into a school building, our child may need a quiet space in school to decompress. Just as a child who is blind may need instructions in Braille, our child may need instructions to be given in specific ways that work for him or her.

A child with a mobility disability may need more time to get around. When their pain is bad, they may not be able to get around at all. In the same way, our child may need longer to complete a task at school. When their anxiety or emotional pain is bad, they may not be able to complete the task at all.

Just as anyone caring for a child with diabetes will need to check blood sugar regularly and adjust what they are feeding them, anyone caring for our children may need to check their anxiety levels regularly and adjust what they expect them to be doing accordingly.

This brings us to the second word we need to thoroughly understand, 'hidden'.

HIDDEN

What makes our children's difficulties particularly challenging to deal with is the fact that they are often invisible to others, that they are hidden disabilities. When people cannot see something, it is very easy and tempting to pretend or imagine that it does not exist.

We all do this to some extent. Most of us are more likely to prioritise a problem that we can clearly see and where it is obvious what assistance is needed. When our child falls over and has a bloody knee, we can see clearly what the problem is and why our child is crying.

Without the bloody knee, it can be tempting to conclude that our child is crying 'without any reason'.

When we see someone walking down the street using a white stick and a guide dog, there are visual clues that the person is visually impaired and we may offer helpful assistance.

This is why when our daughter is crying out in emotional pain, it is all too easy to conclude that she is crying 'without reason' and to disregard her pain and the assistance that is needed.

This is why our children's disabilities are so often disregarded by others. The fact that people cannot clearly see their disability is often used to justify not helping and to refuse them the adjustments they need. This is why we are so often not believed when we try to explain our child's needs.

Many of us will be familiar with being told, 'Well, he doesn't *look* autistic!' To which, if you are quick off the mark you could reply, although maybe not out loud, 'Well, you don't *look* ignorant, but here we are!'

So, in a sense, our children have a double disability. Not only do they have all the challenges of the disability itself, but they also have the additional burden of the disability being denied or ignored because it is hidden or not immediately obvious.

Not only are we fighting for our children's disability rights, but we are also fighting for the right of their difficulties to be considered disabilities at all.

I have found that making the comparison with visible disabilities often helps people to understand. For example, if a teacher is expecting our daughter to do something that will trigger her anxiety, we can say, 'Would you expect a child using a wheelchair to walk up those stairs?'

This is why it is often easier to get support for a child with severe or 'classic' autism than for one who has high-functioning autism. Severe autism is rarely a hidden disability because people can usually see it, either because the person is non-verbal or due to unmistakeable behaviours. This makes it easier to 'get it' and harder to deny that it exists.

GOOD AND BAD DAYS

As well as its invisibility, the fact that our children's symptoms vary over time makes it harder to recognise as a disability like any other. Many disabilities, be they hidden or visible, have symptoms that change and can come and go. Even someone who is a wheelchair user or has other visible difficulties can have good days and bad days. Symptoms are rarely 'all or nothing', they are a complex spectrum of colours that are affected by many things in our children's lives.

The fact that our children may be able to do something one day and not the next does not mean that they do not have a disability. Like everyone else, our children will also have good days and bad days.

I have a friend with multiple sclerosis who is able to walk unassisted on some days but needs to use a wheelchair on others. No-one would deny that she has a disability. Our children's hidden disability needs, however, are often denied for exactly the same reason, that their symptoms vary from day to day.

How many of us have been told that because our child was able to complete homework on one day proves that she should be able to do it every day?

This confusion means that demands can be put on our child that would never be put on a child whose disability is visible.

This is not just a problem with other people and their ignorance. It can cause confusion for us too. It can be very hard to accept that although our child may be *capable* of tidying his room, his disability may make it impossible *at some times*. When I struggled with this it helped me to remember my friend with multiple sclerosis. Yes, she is able to walk, but on some days her disability makes walking very difficult indeed.

DIFFERENT TYPES OF HIDDEN DISABILITIES

Hidden disabilities are often divided into being either brain-based or physical-based.

So long as they meet the legal definition of disability, brain-based ones can include psychiatric conditions like bipolar disorder, chronic depression, anxiety disorders and OCD (obsessive compulsive disorder). They can also include autistic spectrum disorders like Asperger's and PDA (pathological demand avoidance), conditions like ADHD (attention deficit hyperactivity disorder), ADD (attention deficit disorder) and conditions such as dyslexia and dyspraxia.

Brain-based hidden disabilities obviously also include brain injuries that may have happened at birth or as a result of accidents. The effect can have a huge impact on a child's behaviour and learning but not be visible to the outside world.

The physical-based hidden disabilities include any bodily disability that people cannot see easily. So, this could include chronic fatigue, diabetes or a heart defect. Anything to do with bowels, such as colitis or fibromyalgia, is particularly likely to be kept hidden for obvious reasons.

Unless hearing aids are worn in a clearly visible way, many deaf and hearing-impaired people also have the additional burden of their disability being hidden. The increased use of 'invisible' aids may help people feel less self-conscious but may also make other people less aware of their needs.

As we probably know with our own children, this is often not 'either/or'. Many people have both brain and physical hidden disabilities and often they are interconnected.

Conditions considered to be 'physical' disabilities such as chronic fatigue, Parkinson's and multiple sclerosis often affect the brain too. Those affected may have particular trouble regulating their emotions at times.[5]

Numerous studies show that people on the autism spectrum are more likely to have ongoing digestive and bowel difficulties. They are 67 per cent more likely to have a diagnosis of colitis or Crohn's and four times more likely to suffer abdominal pain, constipation and diarrhoea.[6]

People on the autism spectrum are far more likely to be diagnosed with hypermobility, including Ehlers-Danlos Syndrome, and have problems with walking as a result.[7]

Additionally, our children may be on medications that produce physical and mental health side effects. One of my children was on an antipsychotic drug for bipolar disorder that caused so much bone pain that walking became very difficult. A friend's child took a medication for a bone pain disorder that produced severe anxiety and mood swings, reminiscent of my child's bipolar. Cause and effect can get very blurred.

This shows what a huge over-simplification it is to separate the brain from the rest of the body. At the end of the day, the brain is just another organ in the body, like the heart, lungs or intestines. If there is a chemical imbalance or difference in the brain, this is as physical as any other disability. In this respect, we could say that all hidden disabilities are physical.

The causes of hidden disabilities, whether they show themselves through physical or mental symptoms, are still not very well understood. However, the medical world is pretty clear that they are largely inherited by our children in their DNA, which is why so many hidden disabilities run in families. There is also some debate about whether some environmental factors could trigger the hidden disabilities or make the symptoms better or worse.

Science is completely clear on one important thing.

Hidden disabilities are *not* caused by bad parenting.

You may need to re-read that sentence a number of times, especially if you sometimes catch yourself wondering what you have done wrong. Many of us consider our child's hidden disability symptoms to be a sign that we are hopeless parents. So here it is again.

Hidden disabilities are *not* caused by bad parenting.[8]

Bad or cruel parenting can cause our children to be screwed up and have many emotional problems, but they will not cause the hidden disabilities. This is why we need to be clear about the difference between hidden disabilities and mental illnesses.

MENTAL ILLNESS AND HIDDEN DISABILITY

A mental illness is a temporary state, usually brought on by something particularly stressful happening in someone's life. A person, including a child, may become mentally ill as a result of a bereavement or as a result of being bullied. Anyone can become mentally ill when faced with a sudden life change, such as losing a job or losing something that is important to us.

Most of us will have experienced depression, anxiety or low self-esteem in our lives. Sometimes it can be severe and need medical assistance. Some of us will have had breakdowns.

The easiest way to understand how this is different from our children's conditions is to remember that:

- illnesses are usually temporary and can go away
- disabilities are usually lifelong – they cannot go away but the symptoms can sometimes be managed.

So, if I have the flu, this is an acute illness and will most likely resolve in time, maybe with the help of medical treatment. But if I have heart disease or arthritis, this is likely to be a disability. Treatment will be about controlling it as it is assumed that it cannot go away.

If my son breaks his leg, he is likely to have temporary problems with walking. But if he has a brittle bone condition, his mobility problems are likely to be a lifelong disability.

In the same way, if our daughter is depressed, this could be mental *illness* due to something that is really disturbing her. If this is the case, with the right counselling or other treatment, our daughter can recover completely.

Alternatively, depression is also a biological symptom of many hidden disabilities, especially bipolar or autism spectrum disorders. For some, ongoing depression (known as chronic depression) is a *disability* in its own right.

As these are usually lifelong conditions, our child will not recover after a few counselling sessions. In these cases, it is necessary to recognise the depression as part of the disability.

Where a hidden disability is diagnosed or recognised, there is generally not a 'fix' for it. There is not a cure to make it go away. If it were fixable or able to go away by itself, it would be an acute illness and not a disability. Treatments for disabilities tend to be about managing symptoms and teaching coping skills, again with varying success.

Many of the problems we have when figuring out how to parent our child come from the confusion between illnesses and disabilities. It is also the source of a lot of misunderstanding by teachers, family and friends.

Many people believe that our children's disabilities can be 'fixed' by treating them in the same way as if they were a temporary mental illness. I have heard schools telling parents that they will only make adjustments to school procedures for their child for a short period of time, while the child is 'getting better'. Or else we are told to see the doctor to obtain a pill to 'fix' or 'cure' our child, making it unnecessary for the school to address their ongoing needs.

Again, if we are clear about the difference between a disability and an illness, we have some tools to question this. Would a blind child be denied books in Braille after a period of time as they 'should be able to see by now'?

This confusion is not helped at all by the fact that our medical services tend to lump mental illnesses and hidden disabilities together. They are often all called 'mental health' services without distinguishing between illnesses and disabilities.

This confusion can make it very hard for our child to get the diagnosis and help she needs. A child who is desperately in need of assessment for autism, ADHD or psychiatric conditions may be sent for counselling instead.[9]

To understand how this can happen, we can imagine that someone with cancer would benefit from counselling to help them deal with the emotional impact of their condition. Saying that, I don't think anyone would suggest that the counselling alone is a substitute for diagnosing and treating the cancer.

To confuse things even more, some professionals use the term 'serious mental illnesses' to refer to psychiatric disabilities such as OCD, bipolar or anxiety disorder. This gives the impression that the difference between a mental illness and a disability is one of 'severity', whereas in fact they are completely different things. They have different causes, have different outcomes and need different treatments.

This also belittles mental illnesses as it gives the impression that they are somehow *less severe* than the hidden disabilities. Anyone who has suffered a mental illness will know just how devastating it can be, and there is no reason to believe that people with a mental illness are suffering any less than those with hidden disabilities.

Although mental illnesses and hidden disabilities are two different things, a child with a hidden disability is just as likely to suffer from a mental illness as anyone else. When this happens it is *in addition to* the hidden disability.

So, if our child with a hidden disability is struggling day in and day out to disguise their challenges in order to fit in, this is going to exhaust them and affect their mental health. If they are being judged and bullied, they are particularly vulnerable to mental health difficulties.

When this happens, we need to be aware that the mental illness could mask the hidden disability. Being aware and clear about the difference helps a lot in figuring out how to manage this.

The sympathetic treatment and understanding of those with mental health problems is an area that is much neglected in most societies. Some of what I share as being helpful for children with hidden disabilities may also be useful for children with mental health difficulties. However, this should not confuse the difference between disability and mental illness.

The confusion between illness and disability is also behind the false belief that parents are responsible for causing the child's hidden disability by bad parenting. Despite conclusive evidence that this is not the case, this view is still very common.

ARE AUTISM AND ADHD ALWAYS HIDDEN DISABILITIES?

If your child has a diagnosis of autism, ADHD or any other ongoing condition, they are only disabled according to the law if they *have ongoing challenges that cause a substantial impact on day-to-day life*.

This means that, regardless of what diagnosis our child may have, if it is not having a *substantial* impact on their day-to-day life, they may not have a hidden disability.

Some people, especially those with high-functioning autism or ADHD, fit into this category. If they are lucky enough for their condition not to cause a substantial impact on their lives, they are not disabled according to the law.

Their autism may show itself as a quirky and unusual personality, amazing talents and passions, and an innovative way of looking at things. Some people on the autism spectrum reject the idea that autism can be a disability because they personally may not meet the legal definition of what a disability is.

Some people in this category argue that it is *offensive* to ever consider autism or ADHD to be a disability. Instead, they suggest that we should consider these conditions to be just *differences*, in the same way as race, hair colour and sexual orientation are differences.

I believe we need to be very careful with these arguments as very many people with these diagnoses *do* meet the criteria to be considered disabled. People have fought very hard for even the most basic disability rights. Twenty years ago there were few disabled toilets in schools. Due to the invisibility of their conditions, people with hidden disabilities need to fight even harder, mainly even to have their disabilities recognised. We need to be cautious about any argument that seems to be invalidating this.

When our children meet the legal definition of disability, they are disabled. If they do not meet this definition, they are not.

This is the case regardless of whether we or our children consider their conditions to be differences or divergences, or whether or not we blame society for many of the problems that our children experience.

If our children have a disability, we are entitled by law to demand that schools and workplaces put reasonable adjustments in place to meet their needs. Just like we can demand a ramp if our child uses a wheelchair, we may need to demand a shorter school day for a child having panic attacks related to their hidden disability.

WHY THIS MATTERS

There has been a huge amount of progress in disability rights over the last 50 years. By law, many buildings, including schools, are now obliged to provide ramps, disabled toilets and even signs in Braille. These 'reasonable adjustments' are not designed to give disabled people an unfair advantage, they are there to even the playing field so that people have more equal access to participation in life. In many countries it is an offence to discriminate against someone due to their disability.

It is estimated that at least 10 per cent of the population benefit from adjustments for mobility disabilities.[10] What they have in common is a disability that is visible.

This progress needs to be extended to people with hidden disabilities such as our children. The equality laws are in place and apply to our children, but lack of understanding about hidden disabilities is still preventing them from getting the same access to reasonable adjustments as children with visible disabilities.

This is why it is so important to be clear about what a disability and a hidden disability are.

One of the most common symptoms across hidden disabilities is sensory overload. Our chaotic, crowded and noisy school environments can be devastating for many of our children. Sensory overload can send them into meltdowns, shutdowns, aggression and a whole range of other symptoms and behaviour. Just as children using wheelchairs are able to access disabled toilets, our children may need to access quiet and calm spaces to calm their sensory overload.

We need to recognise that these are disability rights.

It is estimated that at least 10 per cent of all children have some form of hidden disability, whether or not it is diagnosed.[11] That is a lot of human potential and talent.

When we ask for reasonable adjustments for our children, we are not asking for an unfair advantage for them. Just like for children who use wheelchairs, we are trying to create a more even playing field.

This applies equally to how we parent our children with hidden disabilities. We may need to make some significant adjustments and changes to how we parent them to fully honour and accommodate their disabilities and needs.

This can be very difficult for us if we have been brought up with strong beliefs about discipline and how to treat children to get them to behave as we wish. As we make the changes we need to make, members of our family may look at us aghast, judge us or even blame us. They do this because they do not 'get it'.

This is why being clear about what a hidden disability is and what it means is so important. Unless we can truly 'get it', how can we expect our mother-in-law to? And most importantly, we need to be clear if we expect our children to 'get it' and to learn how to understand their own needs and experiences as they grow up and lead independent lives.

This is why this matters.

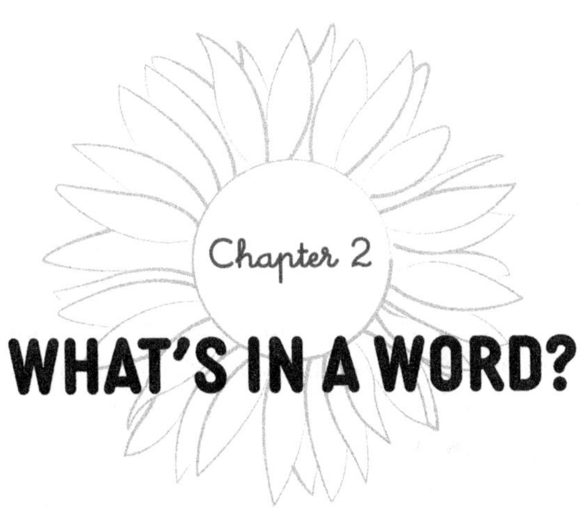

Chapter 2

WHAT'S IN A WORD?

SHOULD I GET A DIAGNOSIS?

Many of us are parenting a child with a hidden disability without a diagnosis. For some, this will be a conscious decision and choice. We may not want our child to have the burden of a 'label' or we may not feel ready to come to terms with a diagnosis and everything this brings with it.

Most commonly, our child's lack of diagnosis is due to the difficulty or even impossibility of getting a diagnostic assessment where we live. Many of us simply do not have that choice.

It sounds so obvious, but it is worth remembering that whether or not our child has a diagnosis, the challenges they are encountering will be the same. The hidden disability may be there regardless of whether or not we have a piece of paper giving it a name. Our challenges when parenting a child with a hidden disability will exist regardless of whether they have a diagnosis or not.

Getting a diagnosis does not affect what our child is experiencing, it only affects how we and others respond to it.

This can cause confusion. When someone says that their son was diagnosed with OCD at the age of 11, it can give the impression that the OCD *started* when he was 11 when in fact the symptoms may have started many years before. Because of this confusion, some people even avoid getting a diagnosis in the hope that it will prevent their child from having a problem. They may think, perhaps unconsciously, that while their daughter is diagnosis free, she is fine and doesn't have a hidden disability.

We may strongly suspect that our loved one has a hidden disability. As our child's parent we are likely to have a special instinct that means we 'just know' that our child has additional needs. We may be pretty sure that their behaviours, reactions and challenges are well off the range of what is considered 'normal'. And we probably have a pretty good idea what we think the diagnosis would be, given the chance to have our child clinically assessed.

Our spouse or family may not agree, frustrating as this can be for everyone concerned.

Our spouse may think that we are overreacting, and that our child is just very badly behaved or extremely active. Our mother-in-law may tell us that there is nothing 'wrong' with our child, only something wrong with our parenting. Our GP may tell us that our daughter's dark moods are just 'normal pre-teen stuff' and that she will grow out of them. Our father may tell us that our son is spending too much time with a particular friend and is 'copying' their behaviour. The school may tell us that we are exaggerating and that a diagnosis is not necessary.

We may even be told, as I was by a counsellor, that the fact that I want my child assessed 'proves' that *I* am the problem and that this means that my child doesn't have a hidden disability.

It is easy for others to tell us not to worry, but deep down we know that something is not right and that our child urgently needs help and so do we.

In countries like the UK, diagnostic assessments within the National Health Service (NHS) may be available but are very hard to access. They often require a lot of fighting to get and many years on a waiting list. Some families have no choice but to fight and wait. Others are able to pay for a private assessment. Others decide not to do it at all.

Many families disagree about whether or not it is OK to pay for a private assessment. This isn't helped by some schools saying they will only accept a diagnosis that comes from the NHS rather than from a private assessment, despite there being no legal basis for this, at least in the UK.[1]

In countries where all medical assessments are private, the cost may simply be too high, especially if insurance is lacking or coverage is inadequate to meet the costs.

And in many places, there is simply nowhere to go to for a diagnostic assessment.

Assuming that we have the possibility to have our child assessed and diagnosed, should we do it? Could a diagnosis make things worse? Could we be forced to accept treatments for our child that we do not want or agree with? Will our child be labelled for life? Will a diagnosis cause discrimination against our child?

Just as many people have strong opinions about whether or not our child has a hidden disability, feelings can also run pretty high about whether or not to get a formal diagnosis.

There are arguments for and against. Ultimately, this is a very personal matter and what may be right for one situation may be totally wrong for another.

People who feel strongly against getting a diagnosis often fear that it will label the child or that it may encourage their symptoms. Others simply feel that a diagnosis is unnecessary as every child is different. They may say, 'Why put our child in a "box" if every child is an individual?'

My view is that in most cases we owe it to ourselves and our loved ones to get a diagnosis, where this is possible. This is why.

ARGUMENTS FOR DIAGNOSIS

IT SHOWS IT IS REAL

A diagnosis validates us in our view that our child has additional needs. It demonstrates that what we are saying is accurate. It shows that we are not 'making it up' to let ourselves off the hook as terrible parents, or to let our child off the hook for bad behaviour.

This is very important when we are up against hostility and criticism when we try to get our child's needs met.

Without the diagnosis it can be very hard to get people to listen.

When other people criticise us and condemn us for how we parent, or refuse requests for reasonable adjustments and help, it will not only be 'our view' that our child has special needs, but that of an official diagnosis by a doctor or psychologist.

Teachers, family members and other people are far less likely to reject a doctor's view than that of a 'mere' parent. It establishes that what we are saying is legitimate.

When asking for support for our child, it can be helpful to say, 'My son was diagnosed by consultant neuropsychiatrist Professor Whatever. I am simply telling you *her* clinical opinion.'

If they still do not want to recognise or address our child's needs, we can then ask, 'Are you questioning medical evidence?'

If we are able to back up the medical diagnosis and recommendations in writing, this will really strengthen our position and make it much easier for us to advocate for our child.

On a personal level, when we have a diagnosis, we know for sure that our child has a hidden disability and that their suffering is not our fault. When we are surrounded by the negativity and judgement of others, it is easy to blame ourselves. The diagnosis helps remind us that this is not the case.

This helps us not to take our child's behaviour personally and helps us to find the most helpful ways to parent them.

Carole, whose daughter has Asperger's, found that:

> During the assessments I felt listened to as a mum and finally vindicated! I now understand that her anxiety is deep and real to her, and this should not be measured by standards applied to neurotypical people.

IT SHOWS OUR CHILD IT IS REAL

A diagnosis *validates our child* as it can help him to understand that what he is experiencing makes sense.

It can give our daughter a frame of reference to understand herself, her gifts and her challenges.

It enables our son to make informed choices about what works best for his needs and to learn specific skills to help him best meet his potential.

It can make it easier for our son to accept and be at peace with himself and ultimately take responsibility for managing his own disability.

Without a diagnosis, our daughter may perpetually be wondering, 'Why am I different?', 'What's "wrong" with me?' and judge herself as crazy, lazy or bad.

IT HELPS OTHERS UNDERSTAND OUR CHILD'S CHALLENGES

A diagnosis helps teachers and others involved in our child's life to have some idea of what his challenges may be.

Although every child's needs will be different and hidden disabilities show up in different ways, the diagnosis is a starting point. If a teacher knows that a child in her care has ADHD, even if she knows nothing else, this gives her some idea that our son may have specific needs around attention, energy, focus and stimulation. It's a helpful starting point, although obviously never the whole picture.

If our daughter has an Asperger's diagnosis, this may help her father to understand that she can react badly to sudden changes in routines. The diagnosis may make it easier for her teacher to understand that crowds and noise may be a problem for her. Again, every child with Asperger's has different needs, but the diagnosis can be a very helpful starting point. If the diagnosis is accepted by her father and the teacher, it can then be refined to the specific details about how it affects our child personally.

IT CAN PROTECT US AND OUR CHILD

A formal diagnosis can protect us and our child if we are reported to social services or the police as a result of the symptoms of our child's hidden disability.

Due to a lack of understanding about hidden disabilities, some people and some organisations believe that our child's symptoms may be caused by child abuse by parents.

When seeking help for our child, it is not at all uncommon for parents to be reported to the police or social services. This is not always personal and does not always mean that the people involved *believe* that we are abusers. Some organisations report parents as a matter of course, perhaps to protect themselves against allegations of malpractice, or simply because they do not know enough about the subject.

I went through this twice and it was probably the most terrifying and stressful thing I have ever gone through. As loving parents, we have an underlying fear of our children being taken away from us to a place where they may suffer and where we are unable to protect them.

Many of my friends who have children with hidden disabilities have also experienced this, including a child support lawyer and an esteemed doctor. We are all at risk and the best way to protect ourselves and our children is by having a diagnosis. As soon as a diagnosis report is presented and a doctor intervenes, the path is often cleared to take our child's needs seriously.

Just as organisations may report us to 'protect themselves', we need to have the right paperwork to 'protect ourselves' and to allow us to advocate for our children.

PROTECTION IF OUR CHILD IS ARRESTED OR EXCLUDED FROM SCHOOL

A formal diagnosis can protect our son if he is excluded from school because of his disability needs or arrested by the police for something in connection with the hidden disability.

As soon as there is a diagnosis, the situation can move from being a 'bad behaviour issue' to becoming a 'disability rights issue'. If the school or the police insist that our child is 'bad' and needs punishment, then the diagnosis is the evidence we need that another approach may be a better fit.

This is not to say that the diagnosis is a 'get out of jail free' card. There may be times when it is appropriate for our child to be arrested or excluded from school. Whether or not this is the case, it is still very important that the hidden disability and all of its implications be taken into account. This is very difficult to argue without a diagnosis.

IT CAN OPEN THE DOOR TO TREATMENT AND SUPPORT

A diagnosis can open the door to treatment and support, if we are lucky enough to have them available to us.

We may or may not choose to accept treatments that are offered, or we may prefer to request different ones, but having a diagnosis is a starting point to getting our child the treatment and support they need.

IT HELPS THINGS TO MAKE SENSE

A diagnosis is a diagnosis. It may be for diabetes, a heart condition or a hidden disability such as ADD or bipolar disorder. The diagnosis can help us to understand what is happening to us but it does not define who we are. It may be a part of who we are, and that may be a small or big part depending on what we are going through.

Just as a person with diabetes may need to avoid excess sugar to be well, a person on the autism spectrum may need to avoid excessive noise or uncertainty to be well.

A child with a diagnosis of a leg abnormality may not be able to run around the playground. A child with a diagnosis of ADHD may not be able to sit still in the classroom.

Both children will have many other aspects to their personality and be unique individuals with strengths and weaknesses that are unrelated to their disability, but they still need their disability needs to be met for them to be healthy and thrive. We are not our medical conditions. However, we need to know and accept what is there so that we can find peace and compassion with ourselves.

Academic publisher Laura James had to wait until adulthood before getting her diagnosis:

> My diagnosis was a vindication: I am not defective. I am autistic. Along with the shock, came a strange sense of comfort. Finally, I belong somewhere – and that somewhere is on the autism spectrum... No one understood why I couldn't cope. Some put it down to my being spoiled or stupid and I didn't have the words to explain the strange feelings no one else seemed to experience. I had tried normal and had failed.[2]

On getting a diagnosis, one of my children drew a picture of the sun on our calendar to mark the day when life started making sense. My child was so relieved that they were neither 'mad nor bad', but just had a condition that could be understood.

We can all identify with this when we are ill and don't know what is wrong. If our doctors are not able to diagnose the problem, we may start to wonder if we are crazy or imagining the problem. Getting a diagnosis that proves that our condition is something real, such as an infection, is extremely reassuring, especially when it is treatable and gives us permission to rest and give ourselves the self-care we need.

We and our loved ones can choose if and when to share a diagnosis. It is ours to use or not as we feel best serves us. If a diagnosis no longer meets our needs or our child's, it can be discarded or replaced with another that is a better fit to our changing circumstances.

Diagnoses are frequently changed, often by different clinicians and at different times. Sometimes this is because of new or changed symptoms. Other times it is because the rules on how particular conditions are diagnosed have changed. In some cases, it can be because a doctor favours a particular diagnosis over another. As diagnoses are so fluid, there is little risk for most people of being 'stuck' with a diagnosis that is no longer accurate or helpful.

Our child may reject his diagnosis and this, in my opinion, is fine too. There are many reasons why our child may not want to accept that they have a hidden disability or they may simply disagree with the diagnosis.

However, having the diagnosis in place means that it is available at any time in the future should they feel that it will help them or support them. And in the meantime, it supports and protects us for all the reasons I have outlined.

ARGUMENTS AGAINST DIAGNOSIS

A DIAGNOSIS IS LABELLING OUR CHILD

The main argument made against assessing for a hidden disability is that a diagnosis is a way of *labelling* our child and that giving our loved one a label is abusive and wrong.

At one of our schools, when I asked for a dyslexia assessment I was accused of wanting to *label* my child dyslexic so that I would not have to face the fact that my child was lazy, of low ability and a low achiever.

I was told, 'We don't like to label children with syndromes. We prefer to treat them as individuals.'

The teacher saw no irony or problem in the fact that she was labelling my child as lazy, of low ability and a low achiever!

Many people who reject a hidden disability diagnosis as 'labelling' are very happy to label our children as bad, mad, stupid, difficult, over-sensitive, aggressive or weird and to label us as bad parents or bad people. A child without a diagnosis may even use these same unhelpful words about themselves.

It seems ironic to me that words like bad, lazy and difficult are considered to be acceptable labels but a medical diagnosis is not.

A diagnosis *is* a label, but so are labels such as intelligent, able, lovely, beautiful, kind, determined and talented.

The reality is that not all labels are bad or negative. When we tell our child that they are worthy and lovable, we are giving them good labels that help them to accept themselves and build their self-esteem.

So what if our child's hidden disability diagnosis is a positive label, one that will help them accept and love themselves, in the same way as the label 'adorable'?

Quite often, there seems to me to be a confusion between the word *label* and the word *judgement*. People may say, 'Don't label me,' when what they mean is, 'Don't judge me.'

We are unlikely to be accused of 'labelling' our son if he is diagnosed with diabetes or a heart condition. In these situations, the diagnosis is simply a statement of medical fact and indication of needs. Diabetes is no less of a label than Asperger's. It is simply a description of 'what is'. The difference appears to be that while diabetes may be considered a *neutral* label, Asperger's may be judged by some to be a *negative* label.

Having Asperger's, ADHD or any other hidden disability is as neutral as any physical disability or illness and does not imply any judgement of the person, only an indication of needs and experiences. The diagnosis is a *description* rather than a judgement.

People who choose to judge others due to their diagnoses are no different from people who judge others due to the colour of their skin, their sexual orientation, their ethnicity or which school they went to.

As Jane, who has multiple hidden disabilities, strongly states:

> If there is a stigma about a particular disability, we fight the stigma, not deny that we have a disability. I stand proud with my diagnoses of Tourette's and Asperger's.

Judgey people judge and that tells us what we need to know about *them*. Meanwhile we can reject these judgements and be proud and strong in who we are, regardless of what hidden disability diagnosis we may or may not have and what others may think.

Some people believe that we can protect our loved ones from being judged by others by making sure that they do not have the diagnosis at all. However, I think we can appreciate that taking away the diagnosis or label does not take away the disability or our child's needs or prevent them from being judged. It is not the diagnosis itself that makes our child different.

Instead of seeing our child's diagnosis as a label, I believe it is far more helpful to think of it as a *tool* at our disposal. Sometimes it may be helpful to use and sometimes it may not be.

When we see diagnosis as a tool, we can pick a diagnosis up and use it when it serves us and ignore it when it is not relevant. There is no need for our child to 'identify' as disabled or with their diagnosis.

As with any medical diagnosis, we and our children can choose when to disclose it. We don't go around telling everyone about every medical diagnosis we have ever had. We probably don't share information about our ingrown toenails with random strangers. In the same way, we can pick and choose when to share our child's hidden disability diagnosis, depending on whether it is relevant to do so and whether or not doing so may help them.

One of my children's dyslexia diagnosis was life-changing, as the assessor presented it as a gift. My child was told that the tests showed that they should be aiming for top universities. They were also told that their challenges were part of this picture and what support they would need. As my child was languishing in the lowest academic group at school, this was quite an exciting revelation! The assessment gave my child the boost they needed, as well as a greater awareness of their needs. Within a year my child had turned around the underachieving and was accepted at one of the top universities in the world.

'MILKING' A DIAGNOSIS

We all know about children (and adults) playing the sick card to get out of doing things that they do not want to do or as an excuse for bad behaviour. Some parents fear getting a diagnosis for this reason, in case it is then used as an excuse by their children.

All parents need to use their judgement on this, not only parents of children with hidden disabilities. Children often get mysterious 'tummy aches' at bedtime or say that they feel ill when they don't want to go to school. We need to figure out what is happening in these situations by using our instinct and reading our children's 'codes' and body language. Sometimes we will get this right and sometimes we won't as there is no objective way of knowing what a child is feeling.

In my opinion this is no different for a child with a hidden disability, regardless of whether or not there is a diagnosis. Chapters 3, 4 and 5 give tips and ideas on how to read and decode our child's behaviour to help us figure out what they might be actually feeling.

I found it very helpful to encourage my children to openly say when they don't want to do something, and if possible say how they feel about it. This meant that my children could ask for a day off school whenever they felt exhausted or overwhelmed. Being overwhelmed is not generally considered to be a legitimate reason to take a day off school, although being 'sick' is. For this reason, it is not hugely surprising that our child may play the sick card. If our child is able to be honest about how they are feeling and what they need to do, there is less incentive to tell us they are sick.

CAN A DIAGNOSIS MAKE MY CHILD WORSE?

Some people are against a diagnosis because they fear that it may make the child worse, as they will 'behave' in a way that is typical of the diagnosis. They may believe that if a child is diagnosed as autistic, they will take on this label and 'behave autistically'.

I have heard this often, especially from grandparents. The idea is that the diagnosis itself may encourage the problem by drawing attention to it. They may believe that if we keep telling our child that they are completely 'normal', they will consider themselves to be 'normal' and therefore behave 'normally'.

It is certainly true that telling a child that she is 'stupid' may affect her self-esteem and cause her to act more 'stupidly'. This is called a self-fulfilling prophecy. However, helping a child to understand how they are wired neurologically, in a supportive and non-judgemental way, can help them to understand and accept themselves. This is much more likely to help them feel 'normal' than denying what they are experiencing and the fullness of who they are.

DIFFERENCES FOR BOYS AND GIRLS

Boys are far more likely to be diagnosed than girls. Figures vary but are usually quoted as being about four to one for autism spectrum disorders and seven to one for ADHD.[3] This can give the impression that boys are more likely to have hidden disabilities than girls.

This may or may not be the case. We need to remember that just because a child does not have a diagnosis does not mean that they do not have the disability.

It is possible that girls may be just as likely as boys to have hidden disabilities, but for a number of reasons, are less able to access diagnoses. As a diagnosis can open the door to understanding and support, this is a problem we need to be aware of.

Girls can fall through the diagnosis net for a number of reasons.

The symptoms and characteristics of hidden disabilities can be different in boys and girls.

Research has shown that boys are more likely to have *external* symptoms such as being hyperactive, impulsive or being very disruptive and possibly aggressive. These kinds of symptoms will draw attention to them and are more likely to flag a possible problem.

In contrast, girls are more likely to have *internal* symptoms such as severe anxiety, depression, eating disorders and self-harm. As these symptoms do not draw attention to our child too readily, it is easier to miss or overlook them.[4]

Additionally, girls may be better at masking and disguising their symptoms in an attempt to fit in. We know that hiding symptoms does not make them go away. Hiding them can add a huge amount of stress to our daughter's life, which is likely to come out in other ways or produce new symptoms that may be more severe than the ones she is trying to conceal.

For example, a girl who is struggling to hide social anxiety due to Asperger's may resort to self-harm by cutting herself or by developing an eating disorder. As she may not be showing typical autistic behaviour associated with boys, her Asperger's may not be spotted.

For example, we know that girls with Asperger's can be highly creative and express themselves through art and creative writing. This is very different to the 'maths geek' stereotype often given to boys on the spectrum as being cold, analytical and unexpressive.

Sarah, mum to a girl with ASD (autism spectrum disorder), found:

> Even after Zara got her diagnosis, the teacher still said that there was no way she could be on the autism spectrum because she makes eye contact. I had to explain that the eye contact thing is less common with girls.

These stereotypes affect boys too. Research shows that both boys and girls on the autism spectrum show higher levels of creativity. However, it does seem to be girls whose needs are more likely to be overlooked.

Another problem is that most research on hidden disabilities is done on boys and the criteria used to diagnose are often based on how symptoms present in boys. This obviously puts girls at a disadvantage during the diagnosis process.

As a result, many people, including teachers and mental health professionals, simply do not know what symptoms to look for in a girl, so vital clues are missed.

WHEN WE CAN'T OR SHOULDN'T GET A DIAGNOSIS

Depending on where we live and the resources available, getting a diagnosis may be very difficult, time consuming or in many cases impossible.

In some places, hidden disabilities are not accepted as existing and some diagnoses are recognised and others are not. Sometimes even neighbouring towns will have a different view on whether, for example, bipolar disorder is an allowed diagnosis in anyone under 18. PDA (pathological demand avoidance) is fully accepted and treated in some countries but dismissed completely in others.

If we are unable to access a diagnostic assessment, figuring out the most probable diagnosis ourself is an effective way to help us to understand, accept and cherish our child by recognising his experiences and his needs. If nothing else, it can help us to better learn how to read our child's codes and to help our child to know and accept himself too.

Even if our idea of the diagnosis proves not to be accurate later, the exercise can help us to connect more with our child and her needs. If we know what the problem probably is, we can still access support through forums and support groups which are usually open to people without a diagnosis.

Maybe we have no idea what our child's diagnosis may be, or even if they have a hidden disability at all? In this situation, the tools in this book will be just as helpful as for those with a diagnosis. This is because learning how to decode our child is especially important when they are struggling or withdrawing for whatever reason.

There are also times when it may be better to figure it out ourselves rather than get a formal diagnosis. An example of this is when an adult has nothing particular to gain from a formal diagnosis.

I have a lot of hidden disability traits myself, but as I recognise my strengths, needs and limitations and have created a lifestyle that works well for me, there is nothing in particular to gain from a formal diagnosis of anything. If I was struggling at school or in the workplace, this would be a different matter.

Another situation is if a child seems to meet the diagnostic criteria of hidden disability, but is happy, functioning well and not suffering, it may be better to not disturb the situation with an assessment at this time.

So, to simplify this dilemma, we can just ask ourselves the question, 'Will a diagnosis help?'

ISN'T IT A DIFFERENCE AND A GIFT?

IT'S A DIFFERENCE

One of the arguments often made against diagnosis is that we should consider our loved one's life situation as a *difference* rather than a disability. The idea is that it is society that is the problem for not 'getting' the needs of people who are wired somewhat differently.

The argument goes that if the world were not so chaotic and noisy, there would be no need for autistic people to have meltdowns. If schools were more flexible and based on individual learning styles, there would be no need for children to be diagnosed with ADHD. Schools and society are the problem, not the children.

According to this view, which has a lot going for it, what many consider to be disorders are in fact *differences*. Some people are simply wired differently and each way of being wired is as *normal* as any other way.

This is why some people prefer to use the word *neurodivergent* when referring to brain-based hidden disabilities, which means in this context 'wired differently'. They use the word *neurotypical* to mean people who are wired in a typical and more common way. This is often a shorthand way to say 'non-autistic' or 'not having ADHD'.

It suggests that rather than their difficulties being our child's problem, they are due to the inflexible thinking of neurotypical people, who discriminate against people who are neurologically different by imposing their way of life on them. They often compare this to discrimination against ethnic minorities or based on sexual orientation.

They also refer to the 'neurotypical world' to mean a society set up to meet the needs of neurotypical rather than neurodivergent people.

While it can be very empowering to see our child's difficulties in this way, we need to be very careful with it indeed. We are fighting very hard to get our children's disability needs acknowledged and met, so saying that they have a difference *instead* of a disability can easily be used against us.

How can we advocate for our child's disability rights if we are at the same time denying that they have a disability?

Unless we are able to change the world so that our children's needs are fully addressed, we do need to continue to argue that their challenges are disabilities, as this is how they are *experienced* by our loved ones, who spend much time suffering because of their conditions.

The same applies to visible disabilities. If our child is born blind, we can consider it to be a visual 'difference' and that many of his difficulties are due to the uncaring 'seeing world'. While this is true, few would argue that blindness is not also a disability. Why would this be any different if a disability is hidden?

I believe that disabilities can be both disorders *and* differences and that neither of these things define us or our child. This applies equally to disabilities that are hidden and those that are visible.

We do not need to choose whether our child has a 'disability' or a 'difference'. We can accept both and use whatever word best helps us or our child in a particular situation.

If our children are suffering from debilitating symptoms, then anything other than the word *disability* would trivialise their pain. Similarly, if we are fighting for their disability rights, we need to use the word *disability* to get them the support they need and to honour their challenges and needs.

However, there are also times when it makes much more sense to use the words *difference* or *neurodivergent*. Examples of this are when we describe our child's quirky personality, unusual creative skills, ability to think outside the box, innovative thinking or their need for ongoing stimulation. Our children may also feel more comfortable using the words *difference* or *neurodivergent* with their friends.

In fact, the word *difference* can be more accurate in any situation where we are referring to our child's *personality* rather than their disability needs.

Just as with a diagnosis label, words like *difference* and *disability* are tools that we can select and use in whatever way best suits us or our child at a particular time.

IT'S A GIFT

Whether it is a disorder or a difference, what is clear is that our loved ones with hidden disabilities have a huge range of gifts to offer. For this reason, some people like to refer to 'the gift of ADHD' or 'the gift of autism'. When we are parenting a child with a hidden disability, it is very helpful to recognise what these gifts are and to value and appreciate them. We can help our child to recognise and value these gifts in themselves too.

Our children may be amazing, resourceful, talented, smart and wonderful human beings. Because they are often hidden in the fog of symptoms and related behaviours, we can fail to see them as they really are, as the fog obscures their beauty and shining light. While we are blinded by that fog, we may fail to see our children's gifts.

It is hard to see the positive while our children are having daily meltdowns, are clinically depressed or are being excluded from school.

Like when we talk about our child having a brain *difference*, we need to be careful that recognising their gifts is not used to deny their challenges and suffering. Having a gift does not mean that their needs are any less pressing.

Our children do not have a gift *instead* of a hidden disability. Their gifts are *as well as* their hidden disability and part of a complex and contradictory whole. Often the gifts only really reveal themselves as the challenges and suffering are relieved.

Many of the gifts of hidden disabilities are the flip side of the challenges themselves. For example:

- A strong passion and focus on a particular interest can, if encouraged, create amazing expertise in that area both academically and professionally. It is no surprise that some of the greatest innovators and talents the world has known have had hidden disabilities.

- Not being wired in a conventional way can make our loved ones super creative. They know that conventional ways of doing things do not work for them so may use their powers of innovation to find ways that do. They may be able to see things that others cannot and come up with fresh ways of doing things, fresh solutions.

- By not being held back by excessive 'mindless socialising', our loved ones may free up time to focus on what really matters to them and may really matter to the world too.
- The passion and energy of someone who is slightly manic or hyperactive can create the drive needed to turn an interesting idea into something that actually happens, be it a successful business or writing a beautiful piece of music.
- Having experienced adversity and being misunderstood, our loved ones can be some of the most compassionate, kind and understanding people we can meet. Knowing suffering first hand, they can be more able to recognise it in others and offer hope and encouragement to those who need it.

Highly successful musician will.i.am talks very positively about his ADHD:

> What's wrong with our society is that we want to pull everything back, stop people thinking out of the box and make everyone the same. I've never wanted to be the same as anyone else.[5]

Another inspiring example of the power of following our passions is the climate activist Greta Thunberg, who has Asperger's and hit the world stage at only 16 years of age:

> Before I started school striking I had no energy, no friends and I didn't speak to anyone. I just sat alone at home with an eating disorder. All of that is gone now, since I have found a meaning, in a world that sometimes seems meaningless to so many people.[6]

Greta sailed across the Atlantic in a small sailing boat in order to participate in the UN climate summits. Rough seas slowed her progress, but her tenacity and passion have inspired millions.

Think of our son 'at his best'. What are his gifts? What are his abilities? What are the nicest parts of our daughter's personality?

What makes us proud of her? This is who our child *really* is, when the fog of stress, anxiety, frustration and anger is blown away.

We need to remember that a child's gifts are not only about achieving things. Our value and worth are not only about *what we do*, they are more about *who we are*.

While it is good to encourage our children to achieve, it is equally important not to define our children by their achievements. In my opinion, the greatest achievement of all is for our child (and us) to have an open heart and an open mind, be happy in our own skin and accepting of everyone's differences, especially our own.

All of this starts by recognising and accepting the challenges of hidden disabilities.

For example, one friend with ADHD holds down a sedentary job by jogging to and from work every day and going to the gym most lunch times. He needs to combine physical activity with time to let his mind wander, without any requirement to focus. If he does this, he can then focus adequately at work. Recognising his challenges and needs helped him to make the life choices that enabled his gifts and abilities to shine.

Many children with hidden disabilities struggle badly with fatigue due to the exhaustion of dealing with their many challenges. If they are aware of this and fully accept and embrace it, they may make career choices that enable flexible working with plenty of rest breaks. This is becoming easier to achieve all the time as more and more careers can be built flexibly with home working. In such a scenario, a person's gifts can fully flourish.

Our loved ones will need to make adjustments in life. This is why their hidden disabilities are a gift and a difference but are also a genuine disability too. To reveal the gift, we have to embrace and accept the disability. They are all parts of the same amazing and lovable whole that is our loved one.

ARE PEOPLE WITH HIDDEN DISABILITIES SMARTER?

The evidence on this is quite uncertain, but I have often heard it said that 'they' (people with hidden disabilities) are very intelligent, perhaps more intelligent than people without hidden disabilities.

I have no idea if this is true, but it seems possible. We know that highly intelligent and accomplished people seem to have a very complex brain chemistry, because there is so much more going on and being processed in the brain. If this is the case, then it is possible that only a slight chemical imbalance would be needed to push the super bright into psychiatric conditions.

Many mental health professionals report the disproportionate number of academics, professionals and creative geniuses among the populations in psychiatric facilities. In fact, the idea of the 'mad professor' persists in our culture and it is often expected that geniuses will have problems with social skills and with moods and sometimes difficulty recognising the difference between different realities. Recent studies seem to back this up. Pitzer College researcher Ruth Karpinski found that people with a very high IQ are over twice as likely to suffer from mood disorders, anxiety disorders, ADHD or autism. She also found that they are three times more likely to suffer from allergies, asthma and autoimmune disorders than the general population.[7]

Karpinski's explanation for this is that perhaps the sensitive brain of the very bright makes them more sensitive to things in life going on around them.

Another point of view on this is that maybe our kids are just reacting to the suffering and adversity that they have experienced all their lives due to the many challenges of living with a hidden disability. You may have heard the expression, 'A smooth sea never made a skilled sailor.'

This is an important truth. We learn to sail well by navigating a choppy sea. Greta Thunberg is a testament to this. In her case she *literally* navigated the ocean in a sailing boat to promote awareness of climate change!

Many highly successful people talk of challenging childhoods, often having to overcome bullying or some other significant obstacle. Obstacles will happen to everyone in life and for many reasons.

Our children with hidden disabilities are facing additional obstacles from a very early age. While this can overwhelm them and make them feel hopeless, these same obstacles have the potential to help them to learn and grow.

We can use our obstacles to learn about ourselves and our needs. We can use obstacles as a way of trampolining ourselves forward. Those who can do this are the people who learn to excel in sailing by learning how to sail on a choppy ocean.

One way we can encourage our children to use obstacles as a way of pushing themselves forward is to model it to them *with our own behaviour*.

We can all fall into the trap of defining ourselves as victims. While recognising that we have been victimised by others, we do not need to *define ourselves* in that way and as soon as we do so, we are stepping out of our power. Maybe we are being victimised by a family member or a colleague at work.

Sharing tales of woe with our child about how awful life is and how nothing can be done about it is a powerful message of hopelessness in the face of adversity.

For more ideas on how we can recognise when we have been victims while still holding on to our power, I suggest you look at the companion book *How to Cope When Your Child Has a Hidden Disability: Self-Care for Parents* where this is talked about in detail.

DO I HAVE A HIDDEN DISABILITY?

Given that we know that many hidden disabilities run in families and have a genetic aspect, it is likely that the answer is yes.

It is very common that while going through the diagnosis process with our children, one or both parents realise that they too share rather a lot of the same symptoms and characteristics. We may have been suffering all of our lives with problems with focus, with mood swings, with sensory overload, with the need to be alone, with being overwhelmed.

We might have spent a lifetime judging ourselves as not being good enough at coping with life. Seeing the lightbulb moment when a diagnosis helps everything make sense for our child may help us also to understand our own life and challenges.

I cannot count how often I have heard parents say, 'I think I need to get diagnosed too' and many do then get their diagnoses after their children get theirs.

As our children's disabilities are on a spectrum, it is possible that we recognise traits and challenges in ourselves that are perhaps not severe enough to get us a diagnosis but have affected our lives nonetheless.

In my case I can see strong traits of both of my children's hidden disabilities in me. I need to spend a lot of time alone and get exhausted by too much contact with people. I become stressed and overwhelmed by noise and crowds. I shut down when I have to multitask or if I am not sure what people expect of me. I cannot read or spell easily but love to write and express my ideas.

I underachieved at school as I wanted to focus on my passions, not what was expected of me. I can see traits of Asperger's, ADD and dyslexia in myself. Realising this has helped me not only understand myself better, but also to have more understanding and empathy for my children.

This has clarified the choices I have had to make in my life, and that my children will also need to make lifestyle choices that *work with* rather than *against* their hidden disabilities.

In my case, if I spend a busy day with colleagues, although I enjoy it a lot I will need at least two days alone to recover. For this reason I cannot thrive in a career that requires daily human interaction. I do great when I am working from home, and thoroughly enjoy seeing colleagues and friends on a time frame that works for me.

I am very proud of my ASD traits and I have no problem with them at all if I am able to choose a lifestyle that works with them rather than against them. My ASD traits have given me a sharp focus in my chosen areas of expertise and are the reason for my success in these fields.

When I recognised my own hidden disability traits, I finally understood why certain areas of parenting were so difficult for me. All parents become exhausted and overwhelmed, but there were things that I found horrific that other parents seemed to cope with well.

Parenting is noisy. Soft play centres, water parks, kids' parties and places where there were many screaming children, often with added background music and splashing (water is sooo noisy) would tip me over the edge. The noise of such places was like a nightmare to me as the sounds reverberated around my brain until I felt I would explode. I would look at other parents chatting happily at these places and feel totally useless.

And the relentless 24-hour care is challenging to all parents, but if we have autistic traits, having no chance ever to be alone and to recharge our batteries can feel like torture. People would suggest I took a break to see friends or go to the cinema, but all I dreamed of was the chance to be in solitary confinement in a white room.

Parenting would have been much, much easier if I had understood these things at the time.

Can you see any traits of hidden disabilities in yourself or other family members, such as your spouse, parent or sibling? Can this help you be more understanding or compassionate with yourself and those people?

TALKING TO OUR CHILD ABOUT THE DIAGNOSIS

For our children to have a happy and productive life, they will need to accept themselves completely. This means accepting their many strengths while recognising their weaknesses and challenges.

Understanding their hidden disability is part of this as it is a part of who they are. This is why I believe they need to know.

At some point we will need to talk to our child about their diagnosis and we will need to use our judgement about the right age and time to do this.

Having gone through this myself with my own children, and spoken to countless other parents about this, some principles became very clear.

If we are going to encourage our child to accept their diagnosis in positive and empowering ways, we need to be sure that *we as parents* accept our child's diagnosis in a positive and empowering way.

If we are feeling bad about the diagnosis or negative or judgemental about our child, this is what we may pass on to our child when we talk to them. If we feel any shame or fear about the diagnosis, this is how our child is likely to feel about it too.

This is why we need to get ourselves clear before we can help our child to accept their diagnosis.

If we are having negative thoughts about the hidden disability, it does not mean that we are a mean or bad parent. Very few parents are going to feel good about their child having a hidden disability. Our highest hope is that our child will be healthy, so it is not surprising that we may feel very upset.

If you are having trouble coming to terms with your child's disability, I suggest you seek help with this. You may also find the companion book *How to Cope When Your Child Has a Hidden Disability: Self-Care for Parents* to be useful as it is about *our* needs and experiences when parenting a child with hidden disabilities.

Before we talk to her or him, we also need to remember that our child already has the hidden disability regardless of whether they know about it and regardless of whether they have a diagnosis. Not telling them about it will not make it go away.

When talking to our child, it can be very helpful to focus on the strengths of the hidden disability. This gives the weaknesses a context.

If our son has ADHD, we can be excited about what a fast thinker he is, how he is able to juggle so many passions, make clear decisions and get so much done. We can point out what a superpower ADHD can be and mention people that he admires who have ADHD. This sets the groundwork for him to accept the weaknesses and challenges too, that fast thinking can make him impatient and restless, that decisiveness may cause badly thought-out plans and recklessness, etc.

You may have heard the saying, 'Without darkness there can be no light.' Strengths and weaknesses are two sides of one coin. For our child this means they will need to accept the dark as well as the light.

If our daughter is on the autism spectrum, we can be excited about her amazing focus and passion about what matters most to her. We can love her creative way of thinking and ability to understand abstract problems. We can really appreciate her ability to see and say things as they are, without frills or fluff. This sets the context for the many challenges that ASD is also giving her.

If we cannot find any 'pluses' for our child's disability, we can focus on all the wonderful qualities our child has like kindness, sensitivity and bravery.

The diagnosis process, on the other hand, focuses on the weaknesses and ignores the strengths. This is because in order to make the diagnosis, enough symptoms need to be ticked off from a list and it has to be shown that our child is suffering severe incapacity as a result of these symptoms.

This negative focus is also necessary when we are looking for the support our child needs. We don't tend to look for support for the 'strength' aspects of our child's hidden disability, so these can easily be overlooked.

Hearing really negative words like 'deficit' and 'disorder' can be very frightening and upsetting. Even though a good clinician will balance this by drawing attention to the strengths, it is not surprising that our child may feel bad and judged by these words and not want them.

It is understandable that our child may feel ashamed of the diagnosis or not want to accept it. Most children desperately want to fit in and be like everyone else. They may be trying really hard to mask and disguise their disability in order to fit in. This is probably exhausting them and making their symptoms worse.

It makes sense that they may be angry or upset about the diagnosis and even angry with us for getting them assessed. It may take some time and maturity for them to come to accept themselves and their diagnosis fully, and the best we can do is be there to support them through this difficult process.

Another thing that I found may help is to tell our child about our own hidden disability traits in a positive way. For me personally, without my Asperger's and ADD traits I would never have had the drive and passion to become a published author and I would not change this about myself for the world. I failed at school because I did not have a diagnosis or understanding, and I would not want my own children to go through this.

Rebecca, who has two children with hidden disabilities, found this helped:

> I said to my son, 'Wow we're really alike in this way aren't we. I also really struggle with some things and I'm thinking of getting diagnosed too.' This normalised things so that it was not so frightening and scary.

It is also helpful to remind our child that the diagnosis is a tool *for them* and that they are in control about when they use it. They do not normally need to tell anyone about their diagnosis unless they choose to or if it will help. They are also free to disregard it if that is what feels right for them.

In these days of 'identity politics', it can be worth reminding our child that having a diagnosis is about recognising their *needs* and does not have to be an identity. They absolutely do not have to 'identify' as disabled.

I have a disability of my knees and to go up or down stairs I need a stair rail. This is a *need* and not who I am. For me, the disability is not my identity.

WHEN OUR CHILD DOES NOT ACCEPT THE DIAGNOSIS

Sometimes, no matter how positive we are about accepting and embracing a diagnosis, our child may not accept it.

It takes a lot of strength and self-confidence to accept something that other people may judge them for. This is especially true in the often-cruel world of childhood and school, where if they do not seem to fit in, our child may feel unsafe and unsupported.

Deborah, whose child is on the autism spectrum, was given this advice:

> My daughter won't accept her diagnosis and a specialist told me that she doesn't need to accept the label. If she acknowledges her difficulties and challenges that is enough.

This is a helpful tip. I would certainly do this if my child was very opposed to their diagnosis. However, in my opinion, accepting difficulties and challenges is not a substitute for having a diagnosis for all the reasons outlined earlier.

For many of our kids, the word 'neurodivergent' can be a better fit for them, as it expresses difference rather than disability. I totally get this and would generally use the word 'neurodivergent' myself in any situation where my child's disability needs, or mine, are not relevant.

So, a child who rejects an ASD diagnosis may agree and feel OK about being neurodivergent. This is absolutely fine as long as their genuine disability needs are not ignored.

However, when we are talking about disability *needs*, and are fighting to advocate for them, this is a time when we need to use the word *disability* and refer to the appropriate disability law in our country.

Ultimately, language is a toolkit. We and our children can choose the word that is the best fit for the particular situation and particular purpose. Knowing that they can choose which word to use and when, and that they are in control of this, can help our children better come to terms with a diagnosis.

Another option is that our child may accept some diagnoses more than others. In our image-conscious world of social media, some diagnoses are more 'socially acceptable' than others. Some attract less judgement and may even have positive connotations, making someone more 'interesting'. Sometimes this is because a celebrity has revealed a particular hidden disability diagnosis, immediately making it a desirable one to have.

A good example of this is bipolar disorder. At the time of writing, research has shown that it is the diagnosis most likely to be accepted by young people.[8] Although accounts in the media about the condition are often inaccurate, the fact that some celebrities have spoken openly about having this diagnosis has helped to destigmatise it.

So, if our child's diagnosis is not currently on the 'trendy list', things can change very quickly when someone popular with our child stands up proudly to talk about having it.

Another scenario is where our child recognises their difficulties but does not agree that their diagnosis is right. They may even later be proved to be correct. In this situation, they may choose to 'accept' a different diagnosis that feels like a better fit to them. This is fine on a day-to-day basis, although we still need to use their original diagnosis documentation when we are fighting or advocating to have their needs met.

Deborah found doing this helped her child:

> My daughter just came home from boarding school and has completely embraced the idea that she has ADHD even though her official diagnosis is autism. The ADHD label works well for her and we are going to go with that for as long as it works. The official autism diagnosis never fitted well with her but she is now acting on her instinct that she has ADHD and working on solutions to deal with her ADHD traits, which is very positive.

MULTIPLE DIAGNOSES

Many of us hope that when we manage to get a diagnosis for our child, their needs can finally be properly understood. But when the diagnosis finally comes, our understanding can be even more confused by multiple diagnoses.

Sometimes it never rains but it pours and our child may go overnight from not having a diagnosis at all to having five or more.

A news article reports a study from the *Journal of Autism and Developmental Disorders* that found that 95 per cent of kids on the autism spectrum also had conditions such as OCD, ADHD, and anxiety and mood disorders.[9] This research is far from conclusive, but it certainly highlights the issue.

Receiving multiple diagnoses for our child can be very frightening. Marisa was quite shocked when this happened:

> I had prepared my head for an ASD diagnosis, but when he got five other diagnoses as well I was totally overwhelmed and panicked. Was my son *that* bad, *that* complicated? Later I realised that it had nothing to do with how bad things were. It was just that his symptoms

overlapped into different categories and most were actually quite mild. It just gives a more complete picture of his needs.

Sometimes the different diagnoses may look like they clash. Let's take the most common pairing, autism spectrum disorders and ADHD, which look like they would produce opposite symptoms. We may have been told that our autism spectrum kids need less stimulation to keep them stable. Then we are told that ADHD kids need more stimulation to keep them focused. What do we do then if our child has both?

How do we cope if our child has OCD (obsessive compulsive disorder) and needs things to be precisely ordered, but at the same time also has ADHD which gives them significant problems in organising anything at all?

Then there is the extra issue of what is a symptom and what is a 'stand-alone' diagnosis? For example, OCD can be a *diagnosis* in its own right, or it can be a *symptom* of an anxiety disorder or of being on the autism spectrum.

How can parents possibly unpick such complicated and confusing needs in this situation? Should we even attempt to figure out which symptom or behaviour comes from which particular condition?

The rest of this book tackles exactly this question. While we absolutely need diagnoses, as parents we need to look beyond them and focus on what our child is trying to communicate with us by their behaviour and symptoms.

This is why the principle of decoding our children is so important. It works regardless of whether our child has one diagnosis, many diagnoses or no diagnosis at all.

Chapter 3

DECODING THE HIDDEN DISABILITY

LISTEN TO THE MUSIC AND NOT THE WORDS

We, as parents of kids with hidden disabilities, have challenges that are beyond the understanding of most families, resulting in just that, a lack of understanding. In the same way, our children are themselves living challenges every day that are beyond the understanding of most 'healthy' people, often including their own families and this includes us.

For our children, their hidden disability is only one of their challenges.

In addition to their hidden disability, they are often dealing with:

- the lack of understanding of their needs by a range of professionals
- the lack of help by teachers, doctors and others in positions of authority
- a lifestyle, such as a school routine, that may make their hidden disability worse
- the judgement and often cruel behaviour of others towards them, including bullying
- the inability to change these things, which are usually out of their control

- the fear that this will never end and that there is no hope.

If we are going to 'get' our kids, we need to see how the hidden disability interacts with these additional challenges. Let's call these additional challenges 'the extras'. What our children experience every day and what we see in their behaviour can be summed up as:

hidden disability + the extras = behaviour

Before looking at how this jigsaw can fit together, we need to start with the hidden disability itself.

As we know, 'hidden disabilities' can refer to many different conditions that produce a range of symptoms and behaviours. They are also likely to have different causes and need a range of different treatments.

Unlike a mental illness, which can be acquired by having a traumatic experience, our children's disabilities are largely biological and inherited.

There are a range of diagnoses out there and the ones that are chosen for our child are rarely clear-cut. There is a lot of overlap of symptoms between the different diagnoses. For example, meltdowns and mood swings are common in autism spectrum conditions, ADHD and bipolar disorder.

The diagnosis our child gets is made by a clinical assessment of symptoms and behaviours. At this time, hidden disabilities are rarely diagnosed through biological markers in blood tests or brain scans although science is moving fast on this. This means that our child's diagnosis will be a clinical *opinion* rather than a *fact*. As we know, people can have different opinions, even doctors!

The result is that our child may receive a number of different diagnoses during their life. Which is chosen could depend on the symptoms that are strongest at the time of assessment, or it could depend on the expertise of the particular doctor carrying out the assessment. The choice may even depend on where we live, especially where different diagnostic guidelines are used. For example, a number of UK clinicians have told me that they would be reluctant to assess for childhood bipolar, pointing out that this may well be different in the US.

Even children with exactly the same diagnosis may show a range of different symptoms. They may also react very differently to the things that trigger their disabilities. For example, the same condition can cause aggression in one person and withdrawal or self-harm in another. One child's autism may cause them to talk incessantly, while another's may cause them to become mute.

You may have heard the expression, 'When you have met a person with Asperger's, you have met *one* person with Asperger's.'

I believe that this is equally true for all hidden disabilities. In fact, it is also true for all people, regardless of whether or not they have a disability. We all respond to things differently. Any parent will be able to point out just how different their children are, especially how some are more sensitive than others.

The main point here is that knowing our child's diagnosis is not enough for us to 'get' them. It is a great starting point, but we need to look beyond the diagnosis to understand what our children are feeling and what behaviours and symptoms this produces.

This is especially important for the many, many children with hidden disabilities who do not have a diagnosis or who have one that we believe is inaccurate.

Whatever our child's diagnosis, their hidden disability is likely to make the world a very threatening and frightening place. Their symptoms, regardless of the specific diagnosis, are also likely to affect how able they are to cope with these challenges. Dealing with judgey people and bullying is tough enough for anyone, but if they also suffer from severe anxiety and depression, these same challenges can become overwhelming for our kids.

The result is a state of severe and ongoing emotional and often physical pain. Regardless of their specific disability, this is something most of our loved ones have in common.

Many parents are also in emotional pain due to the stress of raising children with hidden disabilities. This is something we have in common with our children. Recognising our own pain can give us some empathy with what they are dealing with.

Our own emotional pain can be so overwhelming that it can blind us from seeing and connecting with what our children are going through. This was certainly the case for me. The fact that we may be struggling emotionally with parenting our child does not mean that we are weak or selfish, it means that we are normal. Research has shown that raising a child with a hidden disability causes the same amount of stress hormones to circulate in the body as soldiers in combat.[1] Few people would accuse soldiers of being weak.

This is why it is so important to recognise and treat our own emotional pain at the same time as we are trying to support our children with theirs. Finding ways to do this led me to write the companion book *How to Cope When Your Child Has a Hidden Disability: Self-Care for Parents*, which is about how we can hold it together emotionally when we are caring for our kids with hidden disabilities.

The most helpful advice I heard on how to understand what my child was going through was: 'Listen to the music and not the words.'

These words changed everything for me and have guided my parenting ever since. I got a lot wrong when I was parenting my children with hidden disabilities, but most of what I got right has come from the wisdom of these eight simple words.

What it means is that our child's symptoms, behaviours and words can be *clues* to understanding them. When we are able to see what they are *doing* as clues, we can use our intelligence to try to decode them. Doing this can be like a puzzle, where we need to figure out what the clues mean.

What do we mean by music and words? The *words* are the things our child does or says. When our son says he hates us or is hitting us, these are words. When our daughter is cutting herself, these are words. If our child is destroying the work of another child, this is a word.

In contrast, the *music* is the feeling that is behind the words and shows what the child is really trying to communicate, even if he does not know it. The music could be trying to say, 'I'm really scared' or 'I can't take any more.' For some children, the music could be 'I'm really frustrated' or 'I'm absolutely exhausted.' By learning to hear the *music*, we can develop a real understanding of our child's experience.

The words can be very painful for us to hear as parents, especially when they are disrespectful or really hurtful. The music is less painful. Although we may be upset to know that our child is feeling the way she is, until we can hear the music, we will not be able to respond to our child's needs.

When we are able to hear the music, our child's words will wound us less and make us less angry. This is because we are now able to understand them in the context of the whole musical score.

This is why we need to learn to listen to our children's *music* as a priority. This helps both us and our child to suffer less and understand each other more.

All of this may seem pretty obvious, but it actually goes against much of what we are taught to do as parents. It also goes against our instinct to defend ourselves or fight back when we are under attack.

It can feel outrageous not to react when our child is being disrespectful or is hurting us. It is natural to want to defend ourselves at this time. It is normal to want to force our child to acknowledge that what they are doing is wrong. We may want apologies from them. We may want to punish them and for justice to be done. We may feel that they need to learn right now that what they are doing is unacceptable and to stop it ever happening again. We are parents. We deserve respect and we have our pride.

It is extremely difficult not to react to 'the words'. In fact, we have to be a saint not to do so. I am committed to listening to the music and not the words, but if the words happen when I am tired or overwhelmed, I do still react to them and say and do things that I later regret. We are not saints and we can only do our best.

Meanwhile, a lot of parenting advice is telling us to respond to the words and not the music. We may have been told to 'get tougher' with our kids and to 'teach them a lesson'. We will probably have been told to 'be consistent', which is not all that logical when our children's hidden disability symptoms are not consistent.

When we listen to the music not the words, being consistent takes on a different meaning. It means that instead of having consistent 'consequences' for particular behaviours, we may instead have consistent responses to particular feelings. So, we may have something we consistently do whenever we know our child is exhausted, or frightened or having a panic attack.

Does listening to the music not the words mean we don't call out or discipline bad behaviour?

The answer to this depends on the music we are able to hear when we learn how to decode our child. The key to determining this is learning to understand and decode our child's behaviour.

There may absolutely be times when it is appropriate and right to call out and discipline the child and other times when doing so will make things very much worse.

In some situations, imposing a 'consequence' can teach our child not to do a particular thing, resulting in them not doing it or doing it less. In other situations, the consequence does not teach the child anything and results in them doing the behaviour more. Our child's behaviour can be the same, the consequence can be the same but the effect of the consequence can be the exact opposite at times. This is really confusing to parents who are trying to be consistent.

For example, a 'time out' may sometimes work well when our child is rude to us. They may learn not to speak to us disrespectfully and be less rude in future. But at other times the 'time out' can turn the rudeness into a full-on verbal and physical assault on us, one that is repeated more and more no matter which consequences we impose. How can the same consequence improve behaviour sometimes and add fuel to the fire at other times? Why do they sometimes learn from the consequences and sometimes not?

The difference is that although the behaviour and consequence may be the same in each case, the music is completely different.

One way to start to understand the difference is to think of how we would respond if our child's disability was visible. Imagine our child has epilepsy and is hitting out during a seizure. Would we punish them for hitting out (the words) or focus on preventing the seizure (the music)? If our child curses when they fall off their bike and break their leg, would we focus on the cursing (the words) or the broken leg (the music)?

Our instincts may tell us that we should back off from calling out our child's words when we can see that she is about to explode into a meltdown. We may know that we shouldn't impose a consequence when our child is in the middle of a panic attack. But it can be very hard to put aside our righteous anger.

It takes a huge amount of willpower and courage to listen to the music and not the words. To do it well involves learning to be an expert code breaker.

HOW TO BE AN EXPERT CODE BREAKER

Expert code breakers are at work behind the scenes in our countries trying to keep us safe from threats to hurt us. Great code-breaking can be decisive in who wins a war. For example, we know that the cracking of the Enigma secret German code had a big impact on the outcome of the Second World War.

To crack a code, the code breaker needs to look at the clues dispassionately. They do not only decode the parts that they agree with and ignore the codes that they disagree with or are offended by.

Before making a judgement about whether the message is good or bad, they first need to be sure that they have decoded and understood it correctly. And they certainly cannot plan a course of action until the code is broken.

It may seem obvious, but exactly the same applies to us.

One of the biggest barriers to cracking our children's codes is that we may be judging the code as either good or bad *before* we have decoded it.

We may even believe that if we try to *understand* their code, we are in some way condoning the behaviour.

Understanding something does not mean that we condone or agree with it.

Our children's codes can include meltdowns, shutdowns, aggressive behaviour, school refusal, defiance, food fussiness and computer game obsessions to name but a few. As we get better at code-breaking we will be better able to know which of our children's behaviours are codes.

Just as the code breakers need to look at codes coldly, without emotion or judgement, we need to do the same. This means that no matter how outrageous or 'wrong' our child's behaviour is, we need to suspend judgement while we are decoding it. This is temporary until the code has been cracked.

Our children are in a state of confusion and turmoil. If we ask them why they are doing or saying the upsetting things, they will probably say that they do not know. This is almost certainly honest. Our son will probably not know why he is refusing to do his homework or feels a compulsion to break all the eggs in the refrigerator. Our daughter may not know why she will only eat food that is the colour beige.

They may have no idea what they are experiencing, let alone why it is happening. They simply do not have the language, communication skills or understanding to give us an accurate answer. Why should they? If we don't understand what is happening in their world as competent adults, how can we expect them as children to do so?

It is *our* job to try to figure it all out, and then when the timing is right to help them understand themselves better too. They speak to us in codes as it is the only way they know.

The idea of *suspending judgement* can be very difficult and controversial, especially if we are dealing with negative, destructive or even abusive behaviours. How do we suspend judgement about a child who is hitting us, stealing from us or telling us she hates us?

This is difficult, especially when we are taught to divide behaviour into 'good' and 'bad' and to reward the 'good behaviour' and ignore or punish the 'bad'.

This is our challenge. We have to take our hand out of the fire in order to see and heal the burn.

There is often a misunderstanding about what suspending judgement actually means. It does not mean that we are being weak or passive. In fact it is the opposite, we are putting ourselves into the role of a fair and open-minded judge who needs to hear every side of the story before handing down the verdict.

If we have an unhappy dog or a crying baby, we would not expect them to express their pain through calm, measured language and judge them when they are not able to do so. We would look for clues in their behaviour. As we don't speak 'dog' or 'baby' we may often get it wrong, but with patience and practice we will increasingly get it right.

As an example, I didn't initially get it right last night with my dog

Ruby. I was very busy with my work and Ruby would not stop whining, barking and disturbing me. I kept shouting at her to be quiet as she has been taught to stop barking on command, but on this occasion it seemed to make her worse. She would not let me work and I was enraged by this. I angrily got up to chastise her, then noticed to my shame that she was barking by the door and trying to open it with her paws as she desperately needed the toilet. She had an upset stomach and was unable to wait for her usual toilet times. I had made the mistake of listening to the words and not the music! I had judged her behaviour before trying to understand what she was trying to communicate. I had let emotion prevent me from being a good code breaker.

Part of code-breaking is to remember that as well as decoding the music, sometimes we really do need to focus on the words as well. Our child may be telling us that they are being bullied or that a particular situation has upset them. If we are not careful, we may be so focused on our child's feelings and the context that we may miss the critical words they are saying.

THE PRESSURE COOKER

Whatever our child's diagnosis or the cause of their emotional pain, they are likely to experience what can be called the *pressure cooker effect*. Learning how to 'see' the amount of steam in our child's pressure cooker is the number one skill to master when learning to decode them.

If you have ever used a pressure cooker, the comparison will be pretty obvious. If not, you will need to use your imagination. As the heat is turned up on a pressure cooker, steam builds up inside. This creates pressure inside the cooker. If you try to remove the lid when the pressure is still high, the pressure cooker will explode. When this happens, it will hurl all of its contents into the room, onto the walls and ceiling, and probably all over you too, burning you pretty badly in the process.

There is only one safe way to open a pressure cooker and that is to reduce the steam first. Pressure cookers have a valve on their lids for this and pressure can also be reduced by turning off the heat until the pressure is low. When the steam has cooled down, it is then safe to open the lid and to enjoy a harmonious meal with the beautifully cooked contents inside.

In the case of our children, the stresses of their day-to-day lives is the build-up of heat and pressure which accumulates as the day progresses. If a critical point of no return is reached, an explosion is inevitable and often happens as they walk through the door on their return from school.

This can take the form of an outward explosion like a rage, meltdown or aggression, or an internal one like withdrawal, obsessive or self-harming behaviours or defiance.

As with the pressure cooker, there are only two ways to prevent this from happening. One is to keep the heat turned down during our child's day by avoiding all stress triggers. The second is to make sure that our child has a 'pressure valve' to let the steam escape. Both are likely to be very difficult for our child, especially if they are in mainstream schools where what happens to them there is largely out of our control.

At school, other people may not realise how high our child's pressure has reached. Only those who know our child well will have the code-breaking skills needed to read their pressure gauges.

As our child's disabilities are hidden, people are likely to be unaware of how noise, crowds, changing expectations, stifling boredom, deadlines, lack of rest, social isolation and bullying may affect our child.

Children with physical hidden disabilities such as colitis or diabetes are also affected. They may be in terror of missing a toilet break or a chance to eat and be struggling to hold it all together.

Our children can become absolutely exhausted by the task of trying to cope and fit in.

In the simplest terms, our children's pressure cooker explodes when the amount of stress and exhaustion is bigger than the available coping skills at that moment.

Understanding the pressure cooker is critical to 'getting' our child's experience and explains why their symptoms can vary so much from day to day, and even within each day.

To really 'get' how the pressure cooker principle works, it can help to hear what it feels like from someone who is living it. Michelle Myers describes it beautifully in her blog:

> Imagine yourself as a bottle of pop. Your ingredients include autism, sensory processing difficulties, ADHD, and a hidden speech and language delay. The world's a confusing place, and your difficulties are largely hidden to the wider world, so not many people understand things from your perspective.
>
> This is your day:
>
> - Going to school is just one big worry for you... so give that bottle a shake!
> - You get to school and your teacher says, 'Let's start a new topic.' What does that mean? ... Give it a shake!
> - You don't understand what you have to do... shake it up!
> - You make a mistake... shake, shake, shake!
> - The lights in class are buzzing, and it's annoying or painful... shake it a little more!
> - It's assembly. You have to sit still while your insides are wiggling and jiggling around... shake it up!
> - The timetable changes and it's not math like it should be, it's now music... and shake again!
> - The car gets stuck in traffic, and the wrong radio station is on in the car... that's a few more shakes!
> - You get home and the lid blows off with the pressure! That's the delayed effect. It's a real thing.[2]

We need to remember that stress is not only about difficult or unpredictable things happening. Many kids are stressed by things *not* happening, especially those on the ADHD spectrum who may be bored senseless when their interests are not stimulated and when they are unable to expend their energy. This frustration can feel like many, many shakes of the bottle of pop.

The pressure cooker principle explains why our child may 'appear' to be holding it together at school, only to melt down or fall apart as soon as they get home. We know that the pressure often explodes towards the end of term or during transitions to school holidays. We know it happens in supermarkets and on public transport. And the prize place for it to happen is family gatherings, especially when the most judgey members of our family are present.

When the pressure cooker blows, parents are often blamed personally and told by teachers and other parents that this is due to poor parenting and a lack of boundaries and discipline at home.

There is often a mistaken idea that for our child's behaviour to be a symptom of their hidden disability, it must consistently occur all the time and in all situations. Rosy, mum to an Asperger's daughter, was told by her mother:

> If she can go to school there can be *no reason* why she cannot go to a noisy, crowded restaurant in the evening. Her autism is not an excuse, otherwise the same problem would occur all the time.

This misunderstanding also results in families not being believed when they ask schools to turn down the pressure during the day. Many of us have been told by teachers, 'He is absolutely fine here so there is no problem to deal with.'

Sometimes our children do not make it home before the pressure cooker explodes and it happens at school, perhaps as a violent outburst against another child or the frustrated destruction of property.

Due to a lack of understanding of the pressure cooker principle, I have seen many, many parents blamed and shamed personally for this by teachers who assume that poor or inconsistent parenting is the cause. Not only are we blamed. Very often our child may also be blamed and shamed personally when he is unable to prevent his pressure cooker from exploding.

Michelle Myers describes this idea that symptoms should occur all the time in order to be taken seriously:

> The times over the years I've felt so confused and isolated when teachers have said to me, 'Well, that is a surprise. We don't see any of that here at school.'
>
> Or I've heard, 'Well, he can behave for me, so maybe you're being too soft on him.'
>
> I spent many a sleepless night wondering if it was me. Was it my parenting? My child explodes at home with me because I'm his safe place. I am predictable and calm, and he can really be himself at home. He is fully accepted at home.[3]

Just like our children, we also have an internal pressure cooker. In fact everyone does. Some people are better able than others to withstand more heat before we blow. Our own pressure cooker can explode from the ongoing pressure of parenting a child with a hidden disability, along with all the other 'normal' stresses of life, work pressures, relationships, difficult people and situations.

Most of us somehow manage to hold it together at work, even with abusive bosses, and then explode in rage on the way home at a driver who cuts us up. Or we hold it in all day but find that the pressure blows when we get home and we let it out by being mean or impatient with our partners and children.

We all know that feeling when we simply cannot take any more. There are times when we have simply run out of energy and coping skills. All parents sometimes 'lose it', as all human beings can only take so much pressure.

Like our children, we 'lose it' when there is too much pressure and not enough coping skills available to us at a particular moment. Some parents have more coping skills than others. Even parents with great coping skills can find they are not sufficient when they are really exhausted or overwhelmed.

Remembering how we felt when we have exploded can help us to understand what our child is dealing with. We can remember how powerful it feels when our pressure gauge is heading to 'code red' and we know that we cannot stop it. For us this will, we hope, only happen occasionally. For our child it may be happening every day.

Every time I have lost it with my family, I felt really ashamed afterwards, as 'good' parents are supposed always to have everything under control. The shame would make me want to pretend it hadn't happened and I hoped that my children would not remember the episodes.

Just like us, our children can feel very ashamed when their pressure cooker explodes. Due to the shame, they might also want to pretend it hasn't happened and be pretty resentful if we remind them about what they did or said during the explosion.

UNDERSTANDING MELTDOWNS AND RAGES

When we are learning to listen to the music rather than the words, it is easiest to start with the times when the music is the loudest. For many families, this will be meltdowns and rages when the music can be deafening. Shutdowns are just as extreme, as the music can appear to be eerily silent.

When we know how to decode the extremes, meltdowns and shutdowns, we can then move on to the advanced skills of decoding when the music is quieter. These advanced code-breaking skills are talked about in the following chapters.

A meltdown happens when our child's pressure cooker explodes. That's basically it and it doesn't take a lot of decoding. Understanding this changed everything for me. Up until this point, I was being encouraged to see meltdowns as 'bad behaviour' to be punished or to see them as a sign that I was a weak or ineffective mother.

We can generally see from our child's body language that they are about to blow as the pressure gets past the point of no return. The explosion when it happens can last many hours and can include screaming, ranting, destroying items at home, including their own prized possessions, and sometimes physical violence towards us or their siblings. It is a terrifying thing to watch, especially when it goes on for a long time. We may not know what to do and we may feel that everyone is unsafe.

Meltdowns are an even more terrifying time for our loved one, as they are experiencing a total breakdown of control and saying and doing things that they neither mean nor intend to do.

People who had meltdowns as children describe feeling that their bodies have been taken over by a force they cannot control. They are likely to feel intense shame and fear afterwards, but simply may not have the tools or ability to prevent the rages from happening. Much as we may try to reason with our loved one during a meltdown, although they may hear our voice, they are unlikely to be able to process or make sense of what we are saying.

I will be talking about how we can respond to rages in Chapter 6, but here we need to understand why rages, meltdowns and shutdowns happen and how they feel for our loved ones.

A pressure cooker exploding is not a wilful or defiant act and our loved ones do not choose to melt down.

Meltdowns are extreme symptoms of the hidden disability and need the same love, compassion and understanding as any other medical symptom. We should no more shame a child for having a meltdown than we would shame a child for having an epileptic seizure.

THE HOOK

Many parents find that when the pressure cooker explodes, our child accuses and blames us. They may shout that they hate us, say it is all our fault, and may even try to physically attack us.

The feeling of injustice at being blamed by the person we have devoted our life to supporting stings very sharply. It is very hard indeed not to react to this with righteous indignation. To help us not to take any of this personally, it really helps to understand about 'the hook'.

Very often, our loved one may point to something that is 'wrong' at home, or that we 'did wrong' and make this the 'reason' for the explosion and therefore our fault. For example, the 'wrong' food may be served, a possession of theirs may have been moved by us, or someone had unexpectedly come to the house. On other occasions, a sibling may be the target of blame, accused of touching or ruining something, or simply stated as being the cause of all their suffering.

Sometimes we or the sibling will have genuinely done something wrong and it is understandable how this can add heat to our child's pressure cooker. But this is unlikely to be the cause of the meltdown.

Sometimes a meltdown is triggered by our child hearing the word 'no'.

The things that are 'wrong' are the 'hook' that the anger or defiance is hung on. It is very tempting and very easy to believe that this hook is the *actual reason* for the explosion. We can get sucked in to our child's story about the 'reason' and feel enraged about the injustice of our child's accusations, even if there is some truth to them.

We may believe that the explosion is really about the wrong food, the refused toy or the fact that we said 'no' or whatever the hook is on that occasion. We may believe that if only we can get everything 'perfect' at home, with the right food, itch-free socks and no unexpected visitors, our child's explosions may stop and that it is our duty and responsibility to make this happen.

It is easy for a parent to react instinctively at these times, to want to fight back and demand reasonableness and justice from our child. Sometimes a meltdown can be the final bit of pressure needed to push our own pressure cookers to explode. The result of everyone's pressure cooker exploding all at once is quite a mess, often quite literally when things get thrown around and broken, and also an emotional mess as everyone loses control.

We need to be mindful of 'the hook' and not engage with it, at least not during the explosion itself.

The hook may be what feels like the final straw to our child, regardless of whether the issue is right or wrong, and may be the result of hundreds or thousands of accumulated emotional assaults they have felt during the day.

It is the hundreds or thousands of emotional assaults that are the real issue for our child, and their lack of ability to process or deal with them.

We are just the outlet for their steam. Understanding what our child may be experiencing at these times helps us to avoid *personalising* what on the surface appear to be very personal and wounding attacks on us.

It also helps to stop us from focusing on 'the hook', rather than what our child is really feeling. The hook is the words, it is not the music.

Here is a letter about 'the hook' written to her parents by Chloe Estelle, who has Asperger's, published in her wonderful blog. The piece is called 'Dear Mom & Dad, This Is Why I Can't Stand You', which is a wonderful title. I was particularly moved by what she writes about doing it out of love. Seeing meltdowns and extreme defiance as an expression of love really helps parents to see the bigger picture, and Chloe's posts have helped me so much to understand and develop more compassion for the experiences of children with hidden disabilities.

Dear Mom and Dad,

Never once in my life have I ever thought that my mom or my dad was the bad guy. You guys have always been my mom and dad, not the enemy.

So, I'm imagining the days that I came home from school. Throughout the day, the world reinforced these ideas that 'I am not capable.' All day I had to stifle these emotions and be in a loud sensory filled environment. My breaks were not breaks. I didn't get to curl up for a few minutes in my safe space. Instead I had to walk among 100 other kids who were all yelling over each other and pushing each other about.

So I come home exhausted and overwhelmed to a mom or a dad that I know believes I am capable. To a parent who will never leave no matter what I do, unlike my so called friends at school. I know that I can let all my anger and frustration out on my parents and everything is going to be okay when I'm done. In the strangest way, I yell and scream and call my parents names out of love. I kick and punch at my parents in the way that I wish I could kick and scream at my teachers and my principal and the bullies at school. I take my anger and frustration and fears out on my parents.

Now, I don't know in the moment that's what I'm doing. I feel this strong urge to get my emotions out anyway that I can.

It feels good to scream and kick and punch. Afterwards, when you come and ask me what you did wrong, I'll say 'I don't know.' Because you did nothing wrong. The reason that I blame you is because you do everything right. I can't blame anyone else, not to their face. If I do, I don't trust that they will still be there when I'm done screaming and kicking and punching.

Now, I know in these moments you are going to forget that I told you I do this out of love and it won't make any sense. I know it's still wrong to do this. I feel guilty afterwards every time, but I also don't know how to cope. But I will learn. You will teach me how. Looking back, I understand all of this. In the moment, I don't understand any of what I'm doing. Hopefully you will.

With love, your child
Chloe Estelle[4]

Although this brilliant letter is written by a person with Asperger's, we see similar scenarios play out where people with the full range of hidden disabilities lash out in this way against the people who love and care for them most.

No matter what the disability is, our children's lives are likely to be challenged to the core. Due to the disability's invisibility, it is often only we, the parents, who are fully able to 'see' the disability, 'get it' and love our children anyway. The fact that we can fully see them makes us the safest outlet for their fury.

This does not make their behaviour 'right' in any way, but it makes it possible to understand it. When there is understanding, we can open the door to working on strategies to help our child manage their pressure cooker. Most importantly, we can also work on strategies to help us to not to be so upset and enraged by what is happening with our children.

When we fully 'get' how the pressure cooker works, and how anger is 'hooked' onto seemingly trivial things, it also makes it easier for us to deal with judgemental comments from teachers, other parents or family members. When other people don't understand the pressure cooker, they may accuse and blame us for causing our child's explosions and anger through a lack of discipline or for 'letting them get away with it'.

When we are clear about what is really happening, it becomes easier to ignore or challenge the judgements of other people.

PROJECTIONS

Although psychology terms can be quite irritating, *projection* is one that is very useful to help us to understand what may be happening when we are under attack verbally from our children.

The idea is that when we really do not like something about ourselves, we may accuse others of that thing and condemn them for it. For example, a man who is insecure about his weight may point out the physical imperfections in others.

A girl who says, 'You are so ugly' to another child could mean that she fears that she herself is ugly. We all do this to some extent as a way of dumping emotions we do not want to feel onto others so that we do not have to deal with them.

Not surprisingly, our children with hidden disabilities are particularly susceptible to blaming or criticising us for things that they are not able to deal with in themselves. This is not because of any weakness in them, but because they have so much more to deal with than most children.

So sometimes when our child says, 'I really hate you', it could mean that at that moment they are really hating themselves. 'You are a terrible mother', could mean that they feel that they are a terrible child. 'I wish you were dead', could mean that they are having suicidal thoughts about themselves.

Being aware of this helps us to take verbal attacks less personally as often what is being said is not about us at all and is a coded way of saying how our child is feeling about themselves. This can help us to stay compassionate rather than jump into righteous anger about how our child is disrespecting us.

We do need some caution when deciding that something that has been said is a projection! It can be very patronising indeed when a valid criticism of someone is dismissed as a projection. What our child is saying about us may actually be valid. We need to have the humility to accept that our child may be right sometimes when they criticise us, or at least partly right. Our code-breaking skills will hopefully help us to determine when this is the case.

UNDERSTANDING SHUTDOWNS

Sometimes when the steam in the pressure cooker builds up to being unendurable, the explosion happens *inwards* rather than outwards. In these cases, instead of our loved one having a meltdown or rage, they instead go into shutdown.

People who are in shutdown appear frozen, unresponsive and unable to carry out any activities. Very often the ability to speak or communicate shuts down too and the person may become non-verbal. They are also likely to become overwhelmed with tiredness and may fall asleep or even faint. Listening is also shut down, so even if they are able to hear us speaking to them, perhaps to talk them out of their shutdown, they are unlikely to be able to process what we are saying.

Shutdowns happen when a person is overwhelmed by the world around them. Everything is just too much and they are unable to cope or deal with the sheer amount of information being presented to them at the same time. We need to remember that 'information' here includes noise, images, conversation, expectations and changes to schedules. As their pressure cooker is steaming up, they may be told to 'just carry on' and somehow be expected to study, know what to do and deal with other people.

During a shutdown, everything short circuits as it is all too much. The only way they can deal with the pressure is to pull the plug. Like an overheating kettle, this immediately cuts out the heat and switches them off.

Shutdown is rather like a poorly configured computer having too many applications open at once. Sometimes there are hidden applications working in the background that are robbing the computer of processing powers. When too much is open, the whole computer can crash and freeze as it cannot cope with it all.

It is very important to understand what is happening when our child is shut down. Again, the best people to learn from are those who go through it. Max Sparrow chillingly describes a shutdown:

> My most recent shutdown started off as a meltdown. My brain was going through all its usual short-circuits when some synaptic gap got crossed, or something. One minute I was out of control, smacking myself in the face, as one does, and the next minute I was on the floor, unable to move. I started to get tunnel vision. My hearing began to get fuzzy. My vision closed and closed like turning off an old tube-driven television, closing down to a tiny dot of light that winked out just as my hearing entirely cut out, leaving me alone in the numbly terrifying darkness.[5]

This helps us to decode and understand shutdown in a meaningful way. It is not usually defiance, stubbornness, laziness or 'bad behaviour' as many would have us believe. It makes perfect sense when we understand it as our child's pressure cooker exploding inwards.

UNDERSTANDING PROTECTION MODE

When we can decode the extremes, we are ready to pick up more subtle clues. When our child's pressure is building up in their pressure cooker but is not at a level where it is going to explode, many other codes present themselves.

While a meltdown or shutdown can be decoded as 'my child's pressure cooker has exploded', the more subtle codes can be understood as 'my child's pressure cooker is overheating'.

Sometimes these are signs that a meltdown or shutdown is imminent.

It is also very common for our child's pressure gauge to get stuck at a hot level. It may not be hot enough to explode, but certainly hot enough to cause a range of symptoms and behaviours. When the pressure build-up is high, our child will be suffering and her behaviours can be the clues that this is happening.

The guys from the Asperger Experts use the term 'defence mode' to describe this in relation to Asperger's syndrome. They describe it as:

> a state of overwhelm in which someone with Asperger's is scared, frustrated, or angry, as well as shut down and withdrawn.[6]

This is very helpful indeed and I believe that we can take this idea further to include *all* hidden disabilities, as well as how we feel when our pressure cookers are stuck on a high heat. For this reason I will use the term 'protection mode'.

Protection mode means that our child is trying to *protect* themselves against what feels like a threatening situation. Although they might not be in actual danger, their body may be reacting as if it is. So as the stressors build up, anxiety kicks in and the body reacts as if it were a *life-threatening situation*.

Although the threats are rarely life threatening, the brain chemically sees them as such. As the threats build up on top of each other, the result is that there is simply too much to process at once.

When our child is in protection mode, they will be spending all of their emotional energy on fighting their feelings, the outside world and anything that they feel is threatening. This will give them very little leftover energy for day-to-day functioning.

Our children may be spending a considerable part of their lives in protection mode. They are living with an ongoing stress response, also called 'fight or flight', which severely affects their ability to behave as they would if they were not in protection mode.

Protection mode is caused by stress hormones. It is a biological and chemical reaction to things in their lives that are stressing them out. Our child cannot simply 'choose' not to have these chemicals running through their bodies. Protection mode cannot be 'disciplined' out of our child. As we learn to decode their clues, there are many strategies that can help. As our child learns to understand herself better, she will also be able to decode the clues and take action both to get and to keep herself out of protection mode.

Regardless of their diagnosis, being in protection mode will make their symptoms more extreme. So, if our child has a psychotic condition, protection mode may cause more hallucinations than usual. If she has ADHD, she may be more hyperactive than usual. If he has

OCD, he may be washing his hands even more than usual. A child with anxiety may become unable to leave her room.

There are also other clues. Protection mode affects a lot of other behaviours too. We can often see obsessions, including food and clothing obsessions, tics, computer game addictions, obsessive hygiene or lack of hygiene, self-harm, drug and alcohol misuse, theft and various 'bizarre' behaviours and habits. Our children may fall into low-level depressions, become anxious over 'trivial' issues or may refuse to go to school or do homework. The range of possible responses to protection mode are endless.

We also need to remember that for some children, a major stressor is boredom and frustration. Our kids can be very fast thinkers and get very stressed when lessons at school move too slowly or are not stimulating enough for them. This can show itself in disruptive and defiant behaviour, while others may become depressed.

Obviously, all of these behaviours are very complicated and have many causes. Not everything challenging our child does is due to protection mode. But as we learn to read and understand our child better, we will get better at recognising when it is.

When we understand the clues of protection mode, many of our children's behaviours start to make more sense. Understanding this does not mean that we agree with or accept the behaviour. But as soon as we are able to see the behaviours as *symptoms* of our child's hidden disability, they become much easier to deal with.

Chapters 6 and 7 suggest strategies to help our child both to get out and stay out of protection mode. When they are out of protection mode, many if not most of these challenging symptoms or behaviours disappear, or at least become manageable.

That is when we get to see who our child really is.

To really 'get' what protection mode feels like, again it is really helpful to listen to people who are living it. Danny Raede, who has Asperger's and is CEO of Asperger Experts, explains, using his term 'defence mode':

> When I was deep in defense mode, it felt like I was constantly overwhelmed. It felt like I was constantly being attacked. Every single

> little thing, whether or not it actually had a logical, rational basis for being threatening, changed and colored my entire perspective. So for example: A pen could be threatening in defense mode, not because somebody is throwing it at you, but just because it is there, and seeing it triggers you in some way.[7]

Decoding protection mode can help us to be less judgemental, more patient and, we hope, more compassionate. It can also help us find strategies to help our child that actually work.

To help us understand what protection mode feels like for our children, it is helpful to think about how it affects us. Because of our stress as parents of a child with a hidden disability, we may also be in protection mode for much of the time. As adults, our 'clues' may be more subtle to decode. We may not be having spectacular meltdowns or be refusing to get out of bed. We will have coping skills that our children have not yet learned and we may be better at controlling our emotions.

As we learn more about our child, it is likely that we will learn more about ourselves too and how we react when our pressure cooker gauge is stuck. This may also help us learn more about our spouse and other members of our family who may also get caught up in protection mode.

We and our children may be embroiled in a complex soup of fear, be overwhelmed, shut down, explode and be trying to feel safe. Add a huge dose of love into the mix and the stakes rise off the scales. We are all in this together. They blame us. We blame them. Basically, we all have to get ourselves out of protection mode!

STRESS HORMONES AND PROTECTION MODE

When our child is in protection mode, they are likely to have an excess of stress hormones such as cortisol and adrenaline in their bodies.

Even if they are not literally in 'fight or flight' mode for survival, there are many levels of threat where stress hormones are released into the body.

Stress hormones are a necessary and normal way to keep us safe and efficient. We all need a little extra adrenaline to help us to cross a busy and difficult road. Many of us perform better when we are under pressure. The dump of stress hormones before an exam can give us the extra drive we need. The adrenaline from a work deadline can give us the rush of energy we need to meet it.

As our children have hidden disabilities, they are likely to be wired somewhat differently from neurotypical children. This means that things we may not expect can cause them to have stress responses. Activities that seem totally manageable to us, like going to a supermarket, can cause a dump of stress hormones for them that can tip them over the edge.

While a neurotypical child may be motivated by a deadline, for a child on the autism spectrum the rush of stress hormones may have the opposite effect. It may paralyse them or send them into a full-on fight or flight response.

Most neurotypical children can cope with a level of boredom. But for a child with ADD, being under-stimulated can cause a level of distress which may only be relieved by disrupting the class.

So, as parents we have quite a big challenge on our hands. While a doctor has the benefit of blood tests to know our child's stress hormone levels at a given moment, we will have to achieve the same thing by using our decoding skills alone. Simply from watching and listening to our child we need to be able to tell:

- Are my child's stress hormones excessively high?
- Are they under- or over-stimulated?
- What typically causes this to happen?
- How do they typically react when stress hormones are high?
- What can help?

STUDYING WHEN IN PROTECTION MODE

Getting someone to study or work when they are in protection mode is one of the biggest sources of anguish and unhappiness in homes where a child has a hidden disability.

This can play out as a daily morning battle to get a child into school. Putting on every item of clothing can be a battle, every sock, getting them through the door, every footstep towards the car, getting them out of the car.

While at school, a child in protection mode may withdraw from all study by shutting down or defiantly fighting out. Kids with attention issues may be overwhelmed with demands to sit still or be focused on a task which means nothing to them. A child with bowel issues may not be able to focus on anything other than how they can access a toilet without the bullies getting there first. A child with fatigue may be zoned out and in a trance until home time.

They will not be learning.

After school, the battle can continue to get our child to do homework, another huge source of additional stress. For many of our children, it just becomes overwhelming and exhausting to even go through this daily charade and the result is school refusal.

Evidence is clear on this point. Our loved one *cannot learn* when they are in protection mode, and trying to force or coax them to do so is futile and counterproductive.[8] We already know from neuroscience that when the brain contains stress hormones, it triggers emotions such as anger, fear, outrage and distrust. These emotions divert energy away from the thinking brain causing it to effectively shut down.

Our loved ones' brains are offline when they are in protection mode. They cannot learn, even if they really want to.

Trying to push learning at these times is going to increase our child's stress and push them deeper into protection mode. The resulting battle becomes a downward spiral as they get more stressed and angry and we get more frustrated and furious.

Danny Raede has a great explanation of why we cannot force an overwhelmed child to study:

> Imagine a young soldier crouching behind a rocky outcropping. Bullets are flying overhead and explosions are booming in the distance. She feels trapped. Beneath her mud splattered military fatigues, her arms are trembling with fear and exhaustion. At that very moment, the soldier's elderly grandmother comes hobbling out onto the battlefield. Moving slowly but with purpose the soldier's grandmother

> walks right up to her granddaughter's hiding spot and says, 'Today is the day. It's time for you to learn how to knit! Don't you worry, dear, I've cleared my entire schedule for our appointment today. After all, knitting is such an important life skill and it's time that you learned it!'
>
> How do you imagine our soldier is going to react in that moment? She's probably going to yell at her grandmother and tell her to go away, which is perfectly understandable. In that moment, the soldier is already physically, mentally, and emotionally overwhelmed.
>
> But how do you imagine grandma is going to react? Well, she's going to feel hurt. She might even get angry and start yelling in return.[9]

This explains why we cannot expect our children to behave rationally or to 'learn' during meltdowns. It also explains why unstable kids lack empathy at these times. This is why it is futile to try to have a logical conversation with a person who is being defensive, angry or withdrawn.

It also explains why the 'consequence' we may impose for rude behaviour does not work at certain times. When our child is in protection mode they will not be able to learn our 'parenting lesson on rudeness' as their brains are 'offline' and they are unable to learn anything at all, no matter how important.

To make things even worse, being in protection mode makes our child feel like a failure. They know they are able to learn but may not understand why they are underachieving. They may feel that they are screwing up their lives. Their self-esteem can be in tatters. They may feel hopeless about doing anything about it.

Protection mode is also a downward spiral. You may have heard of the *negativity bias*. This means that we react much more to bad things that happen in our lives than to good things. Apparently, we need five compliments to make up for one criticism. This means that when our child feels like a failure, every negative word they hear can make things feel worse and worse until the cycle is broken.[10]

Teachers may be telling us that our child is falling behind, what they 'should' be able to do at their age, how they 'should' be behaving. No matter how much a teacher complains to us, our child is not going to be able to learn well until they are out of protection mode. There is a lot that the teacher can do to help with this if they are willing.

Understanding protection mode affects how we parent a child with a hidden disability. If our child is already full of shame and low self-esteem, punishments and consequences used at the wrong time can push them deeper into protection mode. This creates a downward spiral and more 'failure' and 'shame' for our child.

It is useful to remember that shame can be an especially big issue for kids with hidden disabilities, who may be hypersensitive to criticism and rejection. It is thought that as many as 99 per cent of those with ADHD are more sensitive than usual in this way, with one in three saying that this is the hardest part of living with ADHD.[11]

The good news is that science shows that when children manage to get out of protection mode, everything changes. Stress hormones are replaced with natural feel-good chemicals. Our children are more likely to want to achieve and do things well because doing so feels really good.

Nothing motivates our children like success.

Fear, frustration and shame become replaced with trust, love, excitement and joy. When these emotions are coursing through our body, the thinking brain can operate at its best.

Free from protection mode, our child is able to learn, not only at school but also all the social and other skills that they will need in life. This is when those parenting lessons on rudeness are likely to actually work.

IS IT A BEHAVIOUR OR A SYMPTOM?

How do we decode if what we are seeing is a behaviour or a symptom? How do we know if it is due to the hidden disability or due to normal childhood ups and downs?

If we cannot tell the difference, how do we stop our children playing us and manipulating us?

The best advice I ever received on this came from one of the parent moderators at the Balanced Mind Parent Network, a forum which deals mainly with mood disorders and bipolar among children and teens. I believe it applies equally to all hidden disabilities.

I was told that if a behaviour happens only when our child's mood is unstable, then it is likely to be a symptom. If it *also* happens when our child's mood is stable, then it is behaviour. If it is a symptom, we treat our child's condition. If it is behaviour, we try to fix the behaviour.

This is so simple and so effective.

So, we ask ourselves, does this behaviour happen when my child is calm and relaxed and not in protection mode? If so, we can go ahead and use rewards and consequences or whatever parenting method we prefer for any child. If our child is clearly in a state of agitation, frustration, anxiety, depression or mania, we treat it as a *symptom* of their hidden disability or a *symptom* of protection mode.

There is a slight problem with this method. It is very hard to apply it if our child is *always* in protection mode. We may not even know what our child is like when they are not. This makes it hard to compare their behaviour when in and out of protection mode.

If we are in any doubt, the easiest way to find out is to do everything we can to get them out of protection mode and then to see if the behaviour persists. This will usually give us our answer. Ideas on how to do this are shared in Chapters 6 and 7.

Before we can figure out strategies, we will need a closer look at how the symptoms and behaviours of protection mode can show up. The next two chapters take us into the more advanced code-breaking we will need to really support and 'get' our child. Firstly, we look at how protection mode can affect our child's behaviour and then how it can affect his or her state of mind.

Chapter 4

HOW PROTECTION MODE AFFECTS BEHAVIOUR

There is no definitive list of clues that our child is in protection mode. There are some very common signs, but every child responds differently to having a pressure cooker that is stuck on 'overheated'.

Not all of these signs 'prove' that our child is in protection mode. There will be times when there genuinely are 'discipline issues'. They may be testing our boundaries or being defiant to test our authority.

As well as having a hidden disability, our children are also human beings. This means that there will be times when the behaviours mentioned below happen for reasons that are unrelated to either their disabilities or being in protection mode. Some are normal in developing children and teenagers.

Here we look at the times when protection mode is a big part of the picture and where a particular behaviour is a *symptom* of the hidden disability itself.

HOMEWORK REFUSAL

'Because of my dyslexia I have to concentrate twice as hard as the others. After school my brain is so tired I'm basically brain dead. My dad tries to make me do homework and I usually end up losing it.' (Simon)

If our child has battled through a day at school, depleting their pot of coping skills so that there are none left, when they get home they are likely to melt down, withdraw, sleep, play computer games or do whatever other protection mode behaviour makes them feel safe.

However it manifests itself, the fact that their pot is empty means that doing homework (or anything involving the thinking brain) can be in functional terms impossible. Stress chemicals may have shut down their thinking brains and they may literally be too exhausted to study. I remember feeling this way as a child myself. I loved studying but my brain had turned to mush by the evening.

Refusal to do homework comes up over and over again on the parent forums regardless of the hidden disability. Parents get frustrated about their inability to 'get' their children to do it. Many say that they feel like failures as parents when even the strongest rewards and consequences fail to get their child to do their homework.

My thinking on this is clear. We cannot get someone to do something that they are unable to do. Whatever their academic ability or potential, a child whose hidden disability causes them to be flooded with stress chemicals after school may not be able to complete a physics assignment or write a book review at this time.

We would not force children with visible disabilities to do things that their disability prevents them from doing. We would not force a child to study while they are having an epileptic seizure. We would not force a child with a bone disorder to go for a run. We need to honour our children's *hidden* disability needs equally.

Most children with hidden disabilities need their time after school to decompress, rebuild their resources and release the steam in the pressure cooker in time for the next day's challenges. They may need time to 'veg out', rest and feel safe. Decompressing may involve computer games. They may need to scream and shout too.

My feeling is that homework should only be attempted when the child has enough energy left and their brain is online. Sometimes, forcing the homework issue, even late in the evening when they have had time to rest, will deplete the child to the point that they will not be able to manage at school the next day.

Many schools push us to force our children to do the homework and will punish them if it is not done. Some, due to our child's special needs, will allow an extension on a deadline. However, this extra time can mean they have to do double the amount of homework the next day to 'keep up'.

This escalation of demands on the child's non-existent energy can be enough to push them over the edge into complete shutdown and school refusal.

When we are able to take our child's pressure cooker reading, we are better able to manage the homework demands.

Had I known about protection mode when my children were at school, I would have been much better at managing this hugely stressful situation. I might have been able to explain to their teachers how the pressure cooker worked and why they sometimes needed complete homework amnesties rather than extensions.

SCHOOL REFUSAL AND ABSENCES

'I just can't deal with the bell. The sound is a dagger into my skull. And everyone looks the same in their uniforms and I don't know who they are. I feel lost and like I'm going to die.' (Alexander)

Unless there is plenty of help in place to support our children, their disability symptoms make it unlikely that they will be able to have a full attendance record.

Being constantly flooded with stress hormones is exhausting and many find it just 'all too much'. This may be expressed as not being able to 'face going in'. When we understand the pressure cooker effect of going to school, we can see that there may be times, especially towards the end of a term, when there is simply too much heat in the pressure cooker to hold the pressure in.

Our child may run out of steam in every sense and to carry on will lead either to an extreme meltdown or to a complete shutdown. On top of this, many of our children also experience bullying and huge social challenges in addition to the symptoms of their specific hidden disabilities.

Schools vary in how accommodating they are on this. Some offer a reduced timetable to help our children manage this pressure or are flexible about drop-off and collection times. Even when schools try to help, many children find these adjustments to be very embarrassing as it makes them stand out as even more different among their classmates.

Our children may be desperately trying to fit in so special rules for them, even when really needed, can draw their classmates' attention to their problems, causing more stress and more protection mode. This really is a catch-22 for our loved ones and something I think we can all empathise with.

Our children's symptoms and feeling overwhelmed can hit them at any time. If they do not have the resources to cope on a particular day, I believe it is wise for them to take a rest and recovery day off school.

This is no different from a child with a visible disability or illness who takes time off school to recover from the symptoms of illness. People do not force a child dealing with cancer or a severe asthma attack into school. When a child has flu it is assumed and expected that they will need to stay home to rest and heal.

Our children's disabilities, although hidden, are just as real and they may need to stay at home when they are having symptoms or feeling overwhelmed, so that their bodies can recover. We need to be flexible to our child's needs on school attendance. Without recovery days as a 'safety valve', complete school refusal becomes far more likely.

Schools, especially in the UK, are under considerable pressure to show high attendance rates in order to gain favourable league table ratings. Many are unable or unwilling to offer the flexibility our children need, and it is not uncommon for parents to be prosecuted for failing to force their autistic children into school.

Understanding how the pressure cooker and protection mode works gives us tools we can use when we are negotiating with schools, along with a knowledge of disability rights law.

Even with help in place, the pressure cooker may just be too hot for some children in mainstream school. As so few schools are able to fully address our children's needs, many parents feel they have no choice but to home educate their children.

Alternatively, if we are very fortunate, we may be able to secure a place in a school that is better equipped to meet the needs of children with hidden disabilities. Such a school may have a less stressful regime and be flexible to each child's needs. This compares to large mainstream schools that may blindly adhere to targets and rules designed for children who do not have hidden disabilities.

Again, the insightful Chloe Estelle can help us understand how school refusal feels and how it can be fuelled by being in protection or defence mode:

> School was the worst. I had days that I woke up and just couldn't go. I know now that I was in defence mode and even when my body was telling me that I was in the middle of a sensory overload, I didn't realise it. Even if I did, I didn't know what a sensory overload was, let alone autism. So I told my parents I was too tired to go to school. Of course they told me that I still had to go. Why wouldn't they? They didn't know what was happening inside me because I didn't know what was happening. Then all of a sudden they became the enemy that wanted me to suffer. I had to fight what felt like a monster in any way I could to not attend school.
>
> It's really scary this moment. It's not a want, it's a need. I needed to stay home as much as I needed food to stay alive. The only way I could convey this was with a series of 'no no no no...' over and over again. It was my only defence against all the bad in the world.[1]

SOCIAL ISSUES

'I need to be completely on my own to recover from being around people. I tell my mum I am suffering from "other-people-ness" and luckily she gets it.' (Manisha)

Many families get frustrated by their child's inability or refusal to socialise. It can be embarrassing when our child stays in his room throughout a family gathering or will not get out of the car when we have taken them to a place of interest. This is particularly common among children on the autism spectrum although others behave in this way too in protection mode.

We have probably taught our children to be polite and to greet visitors to our homes. We may worry that others will consider our children to be rude if they shut themselves away or stay silent in social situations. They may also assume that we are bad parents who have failed to teach our children social skills.

We may also worry that our children are isolated and lonely from the lack of a social life. We know how much we enjoy talking and being with friends and family and want our loved ones to enjoy these things too.

Social anxiety or not understanding appropriate social behaviours are listed as symptoms of a number of hidden disabilities. They can drive our children deeper into protection mode and it is worth understanding how it may feel for them.

Our children can be overwhelmed by all the expectations and pressures of dealing with people socially. It can be exhausting to read body language and work out what to say, when to say it and how to behave. For some, especially those on the autism spectrum, these skills do not come naturally and having to deal with these situations can be exhausting.

If their pot is empty and their pressure cooker is close to exploding, for example after a day in school, any kind of social interaction can be just too much, even with us. They may need to be left alone to rest and recharge their batteries.

Clare, who has various hidden disabilities, gives us some lovely insights not only about how this feels but also into what she would do to release the pressure in her pressure cooker:

> We used to have big Christmas get-togethers where the whole extended family would be invited to my nan's house. Despite the fact I knew everyone and actually enjoyed seeing them all, it didn't alleviate the anxiety I felt around the social interaction. It would get to a point after a few hours that my social quota was full. My social anxiety, that I kept carefully cloaked, bubbled away under the surface and would build until I had no option but to release it somehow. For me this

> meant covertly sneaking off upstairs into the silence and the dark of an empty room, where I would just sit and quietly release the pressure through an overflow of tears.
>
> Once I had sobbed my anxiety level down I was ready to re-emerge and face it all again. I always felt such anguish that even though this was my family, who I loved, being with them still elicited the same anxiety reaction as if it was a group of complete strangers.

There are a number of ways of turning down the heat, of which 'crying it out' is a great example. Another is to build confidence in social skills, thereby reducing the stress about how our child is 'supposed' to perform.

When done well, learning social and communication skills can help our children feel more control in social situations and to trust them more. This can include things like how to greet strangers, what to do with their hands while they do so, how to respond to compliments, how their mouth should be, etc. We may need to watch our children carefully to see if these are things that may be stressing them. This is very easy to overlook when social skills come so naturally to many of us.

When our child does not want to socialise it is not always due to social anxiety. Sometimes it is due to them wanting to do other things instead, perhaps something related to their passions or interests.

Our daughter may not see the point in mindless small talk or engaging with people for the sake of it, especially if she can do something more interesting to her such as play Minecraft®, read a good book or watch a favourite box set. This is something we can respect, especially if they are not lonely and are managing some social contact in other ways, for example with friends online.

We all have different needs for socialising. Some people, who may be extroverts, thrive on being around people and are energised by it. Others, who may be introverts, are exhausted by large groups and are energised by spending time alone.

At the other end of the spectrum is the need to be constantly around people. This is more common in children with ADHD who may struggle with being alone and need the stimulation of lots of people to interact with. For them, being unable to go out or be with other people can push them deeper into protection mode.

In addition, to help us understand our child, it is useful to figure out where we are on the extrovert to introvert spectrum and how much socialising we need and enjoy. Being an introvert myself made it easier for me to empathise with my child's desire to hide away, and I appreciate that this may be harder for a parent who is an extrovert.

As our children come out of protection mode, dealing with socialising will become much easier. A child who doesn't want to socialise may learn how to greet people to be polite, and then know how to retreat without it appearing rude. If the heat on their pressure cooker is low enough, an introverted or previously socially anxious person may happily go to parties, hang out in groups or even enjoy networking events as an adult.

At the opposite end of the spectrum, a child who hates being alone may learn to tolerate and even enjoy his own company when he is feeling sufficiently stimulated in other parts of his life. When the heat is down, many things become possible.

We need to remember that there are positives in not wanting to socialise. It has been suggested that one reason so many of the world's great innovators have hidden disabilities is that they are less caught up in social situations. They may feel less restricted by social rules and pleasing other people. This frees up a lot of time and energy to use more creativity for the thinking up of new ideas.

This could be a silver lining if our children prefer not to socialise. Temple Grandin, who is on the autism spectrum, suggests:

> What would happen if the autism gene was eliminated from the gene pool? You would have a bunch of people standing around in a cave, chatting and socialising and not getting anything done.[2]

TECHNOLOGY AND GAMING

'So we play Minecraft® for twenty hours in a row. It's like, oh my god, I haven't eaten, slept and need to actually do my homework and get on with life.' (Sanjeev)

For our children, the real world can feel threatening, out of control and hard to trust. Due to their hidden disability, they may feel like failures in the real world. They may know that they are bright and able even though others may not recognise it.

It is not a great surprise that the virtual world of technology and gaming may have great appeal to them. They feel safe, technology follows clear rules and is predictable. It is fun and they can do really well at it, show off their strengths and feel proud of their achievements. While they are in protection mode it can give them what the real world cannot – control and trust.

Danny Raede, who has Asperger's, explains:

> When I was in defence mode, I played video games because it was safe. I could pause the game at any point, and if something bad happened to me, I'd just reset and try again.[3]

Many children with hidden disabilities find fun, security, happiness and excitement in the virtual worlds of computer games. Other children do this too of course, but for our children, gaming can take on a whole other dimension, both keeping them in and also helping them out of protection mode. This is a hard one to decode but very helpful when we understand what technology is doing for our child.

It is not uncommon for our children to spend days, weeks and even years immersed in video game worlds. We can understand the appeal, especially when the real world feels so threatening, exhausting and overwhelming to our children.

People stuck in protection mode have trouble getting things done. Even the most loving and caring home life can feel exhausting to our children if there is too much heat in their pressure cooker. There may be demands to do homework, to do chores, to eat, to socialise, to take a shower, to thank someone for a birthday card, the list goes on.

Candice, who has multiple hidden disabilities, explains:

> So I said to my mum, I am just sooo stressed out I just need you to get out of my face so I can decompress. Just leave me alone to play my games. Can't she get that she's making things worse?

So what we need to remember as parents is that our children's computer game world can be their 'safe place' in a scary world. Chloe Estelle graphically explains:

> I locked myself in my bathroom one weekend. I had placed all these pillows in my bathtub and curled up behind my computer screen. I shut a world out that I didn't quite fit into, that was very painful. I locked my parents out who were trying to take my safe place away and keep it barred away from me in a safe. They wanted me to put down my place of safety and escape for a world that was loud and mean and painful. My parents and I fought constantly over these devices that I used to keep my state of mind healthy. We both seemed to speak different languages for they saw my best friend as an enemy and I didn't have the ability to communicate my needs.[4]

For us as parents, this behaviour can look both negative and infuriating. We may worry that our child is addicted to their gaming, as one would be to a drug. We may blame the gaming for their shutdown behaviour, such as staying in their rooms and not wanting to participate in daily life.

We may believe that if only we could stop them gaming, then they would engage with real life and do something more meaningful with their lives. We may yell at them to stop, try to impose screen time limits and try to get them to do other more productive activities.

Our child may not see the problem or what all the fuss is about, especially as they are likely to be enjoying themselves so much.

To balance our worries, we need also to recognise the positives of technology and gaming, and plenty of research backs up the benefits of online play.[5]

- In a video game world, our child collaborates with their friends and engages in a lot of social activity through the game. This helps them to develop social skills and learn to process emotions in a safe way.
- Many of the games involve considerable problem-solving skills and intellectual challenge, along with adventure and creative challenges.

- Many of the games involve dealing with threats, dangers and emergencies. Learning how to deal with these in a virtual world can give our child confidence that can be used later in the real world. Another nice aspect is that in video games, our child is often playing a strong and heroic role which can boost their self-esteem.

When we learn how to understand our child's video game use rather than simply judge it, we can see better how it fits into the wider picture of their protection mode. When our children feel understood it is a huge relief for them. It is really supportive to acknowledge the benefits of gaming for our child and perhaps enter their virtual world with them. This can strengthen our connection to our child. When our child feels listened to and understood it is much easier to negotiate about which games they play and how much screen time is good for them.

If they feel listened to and understood, they are much more likely to listen to us.

And as Danny Raede found, as he came out of protection mode, his interest in computer games greatly declined:

> I realized that after almost two decades of playing video games, killing virtual people no longer appealed to me. Building things no longer appealed to me... So I stopped, and filled my time with other, more enjoyable activities.[6]

FUSSY EATING, OBSESSIONS AND RITUALS

'I can only eat food that tastes of beige.' (Lola)

Protection mode may cause our son to be in a state of ongoing anxiety, fear or frustration. Everything may feel out of his control and this frightens and overwhelms him even more. In this state it is very common to become fixated or obsessed about things being 'right' or 'wrong'.

For many, this can become a food obsession. Danny Raede explains:

> At school I ate a peanut butter and jelly sandwich for lunch almost every single day from first to tenth grade. When I say almost every single day, I mean that I can literally count on both hands the number of days I didn't eat PB&J.
>
> I was one of the pickiest eaters you can imagine. Everything had to be a certain way. EVERYTHING. I had to have a specific brand of bread. I had to have a certain type of jelly. And if you used the same knife to cut my sandwich that touched anything green, it was game over.[7]

Food pickiness tends to be associated with people on the autism spectrum, mainly due to sensory overload when they are bombarded with strong flavours and textures. This is because all of their senses tend to be highly tuned, causing our children to be highly sensitive to noise, smell, taste and touch.

This is why so many of our children have problems with 'itchy' clothing and labels irritating their skin. And this is why noisy and crowded places are so overwhelming and exhausting for them.

In such a situation, where a person feels under threat, it can feel safer to eat only a proven safe item of food or wear a trusted item of clothing. One way to feel safer is to be in control of something. Danny explains:

> I always had to be in control. I was 'invested' in being in control. Of everything. In essence, people with Asperger's are often picky eaters because it is an easy way for them to gain control in a VERY scary world.[8]

This need for control seems to apply to anyone caught in a world of chronic fear or frustration, so is likely to apply to some extent to most people with hidden disabilities, not only those on the autism spectrum. Children with ADHD, for example, can become wound up like a coil as their exuberance and passions are squashed and repressed and feel out of control.

When they are feeling this way, many children wear the same item of clothing day in and day out. They do this because they *trust* it. They will eat the same food because they *trust* it.

When on the brink of crisis, our child may not be in the mood to experiment with new foods, clothes or places. Being forced to do so can be too stressful and may push their pressure cooker to explode.

This is why routines and obsessions can help our child to feel safe and why people are so resistant to change when they are in protection mode. Our children are in survival mode, and this obsessive behaviour makes sense when we look at it from this perspective.

We can probably relate to this in our own lives. When we are under intense pressure, how many of us take solace in eating a particular thing, maybe cake, to 'make us feel better', to make us feel safe? Most of us have our 'comfort foods' to help us deal with stress and difficult times. How many parents reach for a bottle of wine every evening 'because we need it' or feel most relaxed when we are wearing a trusted old pair of tracksuit bottoms and baggy sweater?

If we can think about how we use food, drink or clothing in this way, we can start to get an idea how these things can feel helpful to our child.

Food and body obsession can be extreme and can extend to all food. We see this with food disorders such as anorexia and body image disorders like body dysmorphia where people become obsessed with hating a particular aspect of their body, or even their whole body.

Conditions like anorexia, bulimia and body dysmorphia are of course much more complex than being stress reactions alone. There is, however, an aspect of them that can be understood as an obsessional need to feel control when everything feels dangerously 'wrong'.

The same applies to many of the behaviours of OCD (obsessive compulsive disorder), including obsessive hygiene and the need to check and re-check or order things in a particular way. They help our child feel they have some control and this can help them feel safe.

Behaviours that look bizarre to people who do not understand how protection mode works, such as not walking on the cracks of pavements or not touching something that has been touched by someone else, make perfect sense when understood in this way.

To understand how this feels for our child, we can think of our own rituals. We may need to sit at a particular table in our favourite cafe or arrange our toiletries in a particular way on the shelf. We may feel distressed if a 'helpful' visitor washes the dishes in the 'wrong' way or puts things into the 'wrong' cupboards. I personally am comforted by a very specific morning routine and am not happy when it is interrupted.

Once we understand that obsessive behaviours are at least partially about our child's pressure cookers, control and trust, we can figure out much more effective ways to support them.

Like us, when our loved ones are feeling safe, calm and in control of their lives, their obsessions and fears tend to recede dramatically. In fact, many can be completely overcome. Some people on the autism spectrum completely resolve their food pickiness as they gain confidence and control over their lives.

Saying all of this, we need to remember that many obsessions are very positive for our children, and in fact the world. At their best, obsessions are actually *passions*. We know that following our passions gives us the most satisfaction in life. We are also most likely to succeed at something if we are passionate about it.

People with hidden disabilities have had and continue to have world-changing achievements due to their passionate interests, curiosity and focus on specific things. Albert Einstein, Charles Darwin and Mozart to name but a few are likely to have been on the autism spectrum, had mood disorders or conditions such as ADHD.

Anne Rice sums this up in this now famous quote about the power of obsession:

> Don't bend, don't water it down; don't try to make it logical; don't edit your own soul according to the fashion. Rather, follow your most intense obsessions mercilessly.[9]

When our child is deeply in protection mode, they may be too overwhelmed to see or follow their passions. When the heat goes down, our *real* child can emerge, along with their passions. Following their passions and special interests is an important way of keeping out of protection mode for our children. It gives them purpose, makes them feel great and makes them feel successful.

And most importantly for protection mode, following passions gives them something important that they have control over and therefore something they can trust. I talk about how we can harness the positive side of obsession to support our children's passions in Part 2.

DEFIANT AND AGGRESSIVE BEHAVIOUR

'How many people do I have to punch before you realise that something is WRONG!' (Cameron)

All children can be be defiant, challenge our authority and refuse to do what they are told. Some may also be aggressive to us and to others and disrespect whatever boundaries they are given.

This can be heartbreaking to see if we are trying to bring our children up to be kind and caring about the needs of others. These values are very dear to us and if our children seem to be challenging them, we can feel like failures as parents. It can also press our buttons if we are bringing them up to respect us and the guidance we give them.

We may have clear ideas about how to bring our children back into line when they breach these values. We may get super strict with our children using 'tough-love' strategies. These may help in some situations or they may make things worse in others.

Dealing with defiance becomes more complicated when our child has a hidden disability. This is why before we react, we need to decode what our child is trying to communicate when they are behaving in this way.

As defiance so resembles what we would consider 'bad behaviour', it is extremely difficult for us to take that necessary step back from it. We need to suspend judging it until we have figured it out. Only then can we work out how best to respond.

Our child's behaviour may be a reaction to having an overheated pressure cooker. It may be a severe stress response. It may be a sign that he is bored and under-stimulated. It may be a sign that she is trying to feel a sense of power and control because her life feels out of control. It may be a cry for help or for attention.

Or, it may have nothing to do with their hidden disability and be just about testing our boundaries and the limits of our authority. They may just be acting up in that moment.

Defiance doesn't just offend us and our sense of right and wrong. It also has a big effect on our child and his ability to have a successful and productive life.

Defiant kids will often fight against any rules or authority whether they are ours, the school's, the country's or at work. This can cause them considerable difficulty with school and workplace regimes. They can be disruptive and sometimes aggressive at school and may be excluded or expelled.

At best they are likely to underachieve, which in itself can fuel any low self-esteem they may have as well as a sense that they are 'failures'.

When a defiant child feels that they are a failure and are no good, they may become even more defiant to regain self-respect and because defiance is something they may be very good at. As they are good at it, when they are being defiant, they are not failing! Defiance can give them all the feel-good hormones that come from success. It can feel good. It can feel powerful. But 'success' at defiance is probably the last thing we would want our children to learn!

When a child is defiant, it is very common for parents to be blamed and accused of not being strict enough or told that we are inconsistent, or simply bad parents. Many of us blame ourselves, especially when we try to use conventional parenting techniques, which can often make things worse for our child. Jennifer reached out:

> Please help me I'm at breaking point. My Asperger's ASD son insults me and threatens me and hits his sister. I've done everything. I've taken away his favourite toys, stopped him watching videos, going to parties, done time out, naughty step, reasoning with him, shouting at him. He doesn't even seem to feel pain when he hurts himself. It's hopeless and I feel like such a useless mum.

If our daughter is being defiant because she is in protection mode, trying to punish her using rewards and consequences can fuel the fire. Although she may not realise it, she may be trying to communicate to us in her code and may be hoping that we will understand it. She may not understand her code herself and may be craving our help to do so.

If we are not able to 'listen to the music and not the words', our child may find it necessary to turn the volume up in the hope that then we will hear what they are trying to say with their codes. This can mean worse or more shocking behaviour. It may get worse and worse until we are able to 'get it'. What starts as a whisper for us to decode – for example, mild defiance – can end up as a deafening scream when our child seems to go completely off the rails.

And the frustration at not being understood can add heat to their pressure cooker, causing a vicious cycle of challenging behaviour.

For some children, the frustration of boredom can mean that even harsh punishments can give them the stimulation and attention they crave. As they probably do know the difference between right and wrong, the shame they feel afterwards can fuel this even further. A child may feel so guilty about what they did that they seek more punishment to curb their guilt. And the best way to get this is... more defiant behaviour.

I remember behaving in this way as a child. I felt so bad about myself that I wanted to be punished and the punishment felt nearly as good as doing the 'naughty acts'.

We know that a child in protection mode may look for ways to feel control over their lives and emotions. This is why they often use the obsessions, rituals and repetitive actions talked about previously. If we understand this, we can see how defiant behaviour can achieve the same thing. Sometimes the defiance or aggression rises so quickly in our child that they may not know how to control it. It can become as automatic to some children as obsessive hand washing is to another child.

Just like obsessions and repetitive actions, defiance can be a way to *stimulate* themselves to block out the frustration and feeling of being overwhelmed that is so common in life with a hidden disability. It can be a way of relieving the build-up of pressure and feel good and exciting to them. It can make them feel in control.

It is not surprising that not only are children with hidden disabilities more likely to be bullied but they may also be more likely to be bullies themselves.[10]

When we understand that defiance may be a protection mode

behaviour, we can see it as a way our child is protecting himself from a threat, be it imagined or real. Even if the threat is gruelling boredom or feeling under-stimulated, often the case with ADD and ADHD, the defiance may be a way of dealing with a chemical stress reaction.

As we know, stress hormones shut down the thinking brain, which can make it very difficult to have any meaningful communication with our child at these times as they may not be able to take in what we are saying.

Will, who has ADD, explains how this felt when he was a child:

> I was just so damn bored at school I would do anything to get the stimulation I needed. I needed stimulation like a drug. So I'd disrupt the class, shout things out, throw things around and pick fights. Even the punishments when they came were stimulating and exciting.

When we understand the need for stimulation for children with ADD and ADHD, it is not surprising that so many go on to have problems with addiction and reckless behaviour. We need to read their codes, understand their needs and help them to meet them in a healthy and productive way.

If their 'success' feel-good chemicals come from defiance, our challenge as parents or teachers is to find ways that our child can feel successful in more productive areas of life. This is why we need to focus on their strengths rather than their weaknesses.

Parents and teachers may despair, 'He just won't listen' and 'She just doesn't care about the punishments, in fact they make her worse!' We all know how hard it is to listen properly to others when we are angry or overwhelmed.

Schools often impose extra boredom as a punishment for disruptive children, such as detentions where children are forced to sit in a room without stimulation. Other punishments include taking away stimulating activities such as sports or games. If the cause of the misbehaving is *under-stimulation* and the punishment is more under-stimulation, this can make things worse. Giving the child a stimulating challenge based on their interests may be more effective.

Science backs up the view that defiance can be about how our child reacts to stress. Brain scientist Dr Steven Porges says that many children with hidden disabilities have a brain chemical imbalance that causes them to detect danger where there is in fact none. The brain's ability to distinguish between safe and dangerous situations is called *neuroception*. Porges believes that this faulty neuroception makes a child with a hidden disability genuinely believe that they are under attack.[11]

As they feel under attack, they go into fight or flight behaviour, which is a normal chemical stress reaction to being under threat. For some children, the defiance and aggression is the 'fight' stress response.

Clinical psychologist Dr Mona Delahook explains how using rewards and punishments when a child feels under threat makes things worse:

> If faulty neuroception is to blame, however, behaviors will be a reflection of an immediate, 'fight or flight' response and not purposeful misbehavior. In such cases, punishment can potentially cause more distress, triggering additional feelings of threat rather than safety.[12]

This offers another explanation of why conventional parenting can make things worse for children with hidden disabilities. If we impose a consequence for defiant behaviour, if our child has this brain imbalance, she may consider the punishment to be a threat. This threat provokes an even deeper fight or flight reaction, causing more defiant behaviour.

Understanding this helps us to see the importance of getting our child out of protection mode. When they are feeling safe they are likely to be less defiant. When they are misbehaving our child may well need a de-escalation of pressure, not an extra build-up of it.

Chloe Estelle gives a really helpful glimpse of how it feels to be defiant while in protection mode, and her account helped me to understand how it may feel for our children:

> I remember that feeling of not wanting to do something so bad that I would just repeat 'NO' over and over if not out loud then in my head. 'No, I don't want to go. Don't make me go. I can't go.' over and over and over. There was this fear that was so massive, I can't even explain.

The sad reality of this is that these meltdowns are caused by a world that isn't made for people like me. We have built a world that doesn't build people up, it tears people down. Especially people like me. The world instilled this fear in me that was so intense, I actually curled up in a ball on the floor and shouted NO at it. Repeatedly.

And parents are being told that these kids need more discipline, that their kids are manipulating them. These kids are labeled misbehaving and bad.

No one blames a child for acting out of fear and refusing to go to the doctors to get a shot.

Something needs to change. I wish I knew exactly what.[13]

When our loved ones are having a threat response they can feel like a cornered animal. Once we have helped them to get out of protection mode, their brain is back online and they are able to hear us again. This would be the right time to talk to our kids about strategies to deal with threats and to build resilience. We cannot build resilience in someone who is under fire. We need to build it prior to being under fire, or after the battle, as preparation for dealing better with the next battle.

INAPPROPRIATE BEHAVIOUR

'What is the problem? It's only a part of the body! And it's funny!' (Harry)

Some children with hidden disabilities say or do things that are considered inappropriate in our societies. This could include saying or doing things that hurt other children, hurting animals, inappropriate touching, stalking or being obsessive with another child. Another common issue is personal hygiene as our child may forget to wash or not understand or agree with the need to do so. As our child gets older there may be issues with inappropriate sexual behaviour and respecting the boundaries of others.

All children do inappropriate behaviour sometimes. If we bring our children up to consider the feelings of others, most will stop doing it after a time.

For children with hidden disabilities it is again more complicated. The hidden disability may make it harder for them to read the emotions of others. It may also be harder for them to understand social conventions and rules. This is especially the case for those with autism spectrum conditions.

If our child's hidden disability includes being impulsive, they may lack a filter between their brain and their mouth. Before thinking about the effect of their words on others, they may have already said or done something inappropriate or hurtful. This is common with ADHD and ADD.

Sorting out inappropriate behaviour is essential for both our child and for others. I have seen cases of even really nasty inappropriate behaviour being ignored or dismissed by people saying things like, 'He can't help it as he has Asperger's' or 'We have to accept it as she has ADHD'.

As well as being unfair to the victim of the inappropriate behaviour, ignoring or dismissing it is not going to help our child either. Without a thought-out intervention, inappropriate behaviour is unlikely to go away by itself and may get worse.

Unless it is dealt with, our child is likely to be unpopular, shunned, bullied or even feared. The more others shy away from our child due to the inappropriate behaviour, the more alone and misunderstood he may feel and the more angry he may become with the world.

The good news is that there are ways to deal with inappropriate behaviour in children with hidden disabilities. To be successful, our child's clues need to be read and understood along with the very real challenges of their hidden disabilities.

Unlike many neurotypical children, our child may not be able just to 'pick up' what is appropriate by watching the reactions of others. Instead, they may need to be taught how to be appropriate. Appropriate behaviour can be taught in a similar way to learning how to read a book, how to play football or how to play a musical instrument.

If our child tells her grandmother that she is fat and ugly, she may rightly believe that she is telling the truth as she has been taught to do.

Her grandmother may in fact be fat and ugly. Our child can be taught mechanically that although it may be true, saying it will hurt and upset her grandmother. When people are upset by what we say or do, they do not want to be around us.

Just like we need to be taught a foreign language step by step, our child may need to learn how to deal with social situations in a similar way. When we make a mistake in a foreign language, we are unlikely to listen to the correction if we are being *shamed* for the mistake. We learn better when we are being *encouraged*. We need to remember this when we are dealing with inappropriate behaviour and it often helps to imagine that our child is learning a foreign language.

And this brings us back to protection mode. Although protection mode does not cause inappropriate behaviour, it totally affects our child's ability to listen and to learn. The learning part of the brain is at least partially offline when they are in protection mode. This means that until we can get our child out of protection mode, interventions to deal with inappropriate behaviour are unlikely to help.

And there is more. When our bodies are full of stress hormones, we feel less empathy and are less able to read how other people are feeling. This is the case for all of us, not only children with hidden disabilities. When we are stressed we tend to focus on ourselves rather than others. This is a normal survival strategy to get ourselves out of danger. We often need to feel safe before we can focus on the needs of other people.

For our child in protection mode, this means that they may be even less able to read the effect of their behaviour on others. It means that whatever problems they *already* have with reading social situations and the feelings of others can be much worse if our child is in protection mode.

So, getting our child out of protection mode will help them with inappropriate behaviour in two ways. Firstly, it gets their brain back online so that they can learn what we are teaching them about how to behave appropriately. Secondly, they will be less self-centred and more able to understand and read the feelings of others.

SELF-HARM

'I scratch and scratch until it bleeds, then I see the pain coming out in the blood and it's a relief.' (Joanna)

It is really hard to see and 'get' emotional pain. Emotional pain is really confusing for us as it can come out as anger, fear and many other emotions. If we as adults struggle to decode what is happening with ourselves, we can imagine how hard this is for our children.

On the other hand, physical pain is less confusing. If our knee hurts because we fell over, we know precisely what we are feeling and why. Seeing the blood coming from the grazed knee makes it really clear. There is a link between the graze and the pain, and we know what to expect during the healing process.

Many of us have some experience of imposing physical pain on ourselves when we are in emotional pain. When we are overwhelmed with grief we may hit our heads against something or scratch ourselves until we bleed. Some people punch a wall or make themselves sick.

We do this to make our emotional pain physical. We may get some relief from it as it is a pain that makes sense.

Victoria Leatham explains this:

> In hurting myself, I had at last found a way to release the pressure. But it was more than that. I was now different. I felt different. I'd discovered a way to control my feelings. Just because self-mutilation wasn't deemed an acceptable coping mechanism didn't mean I was going to stop doing it.[14]

Our children may be emotionally overwhelmed, and this can be shown in different ways. One child may become aggressive, another defiant and another may shut down or go into a virtual world. Others may make their emotional pain physical by self-harm.

Many children, especially those on the autism spectrum, have considerable difficulties expressing and accepting their emotions in a healthy way. There is also a particularly strong link between self-harm and ADHD, especially in girls.[15]

When Carole's child started self-harming, some family members thought she was doing it out of defiance. Luckily, Carole's decoding skills were more honed:

> At seven we noticed she had pulled all her eyelashes out, leaving a few stray ones in the corners of her eyes. I worked out she was self-harming in this way each night because she would hear us closing and bolting the storm door and in her head she feared we had abandoned her because of her 'bad' behaviour. When we changed how we dealt with doors in our home, my daughter felt 'heard' and things really started to change for her.

It is devastating to see our children harming themselves. We may be terrified of what may happen to them and feel powerless about how best to respond. We may worry that we have done something wrong.

We may be fighting to protect our children from harm from others, only to also have to protect them from themselves.

Self-harm is very frightening. The most common types are skin cutting and head banging. As they get older self-harm can include alcohol and drug misuse and of course our ultimate fear, suicidal acts.

But if we can overcome our own panic and understand our child's self-harm as an expression of emotional pain, the actions immediately make more sense.

It helped me to focus on my own self harm. I know that for many years, whenever I became overwhelmed with my own emotions and unable to process them, I would reach for a cigarette. I didn't enjoy the cigarettes and in fact found smoking to be unpleasant and it sometimes literally made me vomit. Smoking is dangerous and can be considered an act of self-harm. But the act of smoking for me became my way of expressing emotional pain. Regardless of any nicotine addiction, it was a behavioural habit. Whenever I felt overwhelmed or stressed, I would immediately reach for a cigarette.

Cutting and other self-harming behaviours can similarly become habits for our loved ones. As soon as they feel emotional pain, they may rush for the knife to cut themselves in the same way that I rushed for a cigarette.

I stopped smoking when I learned how to identify and express my emotions healthily. When I could do that, it became possible to break the habit. Learning to identify, feel and express emotions is one of the key ways out of protection mode.

I am not suggesting that something as complex as cutting and other self-harming behaviours are completely due to protection mode reactions. However, I do believe that helping our loved ones gain control over their lives and emotions will help them to an emotional place where they will be better able to heal and treat their self-harm.

Another critical word here is *control*. We know that many of the things our children do when they are in protection mode are attempts to gain control over lives that feel frighteningly out of control.

Self-harm can be a way of feeling in control of something, in this case being in control of the pain. This makes perfect sense.

And for some of our children, although they may do the self-harm in private, they may hope we will find out. They may hope that we will see the emotional pain behind their actions and help them. This is why acts of self-harm can be cries for help. To get them the help they need we need to be able to decode what they are doing, to listen to the music not the words.

LYING AND STEALING

'I know it's wrong. But I get scared when I have to tell the truth.' (Ben)

Lying and stealing are probably the most challenging tests for us in 'listening to the music and not the words'. It is extremely hard to decode behaviour that so utterly offends our values of right and wrong.

It is natural that we may want to judge this behaviour and condemn it in the strongest possible terms, backed up with punishments and consequences. Our child appears to be disrespecting us and our values. We may feel that their hidden disability should not be an 'excuse'. If our child has picked up 'wrong' values, these will need to be fixed quickly.

But what if our loved one's lying is not evidence of a character flaw or disrespect?

Before we react, it can be helpful to suspend our judgement for long enough to understand what may be happening with our child. This does not condone the behaviour but until we understand it, we will not be able to find a strategy that will make a difference.

Many children lie and steal and they do so for many reasons. Some do it 'because they can' and weigh up the chances of getting caught and punished. Others get a kick out of breaking a rule, or do it to impress someone else or to get something that they are not supposed to have.

Many of us will have lied and stolen things as children but have grown out of it.

When a child has a hidden disability, there may be other factors at play. Quite often children will lie or steal things for no apparent gain for themselves. They may be taking things that they do not actually want or need. They may be inventing stories or lies that don't seem to help them in any way.

Or perhaps, no matter how much we punish our child for doing these things it only seems to make things worse. How do we decode this and how do we respond? There are many possibilities to consider.

We can start by thinking about times when it is correct and necessary to lie, when we would lie ourselves. No matter how virtuous we may be, most people would tell a lie if we or our loved ones were under threat and telling the truth would put them into danger.

In times of war or persecution, people may have to pretend to be someone they are not to stay safe. It may be dangerous to tell the truth, and a well-chosen lie can literally save our lives.

When a person is in danger, lying as a defence against a threat makes perfect sense and it is something any rational person would do. This can help us to understand lying as a protective behaviour.

If our child is in protection mode, it is not a huge leap to imagine that they may be lying to protect themselves from the threat that is daily life. We may not see the threat but they may well be feeling it, and the body does not distinguish between real and imagined threats. The threat may be that our child is facing complicated emotions that they don't know how to deal with.

Neuroscience shows that lying can be an effective self-preservation strategy when we are faced with feeling overwhelmed and with emotional shutdown. In other words, lying can be a symptom of protection mode, especially in people with hidden disabilities.

In fact, some psychologists take this further and suggest that as well as 'fight or flight', when humans feel under threat we can add another 'f' word, 'fib'. For our kids, the threats may be things like embarrassment, fear, guilt or shame. The threat may be bullying or feeling like a failure or a disappointment to us. Fibbing or stealing may give them relief from these feelings and a sense of control and power.

This is explained by ADHD specialist psychologists Monica Hassall and Barbara Hunter:

> What if your child's lying is not evidence of a character flaw or disrespect? What if his fibs are actually a self-preservation strategy rooted in poor inhibition, emotional regulation, working memory, and attention – all hallmarks of ADHD?[16]

This is an interesting point. We already know that many of our children, especially those with ADD or ADHD, already have problems with impulse control and working memory. This can cause them to act without thinking about the consequences of their actions and also have difficulties learning from their mistakes. When we understand the implications, it makes sense why they may be both lying and stealing.

We also need to remember how good it can feel to get away with something we know we shouldn't do. Getting away with stealing something, even when we do not *want* the thing, can feel like a victory. At that moment we can feel very powerful. It can give us a shot of adrenaline and excitement. This is a big deal for children who feel powerless and out of control in other areas of their lives.

Joel, who has multiple hidden disabilities, used to steal as a child:

> I felt so left behind in life and it felt so unfair that I would use any chance I could to get something back. So I'd take things when I could. Anything. Each time I did it I felt I was redressing the unfairness, evening up the score. The more my parents shamed me for it, the more determined I was to get back at them by taking more things.

I still remember how exciting it was to steal Smarties from Woolworths when I was a child by pushing the tube of chocolates up my sleeve. It felt daring and dangerous, and the chocolate tasted extra sweet afterwards.

As it may make our children feel good and powerful, lying and stealing can become addictive. Like other protective behaviours, it can become a habit. Just as some children may get into the habit of cutting themselves when they are emotionally overwhelmed, others may automatically lie or steal something. Lying or stealing can be similar to reaching for a cigarette or bottle of wine when we are feeling stressed.

As our child is likely to get caught and punished, in some ways lying and stealing can be similar to other self-harm activities. They may give a short-term feeling of power and control. When they are caught there may be the hope of getting help with the overwhelming emotions that they may be unable to process in any other way.

Or they may want to get caught so that they can be punished. Some kids feel that they need to be punished because they feel full of shame about their worth. This can happen when they don't fully accept themselves or their hidden disabilities. If this is the case, being punished can feel like some form of 'relief'.

Maybe they are doing it to get our attention and reassurance that they are still loved when they do something very 'wrong'. Sometimes they may feel that they are 'bad' inside so doing something bad helps everything make sense.

Some of our children not only lie to us but also lie to themselves. They may be struggling so badly with self-esteem that they genuinely believe their own lies as a way to stay safe.

If any of this resonates, and we think our child's lying or stealing may be a form of self-preservation, then punishing them may make things worse. This is especially the case if they *want* to be punished as they feel bad about themselves.

If the lying and stealing is a protection mode behaviour, even in part, it may make sense to focus on getting and keeping them out of protection mode. The chapters in Part 2 suggest how to do this.

If our child's hidden disability causes problems of impulsivity and working memory, we need to take this into account. These are *symptoms* and not bad behaviour and need to be treated as symptoms. We would not punish the symptoms of visible illnesses or disabilities. Our children may need help with how to manage their impulsive urges to act before thinking something through.

Many of our child's symptoms or weaknesses can be channelled into strengths. If we are able to do this, we may be able to help them break unpleasant habits like lying and stealing.

Not all lying or stealing is a response to protection mode. People may also lie for other reasons, including to manipulate and control others, to get things, to gain power or advantage over others or simply to fuel their egos to feel superior. Children with hidden disability are not saints and may be as likely to do these things as anyone else.

By truly learning to listen to the music and not the words with our loved ones, we will be better able to recognise which kind of lying and stealing we are dealing with.

Chapter 5

HOW PROTECTION MODE AFFECTS MIND AND BODY

As well as affecting our children's behaviour, being in protection mode with an overheating pressure cooker will clearly affect their bodies and their state of mind. Hidden disabilities often involve biological differences that cause physical symptoms as well as changes to moods and states of mind. Many of these symptoms get worse when our child is simultaneously dealing with flooding stress hormones. Others only occur when our child is in protection mode.

This is why it is helpful to shine a light on how this may show up for our child. Remembering that everyone is affected differently, this gives some clues on how we may be able to decode what our children may be experiencing.

SENSORY SENSITIVITY

'I'll be OK if you leave me alone. Please don't talk to me or touch me. I would be grateful if you would explain this to anyone who asks.' (Isabella)

One of the most common features of many hidden disabilities is some form of sensory sensitivity. Knowing how to recognise this in our child helps us to understand their needs and how to help them out of protection mode.

Sensory sensitivity is a spectrum. At one end of the spectrum is when our child is extremely sensitive to every noise, touch or smell. Too much of this turns the heat up under their pressure cooker and pushes them deeper into protection mode. This is *sensory overload.*

At the other end of the spectrum is when our child finds that the *lack* of noise, touch or smell turns up the heat under their pressure cooker and pushes them deeper into protection mode. We could call this *sensory underload.*

Sensory overload happens when we are getting more input from our five senses than our brain can sort through and process.

There may be many conversations going on at once, background music, flashing overhead lights, pneumatic drills or a loud party. Our child may be overwhelmed by strong smells, itchy textures, a barking dog, changing expectations, unfamiliar flavours, unfamiliar people.

Sensory overload tends to be associated with people on the autism spectrum and mood disorders but anyone can get it when they are stressed. Most of us recognise that feeling when every sound can grate and put our nerves on edge. Sensory overload makes us irritable, restless and wound up.

As our child is struggling to keep her pressure cooker from exploding, the extra challenge of too much sensory data can be just too much. One noise or smell too many can tip any susceptible child from protection mode into a full-on meltdown, shutdown or aggressive or defiant behaviour.

When we understand how protection mode works, we see how difficult noisy schools and open plan workplaces can be. This is why many of our children do better in smaller, quieter schools. And this is why our children often need to have quiet places to 'turn down the heat' from sensory overload.

As our children come out of protection mode and have more control over their lives, they can become more resilient to the bombardment of the senses. One young person I know who had problems with this really enjoyed working in Hong Kong, which is probably the sensory overload capital of the world. This was possible as their pressure cooker was not overheated at this time and they were not in protection mode.

Equally important and worth looking out for is something that looks like the *opposite* of sensory overload. Sensory underload is rarely talked about and is especially common in children on the ADHD spectrum, although anyone can get it too.

Children with sensory underload may shut down, become irritated or defiant or even out of control when there is not enough going on to stimulate them. They may need a lot of stimulation in order to stay interested and focused on what they are doing.

Children with underload may work best with lots of sensory stuff going on to keep them stimulated. It is not uncommon for these children to study best with the television on, music playing and while having a number of conversations all at the same time.

While most people dislike being bored, for children with sensory underload, boredom is something much, much bigger and can become a symptom of their hidden disability. In fact, the boredom can be so severe that the frustration can push them over the edge into a meltdown or a shutdown.

Jake, who has ADD, describes how boredom feels for a child with sensory underload:

> When I'm bored I just can't do what people are saying I should do. It's impossible. If feels like a massive itch in my stomach or a coil that is winding me up until I feel I'm going to explode. The only way I can cope is to get stimulation. The easiest way is to do something crazy in class which will shake things up for me. Other times I go into a day dream which I can make pretty interesting.

And to test our code-breaking skills even further, some children with hidden disabilities have both sensory overload and sensory underload, although not usually at the same time. They may need to be alone in a totally quiet place to be able to study without overwhelm, but also need to regularly walk around busy streets, listen to loud music and go to noisy parties to prevent the underwhelm that may shut them down.

This can cause a lot of confusion to parents and teachers. On the one hand they may be trying to provide a quiet environment for the child to decompress only to find the same child wanting to listen to heavy metal music at top volume to help them concentrate.

To help us understand this, we can remember that sensory overload and sensory underload are two sides of the same coin. That coin is sensory *sensitivity*. If our child is in protection mode, they are likely to be more sensitive to their senses in whatever way this reveals itself for our individual child.

INVOLUNTARY ACTIONS

'Pull my ear lobe. Now pull it fast. Carry on. Now stop pulling. Think about pulling it. Pull it again. Now stop. Pull, pull, pull. Want to stop but can't. It's on repeat. An endless loop.' (Becky)

Many children with hidden disabilities do repetitive actions. Some may be involuntary and for others there is some level of control. They are often called *tics* or *stims* and can cause considerable embarrassment to our loved ones. They may also have to endure critical comments and judgements from others who do not 'get it'.

The actions can include include body jolts, repetitive blinking, coughing, head banging or repeating a sound or phrase. They can also include rhythmic rocking, flapping hands, jumping or pacing, scratching the skin, stroking particular objects or rearranging things compulsively. At times the actions can cause physical harm to themselves or others.

Repetitive actions are listed as diagnostic features of ADHD, autism spectrum disorders and OCD. They are a central feature of a diagnosis of Tourette's.

Involuntary repetitive actions have a lot of possible causes. They are not caused directly by being in protection mode, but many people find that relieving pressure and gaining control and trust over their lives can reduce the severity considerably.

For this reason, it is very helpful to learn to decode our child's involuntary actions.

A good starting point is again to think about ourselves. Many of us do repetitive and involuntary actions and many are socially acceptable and considered 'normal', although somewhat irritating to others.

We may find it hard to stop ourselves biting our nails, twirling our hair or cracking our joints. Some people continuously tap their pencil, whistle or clear their throat whenever they are bored or upset. No matter how much people point out these habits to us, it can be very difficult for us to stop doing them.

It is useful to try to understand what triggers us to do these things, what type of relief doing them brings us and when we do not feel the need to do them. Understanding our own clues can help us start to understand our child's.

The difference between our repetitive actions and our children's is that for people with hidden disabilities they may not be considered socially acceptable, be more extreme and can go on for a long time. For some people with hidden disabilities, they happen nearly all the time.

For many of us, including our children, repetitive actions are a way of relieving pressure. This is why it can be so helpful to try to relieve the amount of pressure building up in our child's pressure cooker.

They often start with an unpleasant sensation that builds up in the body until it is released by doing the action.

Repetitive actions can feel good for our loved ones, especially when they are overwhelmed, frightened, angry or simply bored and frustrated. They can bring immediate comfort. Some people also find that the repetitive actions help them to focus as they can quieten down racing thoughts and overwhelming feelings.

Alex Lowery, who has ADHD, Asperger's and OCD, describes how it feels:

> When I'm on my own, or even just with my family who accept it, I tend to be very extreme with my movements, which I believe are a mix of both stims and tics. I'll jump up and down as well as run around. These movements together really provide a strong relief for me.
>
> I'll tend to use my whole body as I think about past events and things that make me really excited. The stimming aspect in particular can really provide a strong focus for me when it comes to things I'm interested in.[1]

Thinking about this, the effect seems similar to types of meditation where people repeat a mantra over and over. Many people find that repeating mantras helps to clear the mind, relax the body and create better clarity and focus. Other forms of meditation involve passing beads through our fingers in a rhythmic way. Doing this does seem to be a controlled type of repetitive action.

Maybe our children are on to something with this that we can all learn from? Or maybe the meditation practices give us some clues to other ways our children may be able to calm the racing thoughts and gain the relief and clarity they need?

EXHAUSTION AND PHYSICAL ILLNESS

'Do not confuse my bad days as a sign of weakness. Those are actually the days I am fighting the hardest.' (Michael)

Many parents of children with hidden disabilities report that their children seem to be constantly exhausted and go from one illness to the next. Some of us are so confused by this that we may wonder if our child is making it all up, maybe for attention or to get out of doing things like going to school. This is one possibility, and if we suspect it we will need to look for other clues.

Other explanations are also possible and need to be taken into account. We need to remember that protection mode is when the body is in a low-level fight or flight mode. This means that our child's body feels under threat and produces powerful stress hormones such as cortisol and adrenaline to prepare it to run away or fight. This dump of hormones is supposed to be short term until the danger has passed.

For our children it doesn't pass. Their bodies may feel they are in a threat situation the whole time that they are in protection mode.

As fight or flight hormones are designed to be short term, if they continue our child may very quickly become depleted of all bodily resources and their energy crashes.

When we understand what stress hormones do to the body, it is not surprising that our children are exhausted much of the time.

People in protection mode often cannot find the energy to do even basic things, not because they are lazy or unmotivated, but because they have literally run out of juice as all their resources have been used up on keeping them safe from the threats their body thinks it is seeing. This may be why they need so much recovery time and are so often in a 'zoned out' state.

This not only affects our child with a hidden disability but can affect us too as we may also be in protection mode.

We know that to fuel the extra power needed by fight or flight, other body functions are weakened or shut down. This includes the brain, and this is why our children cannot study and learn well when they are in protection mode.

Another body function that is weakened by stress hormones is the immune system. If the immune system is weak, our child may be more susceptible to any illness going around and it may take them longer to recover than a child with a stronger immune system.

Many of our children are also suffering ongoing physical pain in addition to the other symptoms of their hidden disabilities. Our child may have a range of chronic health conditions in addition to their hidden disability. Common ones for children with ASD and ADHD are joint and digestive problems, sometimes severe.

It is not uncommon for anyone to physically faint or have nausea when they are having a severe fight or flight reaction, as stress hormones direct the blood supply away from the head and stomach. Our Victorian ancestors understood this when they carried smelling salts around with them to treat people who passed out when in shock. Nowadays, people who experience this are more likely to be judged and disregarded.

For some this can be a vicious cycle. A child with chronic fatigue has a medical condition that causes exhaustion. The struggle to carry out their life without the energy they need can understandably make them more and more stressed, anxious and frustrated. This releases stress hormones and can push them deeper into protection mode. The stress hormones produce additional exhaustion on top of what is produced by the illness.

Another important factor that affects our child's energy levels is sleep. Insomnia is a characteristic of many hidden disabilities, and the reasons for this are complicated and not well understood.

One possible factor is again stress hormones. We know that fight or flight hormones are designed to keep us awake to deal with a threat. They would be pretty useless if they let us fall asleep when a sabre-toothed tiger was approaching. Children in protection mode are likely to have a high level of these hormones circulating that may make them too wired to sleep.

They may also have body clock irregularities, racing minds that will not switch off at night or physical pain that makes sleep very difficult. The result is an extra level of exhaustion that can impact every other area of life, including the ability to regulate their pressure cooker, stress and moods.

Exhaustion and protection mode form a cycle that feeds on itself. The more exhausted they become, the more anxious they become about not being able to do something important, such as sitting an exam or holding down a job. Then this frustration can produce a fight or flight response that causes yet more exhaustion, and the cycle continues.

Helping our loved one to get out of protection mode can be very important in breaking the cycle between exhaustion and anxiety.

This might mean allowing them to rest when they are exhausted and teaching them to listen to their bodies and pace themselves accordingly.

This can be very frustrating for our loved ones, especially if there are a lot of things they want to do and achieve but are prevented from doing due to exhaustion.

Understanding and teaching them how stress hormones *biologically* cause extreme exhaustion and that it is *not their fault* can help them to be kinder and more compassionate to themselves at these times. Knowing the scientific explanation for the exhaustion can make it easier for them to both understand and accept it.

It also helps us to be more understanding of, and compassionate to, our children if they need extended periods of downtime.

We need to remember that recovery time is not 'wasted' time. For anyone with a hidden disability it is essential time and just as necessary for productivity as time doing apparently more meaningful activities.

No matter how brilliant and sophisticated our mobile phones are, unless we give them the time they need to recharge and close down applications we are not using, they are not going to work. Our children are no different and neither are we.

MOTIVATION AND FOCUS PROBLEMS

'My ADD makes it hard for me to focus and focus sounds like hocus pocus and I really like magic a whole lot. Abracadabra!' (Daniel)

Our child may spend a lot of time daydreaming, be forgetful and procrastinate a lot. It can be really hard to get them started on a task and they sometimes find it almost impossible to have any motivation at all. Then they may be distracted by the 'wrong' task and seem to have no idea about setting priorities and getting things done.

This could be because our child is tired, overwhelmed or over-stressed. Their pressure cooker may just be too hot and procrastination may be their body's way of giving them the space they need to rest. They may need to avoid doing things to give themselves time to recover.

Just as our thinking brain can shut down when we are flooded with stress hormones, so does our ability to focus on tasks, work out plans of action, and remember the facts and steps we need to carry them out.

Sometimes the problem is finding the motivation for getting started and if we do get started, knowing at what point we should stop a task. Or it can result in an almost obsessive focus on one thing to the exclusion of everything else that needs doing. Or it can result in flitting from one task to another without focusing on anything to the point of completion.

Unless we understand how to decode these things in our children, this state of affairs can cause a lot of suffering and frustration, especially if they feel shamed for it or punished.

Sometimes our loved ones are unable to start or complete a task because they are perfectionists. It may be easier not to do a task at all than risk anything but an A+ grade for it. If they consider anything less than the top grade to be a fail, this hugely increases the anxiety around the task, pushing them further into protection mode. This makes them more likely to shut down rather than attempt the task at all.

If we can relate to this, we can see why telling our child 'just to do their best' may fall on deaf ears when they are in protection mode and can even make them feel worse, as they may despair that mum or dad is just not 'getting it'.

When our child does manage to get started on a task, their lack of focus can become an obsessive focus. They may get so engrossed that they are unable to stop, even when the task is complete or something more important needs to be done.

So, although we may hope that our child will spend half an hour on a homework task to design a book cover, she may still be perfecting the details four hours later, ignoring all the other tasks to be done. Rather than being praised for the beautiful book cover, she may then be punished for not having done her maths.

Although our child may have 'attention deficit' or 'inability to concentrate' as part of their diagnosis, when something grabs his or her attention it can become an obsessive focus or passion.

Our daughter may stay up all night, engrossed in building a model unicorn, but be unable to focus on the task of tidying her room. Completing a challenging level on a computer game can be more important to our son than completing a homework task due the next morning and may even be more important than eating or drinking.

This can affect the physical body too. Our loved one may check out from personal hygiene or from choosing appropriate clothing. Or it can result in the opposite, causing an obsessive focus on getting a hairstyle 'perfect', or having a 'fashionable' body shape or the 'right' clothing.

Motivation and focus problems are not only caused by overwhelm and stress. Many children with hidden disabilities need stimulation in order to be able to focus. If they are not interested in the task or if it is boring or repetitive, they may go to great lengths to avoid doing it as the frustration or boredom may be too much to endure.

Will, who has ADD, explains:

> We had to write up boring lab reports every week and I just couldn't get myself to do it. So I kept telling the teacher that I'd lost my book and I entertained myself by thinking up more and more crazy excuses for not doing it. The teacher's angry reaction gave me the stimulation I needed.

If motivation and focus affect our child in this way, we may need to take steps to find them tasks that are meaningful to them so that they don't need to find stimulation in 'unproductive' ways. They may even be able to build up a 'boredom reserve' to give them enough focus to do the things they may not enjoy so much.

When our child is not focused on the tasks that need doing, we may worry that they lack ambition and drive, are lazy, don't care about their lives or are trying to spite or punish us.

We may feel that they are ungrateful after all the opportunities we have set up for them, all the encouragement we have given, all the sacrifices we have made. Despite everything we are doing for them, they may remain in their bedrooms and not participate fully in life. Our frustration with this is very understandable.

But to support our kids, we need to find a way to replace this judgement with *understanding* of what the behaviour is really telling us, however difficult this may be, however unreasonable it may appear. Within our child's world, much of their behaviour makes sense when we are able to decode the clues.

When our loved ones are no longer in protection mode, many of these focus issues may either reduce or disappear completely. In the interim, they may need extra help getting started on tasks and support with getting organised. We may have to get creative to make tasks more interesting. When protection mode is bad, we may have to be patient and accept that they simply cannot get things done at this time.

We also need to remember the positives. When our child will *only* focus on tasks that really interest them, rather than what they are asked to do, we need to remember this can bring huge and even groundbreaking success to our loved ones.

There is a good reason that so many great innovations are carried out by people with hidden disabilities, especially ADHD, bipolar and those on the autism spectrum. They do so because they focus on their passions and interests, often regardless of other things people may want them to do.

This is why we have the popular image of the brilliant professor, so focused on cracking a mathematical dilemma that she forgets to brush her hair or wear matching socks. Frequently these brilliant people even forget to eat.

Learning to read our own clues can also help us decode our child. What motivates us to get going on a task? What makes it hard to get started? Are we better able to focus on simple repetitive tasks or difficult and challenging ones?

The answers are unlikely to be the same as for our child but doing this can help us to focus on what we need to figure out for them.

CHAOS AND LACK OF ORGANISATION

'I think the dog ate my homework.' (Justin)

Our child may be chaotic, disorganised, unable to plan time or possessions and create mess wherever they go.

Total chaos is politely referred to as *executive function* difficulties by psychologists and even has its own stand-alone diagnosis of executive function disorder. Anyone can have executive function difficulties, especially when in protection mode. For our children it is most commonly seen with ADHD, ADD, dyslexia, dyspraxia and autism spectrum conditions. In fact, it is a listed symptom for some of these diagnoses.

Many neurotypical children are messy and forgetful, especially teenagers, but executive function problems take this to such an extreme level that they can affect every aspect of our child's life.

Our son may be unable to enter his own room due to the mountains of mess. Deadlines for tasks are not only missed but completely forgotten. Our daughter may be too disorganised to get things done and no matter how often we remind her, she cannot remember what to do and when.

Our child may be clueless about how to prioritise, be a scatter-brain, have little concept of time, be constantly losing everything, including passports, keys and school work. They may be really easily distracted and have problems listening, often disappearing into a bubble of chaos.

The chaos drives parents and teachers crazy, and attempts to deal with it through discipline often make things worse.

Psychologist Nicole Carvill explains:

> Dear Parent – I see that you're frustrated. And I see that your child is too. You wish your child would just listen, follow through and complete their schoolwork; stop getting so distracted and stop over-reacting when things don't go their way.
>
> What if I told you that what appears to be a behaviour issue; something worthy of a time-out, lecture, loss of privilege or other such punishment, might actually be a cognitive issue, requiring quite a different response?[2]

Executive function difficulties are due to brain differences, especially in the frontal lobe of the brain that affect our child's working memory and ability to organise tasks.

Our child is probably not being 'naughty' and may genuinely not remember what he is supposed to be doing, especially if he is distracted, upset or feels under pressure.

However infuriating and frustrating this is for us as parents, it is infinitely worse for our loved ones themselves, who become more and more stressed and overwhelmed by the task of getting themselves organised.

Our child is not enjoying this any more than we are.

A room can become messy beyond the point of no return. Homework can bottleneck to the point that it is beyond possible to know where to start.

I have seen children spend hours producing beautiful and amazing work only to get no marks for it and a punishment. This could be because it was lost before being handed in or it had become a wet, screwed-up mess in their bag on the way to school. Or our child may have been so focused on the work that the deadline was missed as he was unable to organise his time. This can result in an automatic fail in the case of exam course work. This is heartbreaking for our child.

In some ways this is like the *opposite* of the obsessive *order* some children do to make themselves feel safe, which in its most severe form is OCD (obsessive compulsive disorder). Creating too much disorder or too much order seem to be opposite ends of the same spectrum. Some children have both extremes, sometimes even at the same time, which is really confusing for both them and us.

The good news is that much can be done to help children with their executive function difficulties when we understand them as a code related to their hidden disability. I had this problem as a child and still do when I am under stress.

There are lots of books and resources to help our child to get organised. None are likely to help while our child is feeling under threat, as she may be far too overwhelmed to be able to engage with what we are teaching.

As protection mode is a reaction to feeling under threat, adding in punishments, pressure and demands is likely to push our child deeper into protection mode, and therefore deeper into chaos, overwhelm and disorganisation. As the chaos gets worse it can feel totally smothering to the child.

Although children with executive function difficulties may appear lazy, sloppy and slovenly, there may be some sort of system in the chaos. They may escape from the pressure of everything they are supposed to be doing, escape from the chaos, by doing something *brilliant* instead.

Without being requested by an adult, a beautiful craft model may suddenly be made, music composed, a poem written, or some software developed with creative coding. Among the chaos, my own son became an amazing film-maker and I became a writer.

As Winnie-the-Pooh says:

> One of the advantages of being disorganised is that one is always having surprising discoveries.[3]

As someone who still struggles with this, I know that when my mind is calm and I feel in control of my life, the thinking brain kicks back in and enables me to work out strategies to compensate for my terrible working memory. This is why getting our child out of protection mode will help with chaos and disorganisation.

If our children are able to recognise and accept that they have this problem, they can take action to help themselves. To have a productive life they may need a life full of lists, flow charts and multiple reminders coming from our technology as well as post-it notes everywhere. I certainly do!

DEPRESSION AND ANXIETY

'My brain is a piece of lead. It's too heavy and I can't think or do anything, so what's the point? But I've got things to do but just can't. That's when I panic and shut down.' (Cameron)

Many of our children with a hidden disability are depressed. This may be for chemical reasons, as may be the case with bipolar disorder or clinical depression. They may also be overwhelmed by the task of managing complex lives and emotions with a hidden disability that is little understood by most people and institutions.

Often the depression can result from our child's frustration at being stuck, inertia and procrastination. They may be frustrated by their inability to get anything done, and judge themselves harshly for this, maybe feeling like a failure and that they have let us down.

This feeling of failure can also be fuelled when unrealistic expectations are made of them, perhaps by teachers or family members. Most commonly the unrealistic expectations are of themselves.

How this feels is summed up brilliantly by an anonymous writer who posted:

> Having anxiety and depression is like being scared and tired at the same time. It's the fear of failure, but no urge to be productive. It's wanting friends, but hating socialising. It's wanting to be alone, but not wanting to be lonely. It's feeling everything at once, then feeling paralysingly numb.[4]

Depression can also result from feeling disconnected with the world and other people, an experience hugely exacerbated if they are also being bullied or do not have a supportive group of friends, a common occurrence among people with hidden disabilities.

Depression can be a downward spiral, as our child sees more and more apparent 'evidence' that they are 'failing' and may lack the ability to take control of anything. They may see other children getting sports awards, being 'popular', getting higher grades, looking cuter, being more 'respected'.

When we understand this, it is not at all surprising that our children often find solace in virtual worlds, daydreaming and withdrawing from life. Things can get to the stage where they feel, 'What's the point?' and this can lead to suicidal thoughts.

Depression and other hidden disability symptoms can become easily blurred. Depression can lead to black-and-white thinking, repetitive thoughts and feeling intensely that they are cut off from life and other people. These are also symptoms of some of the hidden disabilities so it is not surprising how many of our loved ones become seriously depressed.

We need to remember the difference here between *clinical* depression and 'feeling low'. In day-to-day speech, the word 'depression' is often used to refer to feeling down or unhappy about something. For example, we might say that we are 'depressed by the state of the economy' or that we are 'depressed because we failed an exam'.

When we are feeling low or unhappy, we can usually cheer ourselves up by something nice happening, or by distracting ourselves with a fun activity, being with friends, going for a run or having an almond croissant.

But when our child is in clinical depression, this is something infinitely more debilitating and complex. Suggestions about doing things to cheer themselves up can feel really patronising and unhelpful and can make them feel even more misunderstood.

When our loved ones are depressed and also in protection mode, as we know, the logical thinking part of the brain will be largely shut down as the body is in a fight or flight response. Even if we point out lots of positive things, for example that they are beautiful, talented, clever and loved, our child may not be able to hear or recognise the truth of what we are saying at these times.

Depression has a knock-on effect too. It is a big factor in treatment non-compliance, when our loved one refuses to take their medication, supplements, special diets or attend medical consultations. This can result in a worsening of their main diagnostic symptoms, which can again fuel their depression, causing yet another downward spiral.

A similar thing occurs with anxiety. Again, chemical and brain differences with some hidden disabilities can make our children more likely to suffer from clinical anxiety. This is especially true for children on the autism spectrum, especially girls and of course those with diagnoses of anxiety disorders.

Again, we need to remember the difference between *clinical* anxiety and 'feeling nervous'. Clinical anxiety is a chemical response resulting in shutdown, meltdown or any of the other protection mode symptoms.

Shutdown (including fainting) at an exam due to clinical anxiety is not the same as exam nerves that can be overcome with a few breathing exercises and sufficient willpower.

At its most extreme are panic attacks, something I did not fully understand until I experienced them myself this year at a time of big transition in my life. When these happen, you are not aware of either panic or anxiety. Instead, it feels rather like a heart attack with chest pain and the inability to breath. Speech and vision are affected, and consciousness can even be lost. I am grateful that I have experienced this as it helps me understand how it can affect others, especially those with hidden disabilities.

I have found that many teachers are confused about or unaware of the difference between clinical anxiety and feeling nervous. They may also not 'get' the difference between clinical depression and feeling down.

It is important to remember these distinctions, especially when trying to get support for our child. If we are really clear about this difference, it will be far easier for us to explain it to others and to advocate for our child.

The result of this confusion is that teachers or family members may expect our child to do things that they simply cannot do and may punish them for 'laziness' or 'not trying hard enough'. Our child may be expected to walk into an examination room during a clinical anxiety attack, or our potentially suicidal son may be told to 'just cheer up'.

Although clinical depression and anxiety are complicated biological and psychological processes, getting a child out of protection mode will certainly do much to alleviate them. Even an improvement of about 20 per cent may get our child's brain sufficiently online for other psychological support to help them. Unless our child can hear and think straight, whatever help is offered is going to fall on deaf ears.

BEING IMPULSIVE OR RECKLESS

'I just don't get why people expect me to hang around analysing stuff. I know what I want to do and just get on with it. Why is that a problem?' (Anil)

A person is impulsive when they have the urge to act on a whim, with little or no forethought and without taking into account the consequences of their actions.

Any glance at a parent forum for children with hidden disabilities shows that being impulsive is often a significant problem, especially with ADHD, ADD, autism spectrum or mood disorders.

Psychologist Dr Angie seems to especially 'get' this one:

> If out at a restaurant, having to 'keep an eye on them' to make sure they don't hit a stranger, pour the salt on the table, reach across the table knocking someone's glass and so on and so on.[5]

Being impulsive is called 'poor impulse control' by psychologists and is thought to be due to the under-development of the frontal cortex of the brain. The effect is that our child may find it harder to override immediate wants or needs.

While a neurotypical child may be able to pause and think of the consequences before doing something, our child's brain chemistry may make this much harder or even impossible. This may cause them to grab at food or toys they want, abandon tasks or leave their chairs at school to wander around classrooms or out of the house. They may also have tantrums when their wishes are not met as they do not have the skills to control their emotional reactions to things like sadness, frustration or anger.

Although we all can can act impulsively at times, most of us have some awareness of the consequences of our actions and can draw on previous experiences and figure out what the consequences may be. According to Dr Angie, things can be somewhat different for our loved ones:

> I am sure that you would agree that many of our kiddos on the spectrum, as well as those with ADHD, don't seem to learn from their experiences or our parental counsel.
>
> When they have an experience, it seems as if the experience has gone right through them, gone forever. If that is the case then they cannot reflect on the past experience when similar circumstances arise. So they keep doing the same things over and over and keep wondering why they continue to get in trouble.[6]

As parents we are taught to use consequences and rewards to get the behaviour we want from our children. This often does not work at all for children with poor impulse control as they may not be able to learn from the consequences of their actions. This is hugely frustrating to parents, who can be at a loss as to what to do.

Although poor impulse control is a complicated biological thing, it does seem to get much worse when a person is very stressed. Dr Michail Mantzios researched the relationship between worry and impulsivity among military recruits. He found that:

> Impulsivity serves to avoid the stress or, in other words, to release the pressure to cope. Becoming more impulsive is related to damaging behaviours and unsuccessful coping.[7]

This suggests that people who are under severe stress, such as soldiers, can use impulsive behaviour as a way of releasing the heat from their pressure cooker, often with damaging effects. This is really helpful to understand. It seems very possible that a similar thing may be happening to our children who are in protection mode.

We know that the learning part of the brain is offline when our children are in protection mode. When we remember this, it makes sense that this may affect their ability to learn lessons from their past experiences and to be able to calmly imagine all the potential outcomes of an action.

If this is the case, helping our children out of protection mode may help them with impulsivity as it gives them the best conditions for learning and clear thinking.

We also need to remember the positives of being impulsive and, like everything else, that how healthy it is is a question of balance. When being impulsive is healthy, we call it being *spontaneous*.

Without ever being spontaneous, our lives would be very boring indeed. Life would be very predictable and we would feel like machines. There is quite a thin line between being impulsive and being spontaneous.

Spontaneity can be a refreshing and lovely thing, even though it involves some element of risk. Deepak Chopra and Rudolph Tanzi say:

> If you are too impulsive, your anger, fear and desire will run out of control. This leads to rash actions and regret afterwards. If you control your impulses too much, your life becomes cold and repressed. This leads to a lack of bonding with others and with your own basic drives.[8]

Problems with impulsivity improve hugely when both we and our child learn how to decode what is happening. There are strategies they can learn to create the 'pause' time they need in order to reflect on what they are about to do. Tips on this are provided in Chapter 6.

ANGER AND IRRITABILITY

'Everything is wrong. Everything! I scream to get it out. Why can't things be right? Everything is just... Ahhhhh!' (Alicia)

Everyone feels angry to some extent when we believe an injustice is being done or when we feel frustrated that life is not going the way we deserve it to go. It's a normal way of our body alerting us that something may need to be done or changed.

Most of us to some extent learn how to manage our anger so that it does not control our actions and poison our lives.

For our loved ones with hidden disabilities, anger and irritability can reach another level. Their hidden disability may already cause them to have problems with communicating their feelings and distresses. If we add to this all their very real extra frustrations in life, it is not surprising that moods can shift from calm to rage and even aggression very quickly indeed. Our children genuinely have a lot to be angry about and may lack the resources to manage the strong emotions.

Cynthia Kim, in her blog about living with Asperger's, wrote:

> We autistics are apparently an angry bunch. And it's no wonder. As children, the world comes at us with an intensity that is confusing, frustrating and, yes, aggravating. Add to that years of miscommunication, bullying, rejection and being misunderstood and it's not surprising to see the 'angry autistic' has become a deeply entrenched stereotype.[9]

Sometimes this can result in a full-on meltdown or 'rage', or its opposite form, a shutdown (see Chapter 3). At other times, it results in a general irritability and anger that can affect many areas of their lives, especially their relationships with others.

The good news is that I know more people who have overcome their uncontrolled anger and irritability than I can count. What seems to work best is learning to recognise and accept their emotions, including anger. When they are able to do this, they can start to learn how to process their experiences and manage how they are feeling.

Cynthia Kim explains:

> So much of my anger as a teen and young adult was related to feeling vulnerable and inadequate. As those feelings have dissipated I've released a lot of the deeply entrenched anger that built up during those years. I'm arriving at a place of acceptance. I'm slowly dusting off the layers of my adult self, like an archaeologist at an ancient dig site, careful not to damage what I'm uncovering.[10]

We know that protection mode largely shuts down the thinking and learning brain. When our child is in protection mode it is especially difficult for them to learn the skills they need to recognise and manage their emotions and anger. This is another reason why helping them out of protection mode can make a big difference to our child's anger and irritability. The next chapters give some suggestions on how we can help our children in this way.

WHEN IT HAS NOTHING TO DO WITH THE HIDDEN DISABILITY

> *'Although I have bipolar, I am just as likely to be annoyed and angry as anyone else. When I am mad it does not necessarily mean that it has anything to do with my bipolar!'* (Richard)

Although our children have hidden disabilities, first and foremost, like us, they are human beings who are doing the best they can.

Although a whole range of behaviours and responses can be affected by their disability or protection mode, often they are simply normal reactions to the stresses of life. Many of the things our loved one does will be done by any person of their age. Most children and young people get angry, are fussy sometimes with food, spend too much time gaming or at times are defiant, messy or chaotic.

For our loved ones, it can be infuriating if everything and anything they do is attributed to the hidden disability. It can be extremely patronising to explain everything they do as being part of protection mode.

Sometimes they may be playing a computer game simply because they are having fun, not as an escape from the stresses of life. Sometimes they will want to eat carrots every day because they really love carrots and not because carrots are the only safe food in an unsafe world.

One of my children has a mood disorder and when they were a child, there were times when their bedroom door would be slammed loudly. I decoded this as meaning that my child's mood was unstable at that moment. This went on for many years. When my child insisted that it was the 'door's fault', I was more focused on their moods and my reactions than on the efficiency of the carpentry in our house. Years later my child calmly suggested that we oil the door hinges and after doing so it no longer slams.

In this case it really was the 'door's fault' and this is an example of where 'listening to the music and not the words' can be taken too far. Sometimes we need to listen to the words too and not overthink things or draw too many conclusions.

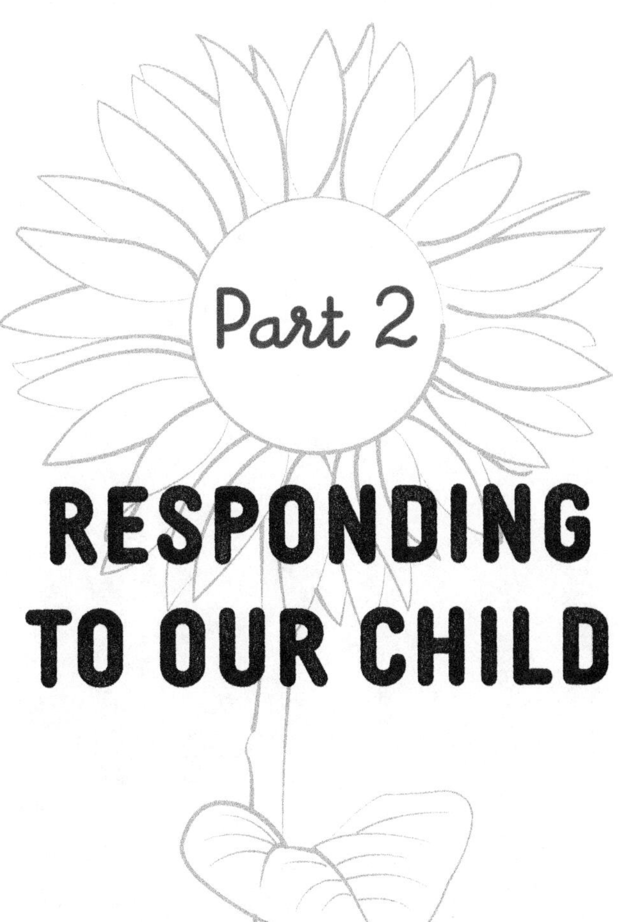

Part 2

RESPONDING TO OUR CHILD

Chapter 6

MANAGING MELTDOWNS AND SHUTDOWNS

This part of the book is about how we can mindfully parent our child with a hidden disability in a way that recognises their needs and experiences.

Whereas the previous part was about decoding and understanding our child's behaviour, this part is about what we can do about it.

Before looking at strategies it is helpful to remember a few principles. Firstly, that there is no magic bullet to solve all of our or our child's problems. We are not trying to change who our child is or make them neurotypical. Instead, we are finding ways to reduce incidents that are destructive to our children and our family life. We are looking for strategies that help our child out of protection mode, so that they can draw on their strengths, shine and meet their potential.

All children are individuals and we all have different family circumstances, environments and levels of support. There is no 'one size fits all' way to get them out of protection mode. We will need to trust our instincts, use trial and error and be prepared to learn from our mistakes.

We also need to remember that children with hidden disabilities may take longer to hit some milestones, like learning to ride a bike, tie their shoe laces, use the toilet, dress themselves or take the bus to school.

When our children are stable, calm and out of protection mode they can often very quickly catch up. Life is not a race.

THE TRAFFIC LIGHT APPROACH

Chapter 3 explained how our child has an internal 'pressure cooker'. When too much pressure builds up from the stress of daily life, like a pressure cooker it can explode with disastrous consequences.

If we cook with a pressure cooker, we will know that we can prevent it from exploding. For a start, pressure cookers come with a release valve on the top which can be used to let off pressure when too much steam has built up. Apart from this, a very quick way to prevent an explosion is to switch off the heat under the cooker to cool it down fast. We can either switch off the heat completely or turn it right down until the pressure comes under control.

Not only does understanding how to cook with a pressure cooker help us to understand meltdowns and rages, it also gives us a key to how to deal with them and also how to prevent them.

This is equally relevant for shutdowns, which are explosions that turn inwards rather than outwards. In fact, shutdowns become more common as a child gets older. As meltdowns can be very shameful for our child, they may develop skills to repress them, directing the explosion inwards instead. The explosion still happens, but how it shows itself will be very different.

Meltdowns, rages and shutdowns are an emotional explosion due to too much build-up of steam. Chapter 3 described how this feels for our child and how a slow drip, drip of seemingly trivial stresses can cause their pressure valve to hit the red.

What we want to do is *release* the pressure before an explosion occurs. This is very different from *repressing* it so that the pressure comes out in another way. If pressure is repressed rather than released, meltdowns may be replaced not only with shutdowns, but also with a range of other serious and self-harming behaviours.

We know that meltdowns usually happen around people our children feel safe and secure with. This means us, if we are caring and loving parents. We are their safe place when they need to explode.

As we are likely to be on the receiving end of them, this also means that it is *we* who need to be super clear about how we respond to meltdowns and help our child to prevent them.

Other people are likely to have their points of views on how to manage meltdowns and shutdowns and may blame or criticise us. This really hurts when we are already being hurt by our child's behaviour. This is why we need to be clear about what we are doing and our reason for doing it.

When we are clear and confident about what we are doing, the judgement of other people will hurt us less. If we have any self-doubt about how to parent meltdowns and shutdowns, the criticism of others can get in through the cracks and be devastating for us.

So that what is suggested here has a context and makes sense, I strongly suggest reading or re-reading Chapter 3 first.

Meltdowns not only drain and exhaust our child, but probably are the number one most stressful thing that parents have to deal with.

Meltdowns are not our fault and do not mean that we are bad parents.

It is important to remember this as many parents tend to blame themselves. Many parents say that they personally feel they have failed if their child is having meltdowns or shutdowns.

Neither are meltdowns our child's fault, and our child is not choosing to have them. They are no-one's fault and just show that our child's hidden disability condition is not yet fully stabilised.

Nothing tests our compassion for our child more than seeing that he has smashed the computer, told us he hates us and attacked his beloved sibling. The screaming may wake up neighbours, and our challenges and our child's are laid bare and exposed for other people to see. When our child is having a meltdown, it can feel like a major crisis.

Family members, teachers or neighbours may think that we are dealing with an out of control, abusive, spoilt brat. They may think that we are weak and 'letting' our child behave in this way. Or they may deny that it is happening at all and accuse us of exaggerating or making it up.

During those moments when our child is saying that she hates us, we can feel horrible emotions that we may not want to face. We are human beings who want and expect justice and respect. Even the most saintly and compassionate of parents will feel our own anger rise when we feel under attack from our children, even if we hold it in and suppress it.

Although we may know that the rage is due to our child's hidden disability, we may still want to take action to restore our damaged authority and pride.

When our loved one is having a meltdown, we can feel under attack, and often have extreme stress reactions just like our child's. With stress hormones running through our body, we can easily go into a fight or flight reaction. The instinct for us can be to either react physically (fight) or get in the car and run away (flight).

The suffering and indignation we feel at this time is intense. But as loving parents, we have to bypass these instincts as it would be wrong to fight our child or to flee from her.

We cannot use our natural stress instincts as we are responsible for our child's welfare at this time, as well as our other children. So, we stay put in the fire and the voice in our head screams, 'What can I do? Someone help me!'

As stress hormones close down our thinking brain, the answer is likely to be, 'I don't know what to do. I can't think!'

Basically, when our child has a meltdown, this can cause us to have one too, although ours may be silent. We are human beings and are as likely to react to stress as anyone else. We also have an internal pressure cooker that can and does explode. As our thinking brain may be offline when our child is having a meltdown, we need to have a planned strategy ahead of time.

The best advice I have heard on managing meltdowns and shutdowns came from some wise parents at the Balanced Mind Parent Network. It is called the *traffic light approach*. A similar approach was also explained to me by psychologists at Great Ormond Street Hospital in London. For me, it is the only thing that both made sense and actually worked.

Conventional parenting advice about rewards and consequences is unlikely to help with meltdowns. Instead, the traffic light approach recognises that our child *does not choose* to have meltdowns and *does not want to have them*.

The starting point is remembering that meltdowns and rages are extreme symptoms of our child's hidden disability and need to be treated as we would any other medical crisis. Meltdowns are symptoms to be treated. They are not bad behaviour.

The traffic light approach involves looking at our child and assessing at a glance what the level of pressure is in their internal pressure cooker. In simplest terms, it will be red, orange or green. This means stop, proceed with caution or go.

This takes time and practice to decode and it is normal to make mistakes along the way.

As our child gets older, they will also need to learn the traffic light approach so that they can take action to stop and prevent their meltdowns and shutdowns for themselves.

The traffic light approach to meltdowns is simply:

- Code red is the explosion, the meltdown.
- Code orange is when pressure is rising fast towards an explosion.
- Code green is when pressure is under control.

CODE RED

In code red, our child is having a meltdown or rage. It is not personal and it is not about us. They probably have little or no control over their actions. Their thinking brain has shut down due to the explosion of stress hormones and they cannot be rational. They cannot hear us. The fire is out of control and any words we say that they do pick up may only inflame it more.

In code red our child is in extreme pain and doesn't know how to stop it. They may be angry with us for not stopping the meltdown or protecting them from it. Our child may be terrified too.

After the meltdown, our child may feel crippling shame, embarrassment and confusion about what happened and why. Afterwards he will probably not remember much or any of what happened or was said, other than the shame.

When our child is at code red, we cannot do anything to stop the meltdown any more than our child can do anything to stop it. No parenting strategy using rewards or consequences will halt it.

It is rather like an epileptic fit that once started has to run its course. In fact, there are forms of epilepsy called *frontal lobe seizures*, which can look very similar to the meltdowns and rages children with hidden disabilities often have. If our child has a lot of meltdowns, our doctor may have already done tests to make sure that she does not have this form of epilepsy.

Punishing a child with a 'consequence' for having a meltdown or giving them a reward for not having one may increase the shame our child already feels, as it gives them the idea that they are responsible for the meltdown or that it is their fault.

Having a meltdown is no more our child's fault than it is for a child with epilepsy to have a seizure. Similarly, we would not blame a child with food poisoning for vomiting on the carpet.

Knowing that it is not our job or even possible to stop the meltdown in code red is a big relief.

As parents, we only have one thing to do during a meltdown, and that is to do our best to *keep everyone safe*.

If the explosion is happening or is imminent, our job is purely practical – to get knives out of reach, to quickly protect valuables that can be broken like laptops, to send siblings to another part of the house. That's it. There is nothing else to do, other than giving our child space and staying close enough to keep them safe.

For most children it is best not to touch them during a meltdown or to say anything other than to agree with whatever they are shouting. Apart from keeping people safe, our other job is not to say or do anything to inflame the rage as this will prolong it and make it worse.

This means resisting the urge to criticise our child, shout at him to get him to hear us, grab him or try to restrain him. He will not hear us and it can make things worse by appearing to turn up the heat, regardless of how kind our intentions are.

Rachel, whose son has Asperger's, remembers:

> One time I could see the rumblings of a meltdown, but his dad couldn't and by not giving him space it quickly escalated and I had a child at the top of the stairs going crazy. His dad was trying to comfort him and go to him (natural instinct) but this made it worse so I had to get

> dad away and stand at the bottom of the stairs to catch my son if he fell. In reality it was probably only for a few minutes but it was the longest few minutes of my life. Helpless doesn't come near to describe what that was like!

Obviously if we are unable to keep our child safe, there may be times when we need to use restraint or to call the emergency services. This would be for safeguarding our families, not as a way of 'treating' or 'punishing' the meltdown.

We need to keep reminding ourselves that our child is having a meltdown. Meltdowns are an extreme symptom of our child's hidden disability. It is not personal. She does not mean anything she is saying or doing, and it will end. We need to remember that it is not bad behaviour and it is not 'naughtiness'.

Our other children may be very frightened by what they are witnessing. They will also need reassuring that their brother or sister is not bad or evil, that the meltdown is part of their hidden disability and that their sibling does not know what they are saying.

If we do not inflame the fire, the meltdown will eventually start to wane and then end. This can take minutes or hours.

As a meltdown is waning, this can be a good time to comfort and reassure our child and many will accept cuddles as they are coming out of code red. Our child will be feeling very vulnerable, and I believe our job at this time is to remind them that they are loved and to reassure them that the meltdown was not their fault and that we are not angry with them.

We also need to allow plenty of recovery time. Meltdowns use a lot of energy and are extremely depleting for our child, as Rachel found:

> When Matt has a meltdown, he is exhausted afterwards. Sometimes he just lies on his bed for hours on end, doing literally nothing, just lying there.

We all have code reds when the pressure and pain is bigger than our ability to control it. Many mothers have code reds during childbirth and labour. Remembering how this feels can help us to respond to our child.

During childbirth, when in intense pain, it is very common for mothers to scream angrily, hurl abuse, blame everyone and to swear in a way not dissimilar to a meltdown. During childbirth, this rage is often directed to our husbands and partners, who 'got us into this mess' in the first place. At other times it is directed towards the midwives and others who are supposed to be there to help us.

Most mothers will have screamed and cursed during labour, even those who are saintly and would normally never dream of causing offence or a fuss. It just comes out due to the extreme pain, and the pain is so strong we cannot stop it. How many of us can actually remember all the things we said and shouted during labour? Once it is over it is over.

When we get the urge to get angry at our child for having a rage, or to punish him afterwards, it is helpful to remember times when we have had an equivalent of a meltdown.

How would we feel if we were held accountable for screaming during childbirth and perhaps punished with a consequence after the birth? How would we feel if our midwives or partner abandoned us during labour, when we are at our most vulnerable, for saying a bad word? Our children are probably experiencing similar levels of emotional pain when their explosions happen.

We cannot stop meltdowns when they have started. But there is a lot we can do to prevent them from happening. These strategies can be attempted when our child is at code orange.

CODE ORANGE

Code orange is when our child is at a high risk of having a meltdown. They are very stressed indeed and the pressure in their pressure cooker is dangerously high but is not yet at the point of explosion. There is a tipping point where a meltdown cannot be prevented, but at code orange they have not reached it.

At code orange, an imminent meltdown can be stopped.

Stopping a meltdown in code orange is the priority for the welfare of our child, for us and the whole family. Our job during code orange is to do whatever is necessary to *prevent the meltdown from happening*.

How we do this goes against most parenting advice about rewards and consequences, never giving in to demands and always being consistent. This means that doing what we need to do to prevent a meltdown can make us feel like bad parents or look that way to others.

In code orange, our child can still hear us and control their behaviour to some extent. So, what we say or do can influence whether the pressure is released harmlessly and peace resumes or whether it accelerates into a full-blown meltdown.

For many children in code orange, saying the word 'no' can send them into code red, often within a fraction of a second. Much as we do not want our child to manipulate us, the single best way to prevent code orange from escalating is not to say no or refuse a demand when we can see that our child's pressure cooker is at risk of exploding.

Rebecca found this:

> When my son was close to blowing, when he heard the word 'No', for him it meant rejection and abandonment exactly when he was crying out for help. It would push him straight over the edge.

Our child may be demanding a particular food which we do not have in the house. He may be demanding that we rearrange the furniture a particular way or that a sibling leave the room. Often the child doesn't even really want the thing but will demand it anyway. If we say no, it can result in a meltdown. If we say yes and keep saying yes, a meltdown can be avoided.

The word 'yes' can be like turning the heat off under their pressure cooker. It can cool our child down so quickly that the demand may be forgotten. With the heat right down, it may also be possible to talk about the demand in a reasonable way as their brain may come back online.

The demands may be completely unreasonable and our love of justice and desire to be treated with respect may make us really want to say no! Saying yes when we want to say no can feel weak and wrong.

If we feel that way, it is worth deciding if our love of justice and respect is more important to us than helping our child prevent an emotional explosion. If we put our child's welfare above our need to be right, then we will swallow our pride, say yes and prevent a meltdown.

Being at code orange is not about being 'naughty', wilful or defiant, even if it looks that way to others. Code orange is a fight or flight reaction and our child's body is full of stress hormones. As was explained in Chapter 3, when this happens, two other things also occur:

- The thinking brain shuts down.
- The ability to learn shuts down.

This means that when our child is in code orange he will not be able to learn any parenting lessons we wish to teach him. So, if we say, 'No, you can't have a chocolate bar' during a code orange, he will not learn that it is unacceptable to demand chocolate bars. This is not because we are a bad teacher about right and wrong, but because his brain is shut down to learning during a stress crisis.

It also means that if we try to explain why we are saying no to his demand, he will not be able to understand us or process what we are saying. This is because the thinking brain has shut down. He probably won't remember what we have said after the crisis has passed anyway.

'You are disgusting and I hate you!' Yes.

'I must have ten thousand chocolates now!' Yes.

'It's all your fault.' Yes

'I won't ever go back to school'. Yes.

Saying yes to a child in code orange does not create a spoilt and indulgent brat who always gets his own way and gets what he wants. This is because code orange is not the time for learning lessons about life.

We need to save our parenting lessons for when our child is in code green.

Other things can help to de-escalate a code orange and bring it back into the safety of code green. These include distracting our child quickly with a fun activity, making them laugh by doing something silly or telling them a joke.

Code orange is also a time when assistance dogs can be helpful. Many animals are very sensitive to people's moods and intuitively know how to give comfort and support when someone is highly stressed. A loving dog may run away during a meltdown but demand strokes during code orange, helping our child to calm down. Trained assistance dogs are taught to offer loving restraint and to try to stop rages. Other animals, especially horses, can have a similar effect.

Michael, whose son has multiple hidden disabilities, said:

> Roxy, our Golden Retriever, would lie on top of my son and kiss him when he sensed a meltdown was on its way. My son never lets me touch him, only the dog. Mostly this would stop the meltdowns. If Roxy couldn't stop the meltdown, she would come and get me and then run away to hide.

CODE GREEN

When our child is in code green, he can hear us, he can talk to us and he can learn. His brain is online and whatever parenting strategy we prefer has a good chance of working.

Nearly all the parenting advice out there is designed for children in code green. So, if we like sticker charts, the 'naughty' step, taking away computer games for 'bad' behaviour, limiting screen time, encouraging them to learn and study, giving them explanations and everything else we hoped to achieve as a parent, make the most of our child's time in code green to do it.

When our child is in code green, it may be reasonable to get her to go to school, to do homework, to accept no for an answer and to share her toys. If our child is in a very good place, it is the time to introduce new things and to help her to grow and learn.

Code green is a time to teach social skills and to encourage our child to follow interests. This is when our son may be able to socialise with people he likes and to enjoy learning and following his passions.

Code green is our real child. It is who they really are.

Code green is a big banding and there are many shades of green. As we get more practice with this, we learn to recognise which shade of green our child is at, and what we can reasonably expect from him or her at that time.

Some parents use the lower ends of code green to unpick meltdowns with their child and help them and us to understand what may be triggering them. Saying this, meltdowns and rages can be so shameful for a child that even mentioning them can send them straight back up to code orange or even straight to red. We clearly need to use our instincts and discretion on this, just another of our decoding challenges!

Many children at the higher end of code green are quite close to code orange or will tip into code orange if too many demands are made of them. These children are in protection mode, which was described in detail in the previous chapters.

WHICH COLOUR ARE THEY AT?

Every child will present their own codes to show us if they are at code red, code orange or code green. As our children grow up and change, their codes will change too. It is not always possible to get this right.

Clues to look out for include:

Code red: Meltdowns look like wildfires that our child seems unable to control. He is unable to hear us other than to pick out odd words. The shutdown version of this could be that our child becomes mute and unable to speak at all. Our son may become frozen, shut away and rock or bang his head. He may not seem to hear us at all and may keep repeating the same thing over and over again.

Code orange: Our daughter may have a 'wild' look in her eyes that shows us that she is holding in her rage or anxiety. Our son's body may be rigid and his movements may not look natural or relaxed. He may be arguing with us without properly hearing what we are saying. Our daughter may be provoking us by making more and more unreasonable demands that don't seem to make sense. Our son may be refusing to do his usual activities, see friends or do things that he would normally be able to do.

Code green: Our son is able to respond to 'normal' rewards and consequences. We are able to talk to him and explain what we

> expect from him. He can hear us and take on board what we are saying. Our child may be 'naughty' to test us or herself or for any of the reasons that a neurotypical child would at times be defiant. Our daughter is interested in following her interests, doing things and communicating with us and others. She is probably able to go to school, see friends and do homework without excessive coaxing.

I am so happy to share the traffic light approach. Parents, including me, have received some truly horrible advice about meltdowns. Some are told to punish their child, use physical restraints or to call the police to get them arrested 'to teach them a lesson'.

Maria, mum of a child with bipolar disorder, is still haunted years later by advice she received from a psychiatric nurse. She followed the advice as at the time she believed an 'expert' would know best:

> My talented son had spent weeks painting an amazing picture that he was really proud of and so were we. During a bad rage he ripped it up, which was devastating to him and all of us as we loved that picture. The so-called 'expert' told me to display the torn-up painting to shame my son so that I could point out daily what he had done. This was to remind him of how destructive he was so that he wouldn't do it again. I still feel so guilty for carrying out what I was told to do.

We cannot underestimate the shame of a meltdown. I have a number of adult friends with hidden disabilities who had nasty rages when they were children, as is normal and would be expected for children with these conditions.

They are so embarrassed and humiliated by memories of the meltdowns that they choose to shut down memories of their whole childhood, including the happy memories, just to avoid the shame.

This is a reminder to us of how important it is to reassure our loved ones when too much pressure builds up that there is no need to be ashamed. They are doing the best they can under really difficult circumstances. We are proud of them and we all have internal pressure cookers.

Chapter 7

OUT OF PROTECTION MODE: PRACTICAL STRATEGIES

Many of our children spend their lives stuck in code orange. Even when they are not having meltdowns or shutdowns, their bodies are still full of fight or flight hormones. Their internal pressure cookers may not be hot enough to explode but are still steaming enough to cause a variety of problems for our children. This state is protection mode, also known as defence mode and is described in detail in Part 1, along with examples of how protection mode can affect our child's behaviour, their health and their state of mind.

This chapter and the two that follow suggest how to get and keep our children out of protection mode. Here I explain the general principles and offer some practical strategies. Chapter 8 provides emotional strategies, while Chapter 9 suggests attitudes that can help our child stay out of protection mode for good.

In my opinion, helping our child with a hidden disability to get out of protection mode is one of our greatest roles as parents. Sadly it is rarely talked about. Asperger Experts call it defence mode and talk about some behaviours in relation to Asperger's.[1] What I call protection mode extends this to children with *all* hidden disabilities. It includes the full range of behaviours that are affected by a long-term flood of fight or flight hormones.

When our children are liberated from the restriction of protection mode, it is possible for them to fly and more than make up for any 'lost time' in their learning, be it academic or life-skills training.

Some of the most successful people I have ever met lost years of their education to school refusal or low attainment during childhood due to being shut down or in protection mode. Success is of course much, much more than our usual ideas of achievement. It is about our child being comfortable about who they are, making healthy choices, following their passions and living their lives in the way that feels right to them.

We need to remember that protection mode is *in addition* to our child's hidden disability. Protection mode makes their symptoms worse and life much more challenging for them.

Helping them out of protection mode is not a substitute for treatment for the hidden disability if this is needed. It is certainly not an alternative to the reasonable adjustments our child may need in school and in life. In fact, some of the adjustments themselves may be part of the strategy to get our child and keep our child out of protection mode.

When we are considering treatments for our child's hidden disabilities, until we are able to get them out of protection mode, it is hard to see which symptoms are from the hidden disability itself and which are the result of the long-term circulation of fight or flight chemicals in the body.

Once we remove protection mode from the equation, we can see what issues remain that may need treatment. Chapters 12 to 14 discuss the range of treatment options for hidden disabilities.

TREATING OUR OWN PROTECTION MODE

To help our children, a good starting point is to recognise that we too may be in protection mode. Raising children is hugely stressful and when hidden disabilities are in the mix too, our stress levels can hit the roof.

If we are going to expect our children to take responsibility for their own wellbeing, we need to teach them this by being good role models. This means we that we need to take responsibility to get and keep *ourselves* out of protection mode.

My companion book *How to Cope When Your Child Has a Hidden Disability: Self-Care for Parents* is specifically about how parents of children with hidden disabilities can get and keep ourselves out of protection mode while dealing with our many challenges. It shares techniques on how we can stay strong, calm and at peace regardless of the storms raging around us and fights we need to pursue.

This is one of my favourite quotes of all time:

> Thousands of candles can be lighted from a single candle, and the life of the candle will not be shortened. Happiness never decreases by being shared.[2]

So when we are calm and happy and free from protection mode, our presence can light the candle of happiness in our family too, without diminishing our own.

In the same way, if we are stressed, angry and bitter, we could without realising it be lighting the candles of stress, anger and bitterness in our children, without relieving our own unhappiness. As our unhappiness candle can light others without diminishing its own flame, we can easily be spreading the unhappiness around.

There is no virtue in holding on to our pain. It will not help our child and it will not help us. We need to remember:

- When children are in protection mode, they cannot learn or listen.
- When parents are in protection mode, we cannot teach or understand.

Like all suggestions and advice, take what feels right and discard what doesn't. If something does not feel right for you, it may help someone else.

There is no need to implement all of these suggestions, only those that feel right at a particular time. Sometimes just being aware of these strategies helps us to make subtle changes that support our children. Often it is the small changes that can make all the difference.

TURNING DOWN THE HEAT

Protection mode means that our children's pressure cookers are stuck at a level that is too hot and in danger of explosion. This can affect every area of their lives.

The simplest way to reduce this pressure is to turn down the heat. This is ridiculously obvious but very easy to overlook.

We overlook this because we are constantly being told that our children 'should' be able to do certain things at a particular age. We may think that they 'should' be able to cope with school, they 'should' learn to swim, 'should' have enough energy to do homework, 'should' attend playdates, 'should' socialise at family events, 'should' be potty trained, 'should' be able to tie their shoe laces. The list goes on and on.

What if the opposite is true for our children? What if, rather than that they 'should' be doing these things, maybe instead they 'shouldn't' be doing them?

Being actively encouraged *not* to do these things is a very simple way of turning down the heat on our child's pressure cooker.

This does not mean that our children will never learn to swim or do homework or socialise. It just means that we do not *require* them to do these things, or anything else for that matter, when they are tired or stressed.

We need to remember that school and work schedules are artificial and usually designed for neurotypical children. Things may simply need to happen in a different way for our children.

When they are tired and stressed, there is only one thing a child should be doing, and that is whatever helps them to recharge their batteries, recover and build up resilience for the next day. That may be sleeping, watching TV, playing video games or building a model kit.

If a child with a hidden disability has no pressures on them whatsoever outside of school, many are able to stay in mainstream education.

Turning down the heat is like recharging our mobile phone when it is out of power. We do not usually expect them to keep working while they are charging. We usually give them a break at these times.

Turning down the heat can be easier said than done. Many schools are not supportive of this idea and may continue to insist on homework and complete attendance and other demands that turn the heat up rather than down.

Schools that 'get it' will try to keep the heat down on our child's pressure cooker. This could include a reduced timetable, homework amnesties, chill out spaces, and clear and predictable routines. For some, keeping the heat down can mean making sure that our child is sufficiently stimulated with activities that are meaningful to him or her.

Turning down the heat does not always mean that our child will do less. Sometimes finding the *right* activity will help them to release the pressure and cool them off.

As an example, a school that 'gets it' may realise that if a child's pressure cooker is heated up by being under-stimulated, as is often the case with ADHD, putting them into detention may cause even more under-stimulation. This is adding fuel to a fire. In this situation, giving the child an exciting task instead may be needed to turn their heat down.

When schools are on board with the idea of cooling down our child's pressure cooker, helpful conversations become possible. There are many possible ways to do this which may be different for each child. The starting point is recognising the need to turn the heat *down* rather than up.

This made all the difference to Rachel's son:

> Throughout primary and the first years of secondary school Matt was a school refuser. When we got pressure taken off at school, like not having to attend registration which he found stressful in the mornings, his attendance went up, he began enjoying school and is now looking forward to uni!

Some schools are great, but with others getting them on board with this can be a battle. Many parents fight and win the reasonable adjustments they need or manage to get their children into another school that does. Others, including me, did not have the time, money, expertise, energy or emotional strength to spend years fighting.

Saying that, at the time I didn't know that disability laws included my children or that schools had a legal duty to make 'reasonable adjustments'. If I had known about these things, the outcome may have been different for my family.

Whatever we do, sometimes this is a battle that we are unable to win. In many countries where awareness of hidden disabilities is limited, it may be impossible.

If we cannot get the heat turned down at school, we can do everything in our power to turn it down when they come home.

Ideally what Michelle does for her son who is on the autism spectrum will not be necessary:

> If I try to force Zack to do homework he goes into a meltdown he can't control. When I see this coming I can't force him to do homework. The school punishes him if he doesn't do it and says I'm making excuses for him. My son comes first, not the school's opinion so I do his homework for him when I have to. I hate doing this and wish it wasn't necessary. I feel like such an awful mum.

I sometimes had to do this too and like many parents I was worried that it would affect my child academically. It helps to remember that our child cannot learn well or at all when they are in protection mode, so sometimes we need to lose a battle to win a war. When my children got out of protection mode, their brains went into turbo charge and they both ended up at top universities.

If the heat cannot be turned down at school, many parents choose to home school, so that they can control what demands are put on their child and when. They can then read their children's codes and see when they need more stimulation or less.

Home schooling is not an option for most families. Parents may need to go out to work or not have the skills or resources to do it. A frazzled parent may desperately need their child out of the house at school to give them a break and to prevent their own pressure cookers from exploding.

Whatever our circumstances, it is wise to stop and think, 'What would turn down this heat for my child?' There is always something we can do.

Sometimes this means doing something for our child that they are perfectly able to do under other circumstances. This would reduce their load to make them better able to cope with other things they need to do.

When their pressure cooker is steaming, this could mean taking on an admin task for them, driving them somewhere that they would normally get to on their own, helping them to dress, picking up their toys when we would normally expect them to do it. It may even mean helping them in the toilet when they have long been independent in that area.

When the pressure cooker is very hot, they sometimes need to feel like babies again, being totally looked after and protected without any need to do anything for themselves. Some children show this by sucking their thumbs or rocking like a baby at these times. Others use different clues to show that this is what they need. I must admit that I also often feel that way when I am very stressed. I want to check out of being an adult and just be held and looked after.

If we take the heat off our child by doing things for them when they need it, other people may judge or criticise us. They may accuse us of being over-indulgent or of preventing our child from being independent.

Just because our child *can* do something does not mean that they *have to* do it on every occasion.

As well as changing our expectations about what our children *should* be doing or achieving, there are simple practical things we can try to keep the heat down. These include:

- finding clothes without itchy seams if this is a problem
- keeping routines as predictable as possible as changes are an extra stress
- keeping food simple and predictable (introducing new items only when they are coming out of protection mode)
- joining them in whatever activity interests them
- prioritising fun and making them laugh
- letting them eat alone if they need to

- letting them guide us about what they need
- encouraging them to spend time outside and doing exercise if they can manage it
- not forcing homework or social activities
- letting them become engrossed in something that interests them, even if other tasks do not get done
- allowing them to do whatever calms them down, including computer games and screen time if that is what they need
- allowing them to connect with other people in a way that turns the heat down – this may be online rather than in person.

GETTING ENOUGH SLEEP

One thing I found very patronising was when experts told me to make sure my child gets enough sleep. Wouldn't it be wonderful if it was that easy, that our child would sleep simply because we 'make sure' they do? Sleep is a massive issue for many children with hidden disabilities. No matter how strict our bedtime routines are, many of our children cannot fall asleep easily or stay asleep.

Our children are dealing with huge challenges that we can barely comprehend. This can affect their brain's ability to switch off at night as they may still be processing and making sense of their experiences and challenges. Sleep problems are so common among our children that there may well also be other biological imbalances involved that are related to their hidden disabilities.

Some of our children also have night terrors, causing them to become paralysed with fear and not know what is real and what is not. This is so traumatic that some children are afraid to let themselves fall asleep.

Not getting enough sleep sends our children deeper into protection mode. It means less available energy and emotional resources to deal with the pressures of life. It becomes a vicious circle. The deeper into protection mode they go, the harder they find it to sleep as they are more wired and stressed.

If our children are not sleeping, it is likely that we are not either. Our exhaustion and resentment can easily feed back to our children, turning up the heat on all of our pressure cookers.

Dealing with sleep is a priority and an important way to help our children out of protection mode. There seem to be two ways to do this:

- getting them to sleep at night
- adjusting their lifestyle so that it does not matter if they sleep at night.

As we live in a culture where we 'do things' during the day and sleep at night, it makes sense to do what we can to try to help our children to sleep at night. Many parents have success with this, at least some of the time. Forgive me for stating the obvious, but these include:

- plenty of exercise to wear the child out
- a hot bath with calming herbs in the water, such as chamomile, lavender or lemon balm
- infusing calming oils in a burner (chamomile and lavender are top choices)
- giving our child a massage before bed
- a weighted blanket to help our child feel safer at night
- letting our child sleep in our bed
- bedtime calming meditations
- special stories to help wind down for sleep
- recordings of calming music or sounds
- singing lullabies to our child, even when they are older.

Some parents help their child sleep by giving them melatonin, magnesium or gentle herbal remedies to promote deep relaxation. My thinking on this is to do whatever works as long as it doesn't hurt them.

For some children nothing works. For others nothing works some of the time. This is when we need a plan B.

After trying absolutely everything, I had to go over to plan B in my household. This involved removing all expectations that my children would sleep at night.

Making the decision that my children did not have to sleep at night was a big relief. A lot of the stress for both my children and for me was that they 'should' be sleeping and that it would be disastrous for everyone if they did not.

Worrying about my children not sleeping was adding heat to both my pressure cooker and theirs. Taking away that expectation took the pressure off bedtime. If they did manage to sleep it was a bonus, but not something I expected or needed to happen.

I was inspired in this by my time living in cultures where children do not have a 'bedtime'. In some places, children are able to hang out with the adults and fall asleep whenever sleep happens naturally. Parents would then scoop the sleeping child off the floor or wherever sleep happens and pop them into a bed. The children may also fall asleep after school for a siesta. There is no real reason why all the sleep must happen at night and particular times. For some families it works better if it is broken up into different times.

Joseph tried this with his two children, one with ASD and one with ADHD who could not sleep well at night:

> Both my kids fall asleep effortlessly after school. I used to wake them up so they would sleep at night, but they just got more and more wired. Bedtime was like a war zone and one we were losing. So I tried leaving them to sleep after school. They still don't sleep much at night, but at least now we have lost the night time drama that was ruining our lives and we are all now getting enough sleep!

I liked this as it removed the drama of trying to force sleep to happen and the panic when it does not. If the body wants to sleep it does and if it doesn't it doesn't.

In my household I modified this as I had to work in the evenings undisturbed. What worked for us was to do the regular bedtime routine of bath and stories, but instead of making them go to bed, they would stay in their rooms and do whatever they wanted, which may or may not include going to sleep. Sometimes they would sleep and sometimes they wouldn't. Beautiful artwork would be produced during the night, stories would be written and games invented.

Without forcing anything, my children caught up on sleep during the afternoon. This pattern happened naturally and stress was reduced. This arrangement was not ideal but worked for us.

FINDING THEIR TRIBE

Many of our children's challenges involve dealing with feeling and being different. They may be comparing themselves with others or feel that others are judging them. Many are dealing with hostility and bullying from other children. Teachers and others may be expecting things from them that feel nearly impossible.

When our children are able to find their tribe, they can finally feel part of something and accepted for who they are. Although they may feel different from 'the outside world', within their tribe they feel like everyone else. That's a really good feeling!

Among our tribe we feel understood and seen. Being around people who 'get us' is such a relief. It releases huge amounts of heat from our pressure cookers. We don't have to struggle to fit in or to mask our symptoms. Among our tribe, we can 'just be' and know that this is fine.

We all find huge relief in finding our tribe. Many parents of children with hidden disabilities also feel different, left out and misunderstood. Finding other parents who 'get us' is very liberating.

Helping our child to find his or her tribe is an important way to get and keep them out of protection mode. These people may be friends, family or professionals. Ideally some of these people may have hidden disabilities themselves. If these people accept themselves and are happy in their own skins, they can be great role models for our children. The 'tribe' may also include neurotypical people who share our child's passion for a particular subject or interest. In fact it can include anyone who is a great listener, open hearted and 'gets' our child.

Whatever their interests or disability status, our child's tribe will accept and cherish them exactly as they are, welcome every quirk of personality and have compassion and understanding for the challenges they have.

Writing in her blog, Emma Pretzel, who has ASD and ADHD, feels that it is important to be around other people with hidden disabilities:

> Autistic friends, autistic friends, autistic mentors, autistic friends, autistic pen pals, autistic role models, autistic relatives, autistic friends, autistic fan-fiction head canons; seriously just as much autistic presence as possible, really though.[3]

Although Emma uses the word 'autistic' rather a lot here, this applies whatever the hidden disability is. The principle is for our child to have as much contact as possible with people who have 'walked their walk' or are on a similar page to our child, be it in interests, outlook or temperament.

We would probably do something similar if our child is the only member of an ethnic minority in class. Standing out as different can be exhausting, so we may want to find situations out of school where our child can have the relief of blending in.

Interestingly enough, the idea of having children with hidden disabilities in mainstream schools is supposed to be about *inclusion*. In practice, for our children it can feel more like *exclusion* if they do not feel that they fit in.

Although there are many arguments against specialist schools for children with disabilities, they do have the advantage that while they are at school, they feel neither different nor an outsider. It may be easier to feel that they are among their tribe when their classmates share their hidden disabilities, strengths and challenges.

On the downside, as soon as our child steps outside the school gate, they may be ill prepared to deal with mainstream society and the 'neurotypical' world. This too can affect their self-esteem and confidence to go after their life goals.

Most of our children will be in mainstream school, whether this is by choice or by necessity. If they are very lucky, there will be members of their 'tribe' at school, even if this is only one trusted friend.

The tribe may be a group of kids who love a particular video game and enjoy getting together to play it. It is common for children who hardly speak to each other at school to get together online to play games together.

Many of our children find it easier and less stressful to communicate online than in person. We obviously need to put safety first and check out who they are speaking to or playing with. Assuming it is fine, a tribe is a tribe and the benefit is there for our child regardless of whether they meet in person or not.

The tribe can include adults. A relative or friend of the family may share our child's passion for chess or a particular football team. I know one boy who is happiest and feels most included amongst a group of local model aeroplane enthusiasts, even though most are the same age as his grandfather. Their common interest and knowledge of aeroplanes seems to eclipse everything else and binds them together as a tribe.

There may also be activity clubs, youth clubs or camps that are designed for children with our child's hidden disabilities. Some hidden disability support groups have family activity sessions or clubs for our children. Going to these can give our child the experience of being one of the majority and 'normal' within the group.

Some of our children will not want to be around others who have a hidden disability. If they are uncomfortable about their own diagnosis, being around children with a similar one can make them feel worse rather than better.

For some of our older children, being put together with children just because they share a hidden disability can feel very patronising. It may be far more natural to find a tribe based on a shared interest or attitude to life, which may indirectly bring them into contact with others with similar hidden disabilities, even if they are unaware of this.

I do need to add a caution here to remember that although all children and young people are vulnerable to abusive or predatory people, those with hidden disabilities are especially vulnerable. As they may be feeling lonely and excluded, they can be excited and trusting when someone seems to be paying them attention or compliments.

As their hidden disabilities may affect their ability to read verbal and non-verbal clues, they may be less able to pick up warning signs about people's behaviour.

Although our main concern will probably be about abusive adults, we need to remember that children as well as adults can groom our child into a false sense of security and then expose them to bullying or abuse, be it in person or online.

I have come across other children offering 'friendship' to a child who feels excluded, only then to convince them to share compromising photos of themselves, ask for money or make other dangerous demands.

So, while helping our child to find his or her tribe and considering this a priority, we need to be mindful of risks and take necessary precautions.

To reduce the risks, we can talk to our child and explain that people may not be who they seem to be online. It is also wise to screen and monitor their online contacts and activity as much as possible and check their phone if they have one. It makes sense to keep everything as closely monitored as we need to feel reassured, while trying to respect the privacy of our child.

Monitoring their social life is quite straightforward for a younger child, but older ones may not like this at all. They may feel that we are infringing their freedom and privacy. They may think that we do not trust them. This is understandable and tricky to manage.

'Freedom versus safety' is difficult to balance. My preference is to err on the side of safety and to explain that although we understand how they feel, we are simply doing our job as a parent to keep them safe.

And to make things even more complicated, we need to talk to our children about staying safe in such a way that does not make them fearful or anxious about social interaction.

Because of worries about online safety, the Asperger Experts website has a moderated online platform for our children to play Minecraft® and other games together. It also has a range of moderated online groups for our child to join to interact with others in a 'neuro-divergent friendly' way.[4]

Finding our tribe can also include connecting with people we do not know personally, but who inspire us.

These may be famous people who are open and accepting of their hidden disabilities. Our child may find that actors, musicians, writers or scientists that they admire share their hidden disability and knowing this can help them to feel part of something potentially great. They can also find their tribe in people in history that they admire. Many of the great achievers and innovators in history have had hidden disabilities. Knowing our child's interests, I would recommend researching them and encouraging a sense of kinship with these people.

Our children's tribe does not need to be human. Many find companionship and close friendship with an animal, most commonly a dog or a horse. Many dogs, for example, have an extraordinary ability to read and understand how our child is feeling and they do this without judgement. It is not surprising that so many people with hidden disabilities seek out non-human companions.

In fact, the tribe does not even have to be technically alive, although our child may feel they are. I am referring here to companions who are teddy bears or other trusted toys. We know that building trust is very important when getting our children out of protection mode. It is not uncommon for our child to feel that their toys are their best and most trustworthy friends.

Carole explains how important soft toys are for her child, who struggles with anxiety:

> My daughter's bed is her safest place and over the years we have populated it with a family of bears. She has a very vivid imagination so I fell into a way of soothing her anxiety by doing voices for the bears. She is now fifteen and the bears are a constant in her life. She talks to them every day and I make them talk back. I have even found that she accepts being told what to do by a bear, whereas she would have been oppositional with me.

I still have my childhood teddies now and often get comfort from seeing and hugging them. Some kids prefer less cuddly things and bond very deeply with another toy, such as an action figure. Others have a special blanket that can take on the role of a trusted friend and protector.

FINDING THEIR PASSIONS

It is not surprising that many of our children take a hit on self-esteem. When their self-esteem is low, they may forget that they have abilities in many areas and that there are a lot of things they can be proud of.

An important part of helping our child out of protection mode is to support them with their interests. This gives our child a meaning in their life, stimulates and excites them and also gives opportunities for them to connect with their tribe.

When our daughter finds her passions, she can gain expertise in a particular area. As well as making life more interesting for her, this builds her self-esteem. It makes her feel successful and in control of an area in her life. All of these things help a child out of protection mode.

Nothing motivates like success and doing well in an area of passion can be what is needed to help our child engage with life and study. When the passionate interest is involved, everything has meaning and purpose in life.

One boy I know seemed only to be interested in football, to the despair of his parents. When this interest was applied to other areas of life, they immediately had meaning for him. So he was happy to do maths if it involved adding up or working out goal averages. His reading improved by reading match reports. The more he succeeded in maths and reading, the more his confidence grew and this impacted every area of life.

Helping our child find and follow their passion can be like a magic key.

I know of more cases than I can count of a child's passion leading directly or indirectly to a career or course of study. One of my children's interest in robots as a child influenced their decision to study physics. Another of my children's passion for films led to a degree and career as a film-maker. The boy who learned maths by adding up football goal averages became an accountant.

Finding their passions is not only about study or careers. Apple's Steve Jobs reminded us:

> And the only way to do great work is to love what you do. If you haven't found it yet, keep looking. Don't settle. As with all matters of the heart, you'll know when you find it.[5]

For some of our children, it will be clear what their interest is. This is often the case for children on the autism spectrum who may have a single-minded passion for a particular subject or activity. For other children it may take more trial and error for them to find something that they like. When they find it, it can transform their life.

Examples of passions I have come across recently include clocks, trains, video games, art, kestrels, the yellow dung beetle, horses, astrophysics, Greek mythology, prime numbers, Bolivia, Hitchcock movies, karate, weather charts, jazz, the Second World War, codes, the colour green.

My view is that unless an interest is illegal, immoral or exploits others, we should do what we can to encourage and support it. This is part of accepting our child for who they are and helping them to reach their potential.

The interest may seem utterly boring or irrelevant to us. It may appear that focusing on the interest may take time away from school work and learning in more 'important' areas. Our child may be so engrossed in their interest that they forget to wash or even eat. Our job is to encourage a healthy balance but still to value and fan their interests, as if their life depended on it, which in some ways it does.

Blogger Emma Pretzel, who has ADHD and Asperger's, makes me smile:

> I'm a college student, and live at home with the folks right now. I am nerdy about most things you can be nerdy about in school. I do literary criticism/theory most of the time (about mostly poetry), and dabble in organic chemistry research. I like tutoring and TAing.
>
> I like stuffed animals, cultural theory, poetry, science fiction,

> evolutionary developmental biology, biochemistry, being 'that social-justice-obsessed person who complains all the time,' languages, CATS CATS CATS, dance, symmetrical things, soft/smooth textures, sports, spherical objects, and obsessively accumulating sources and data on everything I'm interested in. I have been referred to as both 'a walking encyclopaedia' and 'a spontaneous TED talk'; if you ask me for sources/information about a subject I know about, you'll make me the happiest creature in the universe.[6]

Very specific interests can often be broadened out. Rachel, whose son has a passionate interest in vintage pocket watches, explained to me:

> Left to his own devices, Matt would have had a much more narrow field of interest, just watches really, whereas with our support he is now an expert on all things vintage and antique from caravans to stamps.

She also discovered that using her son's passion for pocket watches became a natural vehicle for developing and practising social skills:

> At first we would ask sellers about their items (to show him the ropes) and gradually introduced him to the idea of asking so that before long he was haggling prices down and charming the pants off all the sellers!

Things are more difficult if our child is not interested in anything and does not have any passions for us to encourage. Many parents complain about this and find it very frustrating, especially if they are giving their child lots of ideas and providing exciting opportunities.

The first thing to remember is that an interest does not have to be a passion or all-consuming focus or obsession. The idea of an autistic 'special interest' is quite extreme and most children thrive and grow from more modest interests. The interest may be much more gentle, something our child likes 'quite a lot' or quite enjoys. Things may come in and out of favour as interests change or come and go.

If our child really is not interested in anything, he could be too deep into protection mode or depression to be able to engage with the world. If this is the case, he may simply not have the physical or emotional resources to focus on anything other than getting through each day.

Focusing on an interest takes energy and time, which our child may not have. It can take a long time to come out of protection mode, especially if all the stressors such as school are still in our child's life. If this is the case, it may be best to focus on turning down the heat on our child's pressure cooker. When it cools down and our child starts to emerge from protection mode, interests and passions may then start to emerge.

It is also possible that our child has interests that we have not recognised. We may not consider the things in question to be worthy of being interests because for us, they are merely time-wasting activities or distractions.

Simon, whose son has ADD, shared:

> My son says he likes music but I can't get him interested in playing an instrument. He just loses interest. Instead of practising, he just wants to waste his time listening to useless stuff like rap day and night. It drives me mad that I cannot get him interested in anything worthwhile.

In this case, the father may have overlooked his son's interest in rap, which even if not to his taste, is a valid and creative form of music and poetry. It is an interest that can be fanned to develop performance skills, writing skills, creativity, connection with people and also having a good time.

It can be only too easy to let our own interests and judgements blind us to our children's interests. Their interests are theirs and need not have anything to do with our interests or ambitions for our child. Some children shut down to interests because they feel that they are being imposed on them by their parents, rather than being genuine interests of their own.

Educational writer Lee Binz thinks that our child's interests may be under our noses but we do not see them. She believes that when our children are really annoying us, this can be the key to their interest:

> I can't tell you how many times I said 'Stop playing chess!' and 'Put that

> book down!' When a child finds their passion, they pursue it with all their heart and soul – and it can be annoying to mom! We watch them 'waste away' with the things that interest them, instead of pursuing things that WE value. It's a challenge to keep THEIR specialisation OUR top priority.[7]

If our child still does not appear to have any interests, the best we can do is expose them to as many activities and ideas as we can. We need to look beyond school work and academics. Our daughter may find that she loves babysitting or caring for a kitten. She may enjoy collecting shells on the beach or playing softball. Our son may find that he loves drawing cartoons or enjoys reading about how best to do this.

BEING IN NATURE

Many people find that being in and part of nature has a huge effect on a racing and anxious mind. I have heard people with every hidden disability diagnosis say that nature is one of the most effective treatments for their symptoms and a gateway out of protection mode.

According to ADD specialist Lara Honos-Web, 'nature fixes' are so powerful that they can be considered a stand-alone treatment. She says:

> The urge to be in nature isn't just another symptom of your ADD, isn't just another distraction flitting across your mind like a gnat that won't go away. This urge may actually be hardwired into you to help you heal.[8]

Research from all over the world has shown that people who live closer to green space have fewer health problems and live longer. It seems that nature itself is a buffer against stress and helps people cope better with life's challenges. In fact it appears that there may be chemicals in trees that can reduce stress hormones and anxiety. We also know that natural sunlight helps to stabilise our moods, gives us vitamin D and resets our body clocks by affecting our melatonin levels.[9]

These are compelling arguments for trying to get our children outside.

For some, just walking in nature does the job. This is the case for me. I have a lively dog, and our time hiking in nature every day whatever the weather helps my mental health, happiness and wellbeing.

Some children find it boring to aimlessly walk in nature so we may need to make it more interesting for them. We could ask them to look for and document the birds they see or identify trees or rocks. I know children who have got really hooked on recognising different bird calls. I remember one of my children and I having names for each of the owls we would hear at night. We called them Twitter, Roo and Quiver after the sounds they were making.

Some children love to use nature diaries to observe and log what they are seeing and experiencing in nature, especially the changing seasons and the moon and stars.

Others are not interested in documenting and prefer to build or *do* things in nature. This could be as simple as making a snowman in winter, sweeping leaves in autumn, helping to clear a blocked river or cut back overgrowth from a footpath.

For many this includes gardening, especially growing and nurturing vegetables that can later be enjoyed by the whole family. My children and I enjoyed going to a local abandoned orchard to gather plums, apples, pears, apricots and cherries. Whatever we are doing or not doing, we can lose ourselves in the healing power of nature.

Trauma specialist Melanie Tonia Evans sums this up beautifully:

> Nature unconditionally accepts, adores us and heals us. We have the most beautiful relationship with nature. As we breathe out, trees and plants breathe in, and as they exhale, they provide us with the life air that we need. Truly – natural nature therapy doesn't cost anything.[10]

Nature connection is so important for health that forest bathing is one of the cornerstones of Japanese healthcare, where it is called *shinrin-yoku*. Doctors send patients out into forests to smell the air, touch the trees and feel the leaves and soil.

But what if my child won't do it?

When our children are in a very stressed or agitated state, getting them out in nature can feel like just another battle. With so many battles to fight, this one can easily not feel like a priority.

They may refuse to leave their rooms and say no to all our nature suggestions. They may be so stressed that the only place they feel safe is their room. If this is the case, I believe we should respect it.

If getting our child outside feels like a battle, forcing it may be counterproductive.

Any type of battle increases the heat in our child's pressure cooker. This is why we need to choose our battles very carefully, to conserve all available energy.

If our child is unable or unwilling to access nature outdoors, there are still things we can do to bring nature to them:

- We can increase the number of plants around the house. We may be able to give our children plants to care for in their bedrooms, allowing them to choose which ones they like best. One of my children chose carnivorous plants which feed on insects and we all found them fascinating.

- We can teach them how to sprout seeds and beans at home on any windowsill. Things like cress grow really quickly and are fun to watch. They may even be willing to eat them if they have grown them themselves.

- We can bring wildlife into the home, especially if it is really easy to look after. Quirky children are likely to choose less conventional pets. My children chose giant African millipedes. They all had names and were studied, cared for and loved. Other families do similar things with stick insects, ant houses or domesticated rats. Of course, more conventional pets like dogs, cats, goldfish and hamsters may be an easier option for many families!

- A lot of children with hidden disabilities are calmed by being around horses, one of the reasons that riding for the disabled schemes are so popular. I know of children who will only leave their room if they get to ride or be around horses. If horses are not their thing, going to a petting farm or a zoo will often get the most reluctant child out of their room.

- We can hang beautiful pictures of nature around the house. We can ask our children to choose pictures of nature for their room that they find calming. They may even want to paint them themselves.
- We can encourage our children to bring nature into their bodies by choosing natural whole foods such as fruits and vegetables. I know this may be a big ask as so many of our children are fussy eaters, but we can only try, as long as eating does not become another stress for them.

So many parents and adults with hidden disabilities emphasise the importance of dogs that they need a special mention. Carole saw her child's life transformed by her dog-walking business:

> When my daughter is walking a dog on a lead she grows in stature visibly. The connection makes her feel strong and courageous. She has something to control. She is in control plus at the same time receiving huge amounts of unconditional love and acceptance.

Some people are able to obtain trained emotional-assistance dogs. There are also a number of organisations that teach people how to train their own dogs to do this. Personally, I find that most loving dogs offer this service without the need for much extra training. Many of them seem to have an extra sense, rather like an emotion sensor to read what our child is feeling. Our children often feel that their dog truly 'gets' them and loves and supports them without judgement. In other words, dogs can be great decoders and we have much to learn from them.

EXERCISE AND SPORT

Many people find exercise to be essential for getting and staying out of protection mode.

We tend to think of exercise as something we 'should' do to improve our physical health, to strengthen our hearts, lungs or muscles. We may also want to do it to lose weight or to look more attractive.

As well as helping our physical health, exercise supports our mental health and wellbeing too. The healing power of exercise is recognised worldwide, with many doctors prescribing 'gym time' as a treatment for a range of mental health- and stress-based disorders. According to the Mental Health Foundation, exercise has a positive impact on mood, reduces stress, improves self-esteem, treats anxiety and is a stand-alone treatment for depression.[11]

Bearing this in mind, it is useful to think carefully about our attitude to exercise. Is it something we look forward to? Or is it something we prefer to avoid but do because we 'should'? Do we think of it in any way as something unpleasant, like a disgusting medicine that we drink because it is good for us? Do we believe that exercise is for sporty types or those with slim and athletic figures? Are we worried we may have to compete and may feel even worse about ourselves? Do we think we are too fat? Maybe we are too unhealthy to exercise?

If we are thinking any of these things, even unconsciously, it is likely that we will pass these views about exercise on to our children.

How would it feel if we had different beliefs about exercise, perhaps as something to be looked forward to, loved and embraced as part of our wellbeing? Something we prioritise because we know that it is a priority? Something we make time for? Something that makes us feel great? Something we can lose ourselves in to feel peace in the face of all of life's challenges?

There are many different opinions on what exercise is best for which purpose. My view on this is that the best exercise for us is whatever we enjoy and that the best exercise for our child is whatever *they* enjoy.

No, that doesn't include exercising our fingers on a keyboard while posting on social media.

Some children do best with highly aerobic exercise such as running, swimming or active team games like football or basketball. Others are happier with something slower such as yoga or Pilates. Some children thrive on competition and are motivated by it. If this is the case, getting our child into a competitive team or sport is fantastic, competing either in a group or as an individual.

Many children with hidden disabilities are amazing with martial arts and are motivated by going up the levels of belt colours. They find that winning combat situations gives them confidence in their own strength and power, especially if they are feeling powerless in social environments and school.

Other children do not enjoy competition at all. They are not motivated by it and are in fact stressed by it. If this is the case, being in a competitive sports team will ramp up our child's stress levels and turn the heat on the pressure cooker up rather than down.

Many of us prefer to exercise in an individual way. At the moment, all of my family enjoy exercising in the gym where we are able to do our own thing in our own time. Other 'doing-our-own-thing' exercise includes swimming, running and dance. Going to an exercise class is also usually not competitive, although it can be tempting to compare what you are doing with others in the class. Many organisations run classes for children that include yoga, dance and a range of keep fit options.

As success is a great motivator, it may well be that the chosen exercise is something our child is good at, but this need not be the case. If our son enjoys the activity and how it makes him feel, he will be more inclined to do it. He may fancy doing it on some days more than others, but the feeling of wellbeing will ultimately be his motivator.

If we use mood charts to help our daughter track and understand her emotions, it can be useful for her to assess her mood before and after exercise so that she can see for herself the effect that exercise has on her mental health. Seeing the choice of a 'stressed' emoticon sticker before karate and a calm happy face one afterwards is a strong visual reminder to our children about the benefit of the choice they are making.

If our children are in schools that cause their pressure cookers to be at the point of exploding when they come home, it may be difficult to motivate them to exercise. This is because their whole body is telling them to shut down everything in order to recharge their batteries. If this is the case, I would not personally force the issue of exercise. Our child may need to veg out in front of a trusted TV show and there will be times when this needs to be a priority over anything else. Learning to read our child's codes will tell us when this is the case. Other people are likely to have strong opinions on this, but we will know if our child needs to decompress.

At times when our child is unable or unwilling to exercise, one of the most helpful things we can do is to instil positive ideas about how good it makes *us* feel. If they associate exercise with fun and wellbeing, they are likely to be more motivated to try it as soon as they have the emotional resources and energy to do so.

So, when we get back from a run, we can tell our child that we were stressed before going out but are now feeling amazing. When we get back from a fitness class, we can tell our child that we didn't fancy going, but are so glad we did as we now feel great and full of energy. We can tell them that we are tired but in a good way. We can show them the benefit and encourage them to exercise, but ultimately the commitment to do so has to come from them when they are ready to do it.

MINDFULNESS AND MEDITATION

There are thousands of studies that show the positive effect of mindfulness meditation on mood, stress, anxiety, self-esteem, sleep and focus. Due to the extra demands in their lives, our children with hidden disabilities suffer considerably from these problems.

Meditating for even only a few minutes a day can make a huge difference, and meditation is a useful tool in the toolbox to help our children out of protection mode.

For this reason, meditation is increasingly being taught in schools, often with amazing outcomes. According to a review of 15 studies:

> Students who were taught meditation at school reported higher optimism, more positive emotions, stronger self-identity, greater self-acceptance and took better care of their health as well as experiencing reduced anxiety, stress and depression. This was compared to before the meditation programs and compared to peers who were not taught meditation...
>
> Finally, meditation was found to improve a host of academic and learning skills in students. These included faster information processing, greater focus, more effective working memory, more creativity and cognitive flexibility.[12]

So, children who meditate are not only happier and healthier but do better in school too. This is a pretty compelling argument for giving meditation a try, as much for ourselves as for our children.

When we meditate, we learn to detach from what is happening in our brains. We sit quietly and gently observe our thoughts and feelings as they arise. The skill is to observe them, but not engage with them in any way. If we try to fight our thoughts and tell them to go away, we are engaging with them.

Meditation can help people with hidden disabilities accept and be at peace with who they are. Much of the anxiety felt by our children comes from their own thoughts about who they want themselves to be. They can become very frustrated when these ideas of themselves do not match up to their often impossibly high expectations and standards. The anxiety can be a result of seeing themselves how they want to be rather than accepting who they actually are.

Meditation and mindfulness teach us to accept the present moment rather than fear the past or future. They help our children to accept themselves fully for who they are, with less judgement and with more compassion for themselves.

Many people who have tried meditation say that they find it too difficult. Often this is because they think that we have to erase all thoughts during meditation. So, when thoughts naturally occur we believe we have failed.

This is not the case at all. The skill is to sit quietly with whatever comes up for us, detach from it and accept it completely. It is the quiet detachment from our racing thoughts that brings about the benefit. This is how we use meditation to calm our racing minds.

There are many different meditation traditions and techniques, and the key is for our child to find the way that works best for them.

Many people like to use guided meditations where they are directed to focus on different parts of their body or imagine that they are in a particularly relaxing or beautiful environment.

Others prefer to focus on their breathing, and there are practices that include counting or retaining the breath. Working with the breath in this way has a particularly strong effect on calming the mind. Other people prefer relaxing music to help them drift into a meditative state. There are many music recordings available specifically for this purpose.

Some traditions use mantras and people find that repeating certain words over and over helps them to lose themselves into a meditation practice. Other people find it really helpful to look at a flickering candle when they are meditating. There are also walking meditations especially in nature, and in fact forest bathing, which is prescribed by the Japanese health service, is a form of meditation.

Other people, including me, prefer complete silence and meditate better without any additional input at all.

In my experience, most children seem to do best with guided meditations. They may already have active imaginations, which makes it easier for them to lose themselves in what they are hearing. Meditations can be guided by a teacher at a meditation group or they can be recordings. There are lots of recorded guided meditations available for children. It is useful to find some that match our child's interests and the things they love. For example, there are meditations about whales, spaceships, trains and butterflies.

As with exercise, a great way to introduce meditation to our child is to do it ourselves and to encourage our child to join us. They will see how it benefits us and reduces our stress. We do need to remember though that whatever meditation method works best for us may not be the right one for our child, so we need to stay flexible.

Meditation is a skill that is learned through practice. To begin with we may only be able to meditate for a few minutes. This is fine. If we notice that our mind is racing or that we are getting fidgety, we can accept this and try to return our focus to whatever is helping us to meditate (the sound, music, our breath, the recording, etc.). After a time we become able to sit for longer periods. If our child learns to do this during childhood, they will have these skills available to them for life.

Chapter 8

OUT OF PROTECTION MODE: BUILDING TRUST

In the previous part about protection mode behaviours, the word 'trust' came up often. People with hidden disabilities explained to us how they need to build up trust with specific foods, clothes, people, routines and activities. When they are feeling overwhelmed, they find comfort in predictable things that they know they can trust. This is why they may eat the same food, wear the same clothes or follow the same routine every day.

As they come out of protection mode, many become more flexible as their trust increases, not only about trusting specific foods and routines, but about trusting life itself.

This involves our children learning to trust their emotions. Many of our children are terrified of their emotions and what may happen if they are feeling angry, upset or confused.

LEARNING TO TRUST EMOTIONS

When children are in protection mode, many strong emotions may be happening at once and they can feel out of control and overwhelmed by them. Emotions can be so overwhelming that they may shut them down to avoid feeling them or try to drown them out by screaming. In fact, any of the behaviours that get worse in protection mode can be ways of drowning out overwhelming emotions.

Danny Raede from Asperger Experts explains just how exhausting and draining it is to fight against our emotions:

> Before, the thoughts were always, 'Fight the anxiety, fight the anxiety, fight the anxiety, I should be able to do something! I should not have anxiety. I am feeling anxious. But I shouldn't feel anxious. But I shouldn't feel that I'm feeling anxious. So now I'm just stupid, but I know that I shouldn't feel that I'm stupid, and then just more anxiety. Now, I feel guilty for feeling all of these things. And I'm just stressed out. But I shouldn't even feel stressed out.' That was my normal loop, which happened pretty much every waking hour.[1]

One of the most important things we can do to help our child come out of protection mode is to teach them not to fear feelings and emotions. When emotions are welcomed instead of feared, miracles can happen. As soon as we are able to accept what we are feeling, the need to shut down or drown out our feelings disappears.

Most people have problems accepting their emotions and most people fear them. This is logical as powerful emotions can hurt a lot and it is natural to want to avoid pain. We also feel out of control while we are feeling them and cannot think clearly. This makes it very tempting to push them away or pretend they are not there.

We are also often taught that there is something shameful in feeling an emotion that is considered 'negative' or 'bad', like being angry, upset or frightened.

It can be helpful to remember the difference between an emotion and an action. For example, *feeling angry* and *acting in anger* are very different things. The emotion here is anger and the action may be hitting someone. They are not the same thing.

It is perfectly possible to recognise that we are angry and not hit someone. It is also possible to hit and be an effective fighter without being angry. The anger in itself does not cause the hitting. We have a choice about how we respond to our anger. Some people shout when they are angry and others become silent.

So, while we may be ashamed of something we may *do* when we are angry, this does not mean we need to be ashamed of *feeling* the anger itself.

Feelings are pretty neutral and are not in themselves 'good' or 'bad'. They are simply the way our body communicates with us and tells us that something is wrong or right. Feelings are like signposts and are very useful indeed. If we switch off our feelings, we are switching off our internal navigation systems.

Anger may be our body's way of telling us that an injustice may have taken place. Happiness may be our body telling us that something is good. Guilt may be our body saying that we did something shameful. Frustration may mean that something has not gone according to plan. We would be pretty lost in assessing our lives without these emotions. And the more we ignore these messages, the more confused and overwhelmed we feel.

Feelings can be powerful and unpleasant, but neuroscience has shown that as soon as we *recognise* a feeling and *acknowledge* that it is there, it starts to disappear. According to neuroscientist Jill Bolte-Taylor the lifespan of a strong emotion is 90 seconds.[2]

Knowing this is very liberating. As the emotion has done its job of warning us about something, it no longer needs to hang around. If we ignore the warning, by ignoring or pushing away a feeling, the body knows that the message has not been delivered and so intensifies it until we can hear it. This means that suppressing anger in any way is likely to make it come back stronger. Acknowledging the anger makes it disappear as the message has been delivered.

This is rather like an alarm clock with a crescendo function. When the alarm goes off in the morning, we may not like it and not want to wake up. If we ignore the alarm, the sound will get louder and louder until we have no choice but to recognise that it is there.

Painful emotions are a problem when they stick around. Feeling anger, grief and frustration for a long period lowers our immunity and makes us sick. It also pushes our children deeper into protection mode.

Nothing makes a painful emotion stick around more than ignoring it. Nothing makes it go away quicker than recognising it – hearing the alarm and acknowledging it by hitting the off button.

In fact, Danny Raede credits learning to embrace and trust his emotions as one of the keys to getting and staying out of protection mode. On getting consumed with anxiety at a movie theatre, he tried something new:

> So anyway, about three-quarters of the way through the movie I remember thinking, 'I'm done. I refuse to play this game anymore. I'm not going to do the game of trying to fix and resist my anxiety anymore. I quit. If my anxiety overwhelms me and kills me, then so be it. But I am done.'
>
> And the weird thing is... As soon as I had that thought, the anxiety stopped pretty darn immediately.
>
> The profound realization I had during the movie is that the thing I was calling anxiety wasn't the sensation of overwhelm and panic I felt. It was the response of me trying to suppress how I felt, and control it, and deny it, and fix it.
>
> Once I stopped denying it, stopped resisting it, and stopped trying to fight it...the anxiety went away.[3]

Painful emotions also stick around when we focus on thinking about the situation or person who caused them. So as our child thinks over and over about the horrible things said to her by other children in school, she will be prolonging the painful emotions.

Unpleasant things happen, but by releasing the emotion it becomes much easier to figure out what if anything needs to be done.

Pema Chödrön says:

> If we could learn to sit with the ninety second surge of emotion that takes place when we are triggered, we might learn to let go, but instead we fuel it with our thoughts and what should last for one and a half minutes may be drawn out for ten or twenty years.[4]

So how do we help our children to recognise their emotions without doing something they may regret?

My strongest suggestion is to practise for ourselves and then demonstrate to our children what to do.

The first helpful technique is called 'the pause'. When a powerful emotion comes up, we can make a conscious decision to pause for a couple of seconds rather than doing anything about it. This pause helps to separate the emotion from any action.

So, if we get very angry, instead of immediately reacting in any way, we do nothing at all and just sit with the anger and let ourselves feel it. We can try to name the emotion. We can say to ourselves or even out loud, 'I am really angry.'

We let ourselves feel angry and observe how it is affecting our body. We may feel a contraction in the jaw or a pain in the stomach. We let it be and acknowledge it all. For this to work, we have to focus on what we are feeling and not the person or situation that made us angry.

Sometimes, after a minute or so the emotion will change. Anger may turn to sadness. Again, we can acknowledge the sadness, feel it and sit with it until it passes. This is just like telling the alarm clock that you have heard the alarm by pressing the button. The emotion may change a number of times when we are sitting with our feelings in this way. After a little while of doing this, we are likely to feel calm and the stress will pass.

Practitioners of mindfulness sometimes call this 'inviting our feelings to tea'. When painful emotions come knocking at our door, rather than turn them away, we can instead welcome them in and invite them to a cup of tea.

Mindfulness master Thich Nhat Hanh says:

> When an unpleasant feeling, physical or mental, arises in him, the wise man does not worry, complain, weep, pound his chest, pull his hair, torture his body and mind, or faint. He calmly observes his feeling and is aware that it is only a feeling. He knows that he is not the feeling, and he is not caught by the feeling. Therefore, the pain cannot bind him.[5]

When we are able to do this for ourselves, we can start teaching our children how to do it. The easiest way is to regularly tell our children how *we* are feeling so that doing so becomes normal. As long as doing this is not accompanied with unpleasant actions like hitting or shouting, this will help them to fear emotions less. So, we can say, 'I'm feeling really stressed at the moment, so I'm going to wait for it to pass.' After 90 seconds we can say, 'The stress has gone now.'

This is a powerful invitation to our child to start doing the same.

Although we will never completely get rid of emotional overwhelm, 'inviting our feelings to tea' reduces it greatly and helps our children to feel more in control of their feelings and reactions. We know that many of our children's protection mode behaviours are about wanting to feel in control, so learning this can make a big difference.

There are other ways we can help our children to recognise and name their emotions. We can show them emojis or pictures that depict different emotions and ask them to point to the one that most shows how they are feeling. We can then give them a word to describe each one.

We can turn 'inviting our feelings to tea' into a game that is suitable for our child's age and interests. There are various board and card games specifically for this purpose that we can play together. There are also fun apps and computer games that do the same thing. The more fun we make it, the quicker they will learn as they will *want* to learn and beat us at the games!

Another helpful way to is use mood charts. Adults with mental health problems often chart their moods to see if their treatments are helping them. A simple sticker chart could work well for a child, allowing them to select the sticker that best shows how they are feeling at that moment.

There are also some great children's books that introduce children to feelings and emotions and encourage them to journal how they are feeling. I would suggest you search for these and read them with your child. There are also similar books for older children and teenagers, although getting an older child to read them may be more challenging.

EMBRACING FAILURE

Our children have to deal with a lot of failure, or more accurately, what looks like failure to them.

Due to the challenges of their hidden disabilities, they may feel like failures, even though we may try to convince them otherwise. From their point of view, they may fail to fit in socially. They may fail to show what they can achieve academically. They may fail to complete tasks that they really want to do. They may fail to understand what is expected of them. They may fail to control their emotions. They may fail to stop the meltdowns, shutdowns or all the other symptoms of being deep in protection mode.

They may look at their neurotypical schoolmates and see that they do not have problems with these things. They see that socialising and completing homework comes easily to them and that they have the energy to do after-school activities. When they compare themselves with these children, it is easy to feel even more inadequate and useless. They probably know that they are as able as their neurotypical classmates, but everything feels insurmountably difficult, overwhelming and exhausting.

This can make them feel very rubbish indeed. They may feel both a failure at life and a disappointment to us.

Feeling like a failure rarely motivates anyone to try harder. It makes us want to give up. It makes us think, 'What's the point?' It drives our children deeper into shutdown and strengthens their protection mode. It can make them lose any motivation to even try, as the risk and shame of failure is too strong.

According to Justine, who has ASD and ADHD:

> I just feel like it's all useless as I am obviously useless and can't do anything properly. Even the easiest of things I seem to fail at, apparently. My brain goes into this negative loop and I don't just fail at things, I really can't even try them. I don't have the emotional strength left.

As parents, it is important to teach our children resilience in the face of what appears to be failure.

The easiest way to do this is to rebrand failure as *success*.

The reality is that nearly all success happens as a result of lessons learnt from previous failures.

This was summed up beautifully by kung fu master Bruce Lee:

> Don't fear failure. — Not failure, but low aim, is the crime. In great attempts it is glorious even to fail.[6]

We are motivated by successes but rarely learn from them. In fact, the opposite can happen and if everything goes right, we can become complacent. Without the skills we acquire from failure, we are not stimulated to move forward. When something goes wrong, if we are resilient and do not take it personally, we can use the experience to figure out what we would need to do to make it go right.

We live in a world where things often do not go according to plan and we need to be able to embrace this. Every failure brings us one step closer to success. Every failure teaches us something important, if we are open to learning it.

Because our children have to deal with more 'failures' than most children, they have more opportunities to learn and this may be one of the reasons they can fly ahead so quickly when they come out of protection mode.

If our children are able to adopt a mindset in which they can embrace their failures as springboards to success, they can achieve unimaginable success in whatever is important to them. The resilience that children with hidden disabilities can acquire by embracing failure is one of the reasons why they are so over- represented among the world's greatest innovators.

It is useful to point out that Einstein and the inventor Nikola Tesla may have been on the autism spectrum or had psychiatric conditions. They may or may not have been geniuses but they certainly had to face failure after failure and develop the resilience to keep going, even when they felt that no-one understood or cared.[7]

How do we teach this to our children?

We can start by talking to them about *our own* failures. If we are human beings, we will have quite a few to choose from! We can talk about our failures with pride rather than shame. We can tell our child what we *learned* from each experience and how we were able to go back to the same situation again and again with better knowledge, better preparation and better skills for dealing with it. We can show our children how we turned our failures into successes by not taking them personally and by not giving up.

If our child is having a difficult time at school, it may be tempting for her to believe that she has failed in the job of fitting in there. But instead she can learn that school is not the best environment for her to learn in. Knowing this can help her to figure out what sort of environment does work for her to learn in. This can result in finding a better fit. No-one could have known this without the initial 'failure'.

It can be difficult or even impossible for our children to learn the lesson of an apparent failure when they are too close to it. They may be too upset by what has happened to see the lesson with clarity. They may also be too deep in protection mode to learn any lesson, as we know that stress hormones switch off the thinking brain. This is when it is very useful to use the 'inviting our feelings to tea' practices to feel and clear the painful emotions. After that has happened, the lessons to be learned become clearer, as will be the next logical steps to take.

This book was written as a result of hundreds, possibly thousands of parenting mistakes. Learning what doesn't work helps us to figure out what does. One of my objectives in writing this book was to help others learn from my failures, just as I learned from them.

We can remind our child that things going wrong are stepping stones to things going right. We can praise and celebrate every lesson that is learned in this way as a great achievement and success in its own right.

MANAGING TRANSITIONS AND CHANGES

Any kind of change or transition is stressful and adds heat to our pressure cookers, even if we want or choose the change. As our children's 'pressure cookers' are already overheated, helping them to deal with transitions is an important way out of protection mode.

Depending on our child's hidden disabilities, there may also be brain chemistry reasons why they struggle with change. This is especially the case with children on the autism spectrum. If this is so, they will have this problem *in addition to* the challenges with change that come from protection mode.

Change and transitions exhaust our children and this is something rarely understood by teachers in mainstream schools. The arrival of a substitute teacher, the change of a timetabled activity, the moving of tables so that their usual seat is not there, their best friend being absent, something that is meant to happen at 10 am happens at 12 am instead, throwing out plans for the rest of the day, the list of change stressors is endless. The deeper a child is into protection mode, the less they will be able to tolerate unscheduled changes.

In fact, everyone who is under stress becomes less flexible, including us. When I am feeling calm and in control of my life, someone cancelling on me at the last minute would be mildly annoying. But if I am already struggling with stress and feeling overwhelmed, the last-minute cancellation can feel like a catastrophe and be really hard to cope with. This is normal as when there is chaos inside us, we want to hang on to what we know and feel sure about.

There is a lot that we can do to help our child manage transitions and change at home. The most important thing we can do is be aware about how they affect our child.

It is easy to remember to support our child with *big* transitions and changes, like moving house, the death of a family member, starting a new school, divorce, etc. We may need to remember that dealing with the small day-to-day changes and transitions are just as important. Small changes can feel like big ones to our child when they accumulate, one on top of the other.

Stressful changes can include the simple act of coming home from school, a cancelled play date or an unexpected illness that causes plans to change suddenly. For some children, a change in the weather or the season is enough to throw them off. In many parts of the world, the change in the time at which it gets dark is also an issue. In the UK it is dark by 3.30 pm in winter and not until after 10 pm in summer. This in itself is enough to throw off our prepared routines.

Some of the changes can be known about in advance, giving us the chance to prepare our child. The more prepared our child is for the change or transition, the less stressful and threatening it will be. It seems to be the unexpected changes that are the most triggering for our child.

So, if we plan to take our child on holiday, we can tell them in advance where they will be going and when. We may be able to show them photos of the room they will be staying in and tell them what food they will be eating. If we will be flying, it can be helpful to talk them through the whole process, including all the stages of security checks, through to collecting baggage, getting on a coach and arriving at the destination.

Many families use visual timetables, as a lot of children struggle with understanding time, especially when they are stressed and anxious. Some children find that having a favourite toy or a preferred item to touch or smell helps them during the transition times. Older children and adults often find it helpful to play with a fidget toy to distract the anxious mind.

When we are clear on what our children need in order to deal with change and transition, we can do what we can to get others on board. If we have a helpful school, they may be able to tell us in advance if there are any changes planned to schedules or if there is going to be a change of teacher. The parents of our child's friends could let us know when they are going to be absent.

We can never know about *all* the changes and unscheduled transitions, as many are unexpected and unplanned. In any organisation, plans can change at the last minute due to unforeseen circumstances. There are always people who will let us down or not do what they say they are going to do. No matter how much we remind teachers and others to let us know about changes, they may forget or not be able to do so in time.

Realistically we cannot protect our child from all unexpected changes and transitions, and neither should we, and we can only do our best with the ones that we do know about. As it is the *accumulation* of all the changes that causes the problem, any lessening of this load will help our child.

Rachel, mum to a thriving son with ASD, has a really helpful suggestion:

> I know we cannot protect our kids from all changes, so we made up fake ones that we knew that Matt could cope with, so that he had some really positive examples of where he had been resilient to look back on.

I love this idea of building resilience to change in this way. We know that success builds success and by controlling when and how the change happens, we can watch our child grow in confidence and self-esteem at these challenging moments. Obviously, we would choose calm 'code green' times to practise this to give maximum opportunity for success.

One of the most difficult transitions for our child is coming home from school each day, leaving one world with its rules and expectations and entering another with different ones. This is also the time when their internal pressure cooker is at its hottest, their pot of coping resources may be empty, they are exhausted and it can all become too much. This is also the time when children are expected to jump into action with homework and after-school activities.

It is useful to be aware that this, along with other transition times, needs a carefully thought-out strategy, which will be different for each child. The aim when managing a transition is to turn the heat on the pressure cooker not only down, but preferably off altogether while they decompress, recover and adapt to the new environment.

For some children this means TV time. Others need to sleep. Others may need to play football. Some need to run around like crazy to burn off their pent-up energy. Others may need quiet cuddles with us or with their dog. Whatever the thing is that helps, it can become a *ritual*, making it predictable and therefore safe and reassuring.

It is also helpful to encourage our child to recognise what they are feeling at these times and to let themselves feel the upset, anger or confusion until these emotions pass. We know that if an emotion is not suppressed, it will pass in only 90 seconds. The 'inviting our feelings to tea' process can be really helpful at these times.

We can also create additional rituals to help our children with changes. Although life may be unpredictable, rituals can help our children to stay grounded and feel secure.

Rituals can help with bedtime, bath time and meal time routines. Saying a blessing before a meal is a transition ritual as well as an expression of gratitude. Story time rituals mean that we are winding down for bed.

To this it may help to add a special after-school song or dance. Or a special game could be played every Friday to mark the beginning of the weekend. You could play uplifting music in the car every day so that your child comes to expect it. The ritual can change according to the child's age and interests and your child can help to choose it.

Adults need transition rituals too. Some are more healthy than others. Many parents mark the end of the parenting day with a glass or three of wine. For me, my ritual is to treat myself to a long, very hot bath.

For both us and our children, transitions and change bring up painful emotions. When they are able, it can be a useful time to use a feelings chart or doing the 'inviting our feelings to tea' activity described earlier.

We also know that practising mindfulness meditation can help our children to manage change and uncertainty. The Totally Meditation website says:

> Ask anyone with Asperger's what structure and routine means and they are very likely to say it means almost everything. There is always a need to have a plan for the day so when something throws a wrench into that plan, it can be difficult to accept. Meditation makes it easier to stop and assess the situation and then move forward with a modified plan accordingly. This is because meditation naturally helps control the effect that life changes have on someone's mental health by teaching the mind and body how to adapt to change.[8]

HOLDING SPACE

Our children often feel trapped in a chaotic world of exhaustion, self-doubt and anxiety. Often the most supportive thing we can do is not to do anything. Sometimes giving them our *loving presence* is what is needed the most.

Feeling that someone is emotionally supporting us is huge. In a world obsessed with 'getting things done' this is not recognised enough.

When our children are suffering, it is very tempting to jump into action and plan what we are going to do about it to help them. Rather than listening to our children, really listening at the deepest level, we can instead overwhelm them with all the things that need to happen to 'fix' the situation. This can drive them deeper into protection mode as quite often what they need and want is for their feelings and experiences to be recognised.

Sometimes what they need most is for us to listen, understand and 'get it'. This gives a lot of relief. It turns the heat down from under their pressure cooker and helps them out of protection mode.

Sometimes it is necessary to jump into action to fix a problem. Sometimes it is not. Part of our job as effective parents is to learn the difference between these times, a process that takes both time and a fair bit of trial and error!

Holding space is when we support our child to say whatever they want to say. It means we don't interrupt them, give them advice or do anything at all to fix what they are talking about.

We don't barrage them with questions or opinions about what they are saying. We just sit with them and let them communicate, holding them in love while they do so. We let it happen at a time that works for them, so it may be late at night when the house is quiet.

This sounds easy to do but it isn't. It takes a lot of practice, at least it did for me. I still have to resist the urge to interrupt and to jump in with suggestions and ideas. Like everything, learning to hold space is about creating new habits when listening to other people.

Taking the time to really listen without giving advice helps our child feel safe and secure. This builds trust with everything that happens in their lives. We need to remember that it is this lack of trust in everything around them that is fuelling our child's anxiety and causing them to shut down to life.

The more our children are able to trust their lives, the more they will be able to build connections: with people, with places, with activities, with life itself.

I think we can all identify with this in our own lives. We know how good it feels when we speak to someone who really 'gets it'. Sometimes we need people not only to *listen* to our words but also to show that they *understand* the feelings behind the words. Advice is helpful sometimes, but the support of someone holding space for us is priceless.

Danielle LaRock explains how holding space helps her:

> The thought that was driving my meltdown was unintelligible in my brain, due to the crashing waves of my emotional reaction. But somehow, eventually, I found myself able to fully lift my head and stare straight on at my distorted reflection in the stainless steel door of the dishwasher.
>
> The whole while, he sat with me. My endlessly loving partner, Jonathan, held space.[9]

If we interrupt or give advice while our child is opening up, it takes our attention away from them and onto us. This can make them feel abandoned by us emotionally.

It goes without saying that we will need to mute our phones when we are holding space. Taking a call when our child is sharing something sensitive can feel like a physical assault.

We need to figure out how best to hold space for our child. Some will appreciate us holding their hand or holding eye contact. Others find this intimidating and prefer some physical distance. It may be best in a car when we are not facing each other. Some older children feel more comfortable when we hold space over the phone or via messaging.

Oliver, who has ADD and Asperger's, explains this:

> The only time I can really open up about how I feel is to my mum. But for some reason it has to be over the phone. As soon as we are physically together, I freeze up and cannot speak at all. I become pretty well mute. I think the phone gives a bit of the distance I need. It's not just the eye contact that switches me off, it's about being physically seen at all as well as seeing the other person. Over the phone I can just go into my head and let everything spill out.

The essence of holding space is showing our child that we love and accept them unconditionally and also trust their ability, when they have this support, to sort things out emotionally for themselves.

Our children may have extreme emotions and a limited vocabulary. This means that it is often very difficult for them to put into words what they want and need to say.

We need to be aware of this and be as patient as we can. Sometimes what they need to express can come out as anger, as shouting or as crying. We can help them find words for it later, but what matters most is that we listen and do not react, even if they are saying things that under other circumstances would be considered offensive.

Our child may need to insult us to get to what is really bothering them. We can hold space through this and not take it personally. As they gain more tools and learn to understand their confusing emotions better, they are likely to insult us less.

This may involve swearing if this reflects the intensity of what they are trying to express. Swearing is usually 'just words' for our kids. Although they need to learn when it is and is not appropriate to swear, 'holding space' is in my opinion not a time to hold back on using any words they choose to express how they feel.

Another beautiful thing about holding space for our children is that they may learn how to do it for others. At the time of writing this book I am going through a difficult transition in my life. Without knowing what I needed, my children held space for me and this was the best support I could have asked for.

HANDING OVER TO THEM

We can help our children to come out and stay out of protection mode using these techniques at any age. Ultimately though, the greatest achievement is when they are able to take responsibility for this themselves.

As they grow older, they will need to take steps not only to recognise when they are in protection mode but to know what steps to take to get themselves out of it. They will need to know how to take the temperature of their own internal pressure cookers and know when and how to turn down the heat when they need to.

Just as we have to learn to decode our children's behaviour, as they grow older they will need to learn how to decode themselves. Ideally, they will become the experts in themselves.

Learning how to do this is one of the biggest independence skills they will need in life. If they are able to keep themselves out of protection mode, their thinking brains will be switched on and they will be able to learn and practise all the other independence skills they will need.

Rachel saw success in this with her son:

> There is no better feeling than seeing Matt taking himself out of a stressful situation, self regulating and coming back to talk when he is calmer. There was a time when I never thought this would happen.

During their childhood, we need to read their codes and assess the best ways to keep the temperature down on their pressure cookers. As they get older we need to start handing this job back to them. Their reading of their 'internal codes' may be different from our reading of them. Ultimately, the more they learn to accept themselves through holding space for themselves, the better they will be at reading their own internal clues.

With time they will be better at it than us, much better. They will become the experts in themselves. They will accept their strengths and their limitations and be prepared to make the lifestyle, medical and other choices that are needed for their wellbeing, whatever hidden disability they may have.

When my children came out of protection mode in early adulthood, they grabbed back the reins of control for treatment from me. It was a scary time, as I was fearful of some of their choices. Mistakes were made and valuable lessons were learned. Much was achieved that could not possibly have happened without the benefit of these 'mistakes'. Through this process, which took a few years, my children learned many things about themselves and their needs that I had missed while parenting them. I had missed them because I had done my best, but they were the experts on themselves.

This is what one of my children discovered about their needs:

> I discovered that in order to be stable and productive I need to have a regular routine that I can be in control of. I need to avoid excess alcohol and caffeine. I need to be busy with something that really interests and challenges me. If I am not interested in it, or can't see the

> point of it, it will exhaust and deplete me. If I can't control my work flow I will crash, then feel a failure. Then I can fall into depression.

Understanding themselves and their needs has helped my children to make lifestyle choices that work for them. They were able to see without shame or self-judgement why some situations were not working out for them and be more able to let them go.

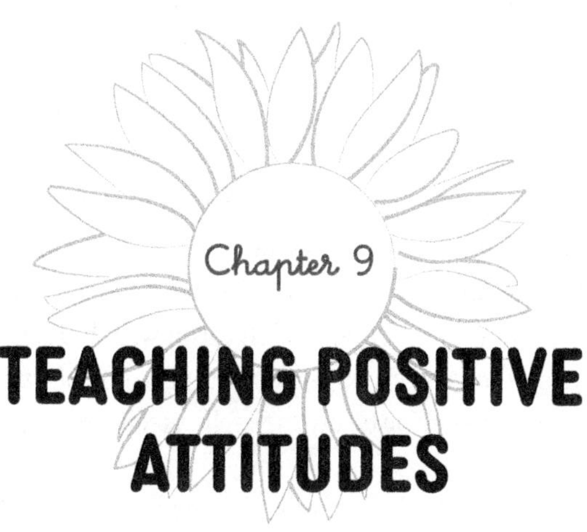

Chapter 9

TEACHING POSITIVE ATTITUDES

While getting our child out of protection mode is really important, if they are to stay out, thrive and have a happy and fulfilled life, they need something more. That something more is a healthy and positive attitude to life. They are dealing with real challenges that they may not be able to control. But they can control how they react to these things and how to react to themselves. This is something we can help them with.

BUILDING SELF-ESTEEM AND SELF-ACCEPTANCE

Most of us at some time will have difficulty accepting ourselves for who we are. We live in a very competitive world where we are bombarded with messages telling us that we are not enough, are too much, not attractive or clever enough, too fat, too thin, not cool, not right. We can easily look at and compare ourselves with others and feel deficient and lacking. This can even become self-hate.

We may scrutinise our 'faults' in the mirror, sit home alone while our friends are out at parties and see the achievements of others that we are unable to match. We can become incensed by the injustice of this and become angry not only with those we cannot compete with, but also ourselves and the world for making us feel so useless.

The growth of social media has fuelled this even further, as people often post a perfect version of themselves and their lives to gain 'likes' and the admiration of others.

Dealing with this is a struggle for even the most confident and strong of people. We can only start to imagine how tough it is for our children with hidden disabilities. In addition to the usual insecurities that young people have, very large numbers of children with hidden disabilities suffer bullying at school, 63 per cent according to one piece of research,[1] something that is shattering to anyone's self-esteem and fuels even more self-loathing.

And even without bullying, our children may feel socially excluded and be aware that they are underachieving in many areas where they so want to do well and prove their worth. They may simply feel *different*, and in the mindset of many of our children, difference simply means that they are *less*.

At an age when *fitting in* feels like everything, it is understandable why many of our children do not want to accept their diagnoses. It makes sense that they may not want to be or feel different and find it hard to accept their challenges as well as their gifts.

It totally makes sense why many of our children have so much difficulty accepting themselves fully for who they are.

We also know that not accepting themselves for who they are is exhausting and pushes them deeper and deeper into protection mode, especially depression, anxiety and rage.

As parents, one of our jobs is to help our children to love and accept themselves fully as they are, regardless of what they look like, achieve, do or not do and regardless of how they feel.

We need to be careful about the word 'acceptance'. Acceptance does not mean that we don't do anything about our challenges. Accepting our symptoms does not mean that we do not treat them or try to improve our lives.

In fact, it means the opposite. Acceptance mean that we fully see and recognise that the challenges are there. When we fully accept them, we can then plan what to do to help ourselves. Acceptance is about our strengths too. It is about seeing the whole package of who we are.

Self-acceptance helps our children to be *resilient* in the face of bullying and the judgey behaviour of others. When someone tells us that we are *less*, this only affects us if we already *believe that we are less*, as it *confirms* our fear about ourselves. If we accept ourselves completely and are happy in our own skin, then the unpleasant behaviour of others may upset us but no longer wound us deeply.

If we accept ourselves fully, any setback in life, of which there will be many, becomes just that, a setback. If we do not accept ourselves, setbacks are devastating, every setback being in our eyes *evidence* of our lack of worth and our lack of lovability.

When we accept ourselves fully, we no longer need to compare ourselves with others as we are happy with who we are, regardless of our appearance, abilities or achievements.

We need to remember though that accepting ourselves does not mean that we give up responsibility for our actions! We are still accountable for what we do.

When we accept ourselves fully, we accept ourselves for who we *are*, rather than what we *do*.

Sharon, who has Asperger's and is the mother of a number of children with hidden disabilities, talks about this:

> For me it's all about respecting who we are. There is so much shame and stigma around. I can't protect them from that outside our home, but I can do my uttermost to keep shame outside the door, make sure that home is the one place where we can be our glorious autistic and ADHD selves. We have lots of challenges, especially my kids who have to deal with school. We try to accept everything, including big emotions like anger and numbing out. It's really hard when I'm being triggered by my kids, but that's my challenge – to put kindness and self-esteem first and that they are worthy of deep respect for who they are.

So, to accept our children fully, we need to be careful of anything we say or imply that could cause our child to feel doubt or shame in their worthiness. We need to show them that we accept them fully even when they misbehave, have meltdowns, a dark mood or fail an exam.

If we can accept them fully at these times, it teaches them that they can also accept themselves, even if they do not like what they are doing or feeling at that particular moment.

Sometimes we do need to judge or punish a behaviour, when they have misbehaved or done something downright wrong. At these times we can try not to judge the child *personally* or make them feel that they have failed us or let us or themselves down.

In these situations, it can help to ask the child to come up with a way to put things right so that we can turn the situation around and offer praise, pride and admiration for how they dealt with a difficult situation.

For example, our child may have been unpleasant to another child. Instead of shaming the child about what happened, we can ask, 'Lena is upset. What do you think could help her feel better? What might put this right?'

Also, as Sharon points out, we need to accept ourselves. When we learn to accept ourselves, we show our children the way. We can rarely change other people, but we can guide them with our example.

I live in the UK, and in our culture it is considered polite to put ourselves down. This is self-deprecation. British people often apologise excessively, even when we've done nothing wrong, and point out our faults to others. It is considered vulgar to mention achievements. While modesty and humility are very sweet, they can easily cross the line into celebrating a lack of self-worth and a lack of self-acceptance.

We need to watch ourselves and our language to see if we are doing this. I certainly was and often still do! If we are unable to accept a compliment ourselves, how can we expect our children to accept praise and good things about themselves?

Jane, who has ASD, explains:

> It took me years to feel comfortable accepting a compliment. Even now I have to stop, think and just try to say 'thank you'. My kids are getting there. It may seem like a little thing, but it actually really matters to our self-esteem.

Every time we criticise ourselves in front of our child, perhaps saying, 'I am so stupid', 'I look awful' or 'Who's going to love an old bag like me?', we are teaching our child to criticise herself. The more we can rise into our own power by accepting ourselves, regardless of our weight, age, relationship status, education level, ethnicity, sexual orientation or bank balance, we are inviting our children to do the same.

Our child also needs to accept his hidden disability fully as *part* of who he is. This will help him to judge himself less and understand more about why he has certain challenges. Fully accepting the hidden disability will also help him to recognise his strengths and have the confidence to act on them.

There are books, podcasts and other resources available for children and young people of different ages to help them understand and accept their hidden disabilities. The best will give a positive balance of the challenges and the strengths. These can be shared with our children as a way of *celebrating* aspects of who they are.

Another thing to remember when helping our child to build self-esteem is the negativity bias. Science shows that humans take much more notice of negative feedback than positive feedback. We tend to dwell on the nasty things people say and do much more than the flattering things. Apparently, it is hardwired into our brains to hold on to horrible memories much more than pleasant ones. I think we can all relate to this. Most of us are more likely to remember an unpleasant comment than a compliment.

As Rick Hanson explains:

> The brain is like Velcro for negative experiences, but Teflon for positive ones.[2]

Our children are dealing with a lot of negative stuff every day and are as affected by the negativity bias as anyone else. Holding on to nasty memories is one of the causes of low self-esteem and negative thinking.

If we are aware of the negativity bias we can try to cheat it. Scientists suggest that one negative experience needs at least five positive ones to be balanced in the mind. This is a really helpful thing to remember. This means that in order to compensate for all the bad experiences they may be having at school, we need to lavish them with positive ones when they get home. When we do need to criticise or punish, we need to offset it with huge amounts of praise, to a value of at least five to one.

AVOIDING A VICTIM MENTALITY

Our children may at times be the victims of unpleasantness, discrimination and other injustices. When people judge them and don't understand their needs they can feel like victims. They may also be the victim of bullying and a world where people simply do not 'get' them.

There is a big difference between being a victim of something and having a victim *mentality*. The victim mentality is when our child considers victimhood as *who they are* rather than as things that *happen to them*.

It is a very easy thing to slip into and most of us do this at times. Our daughter may be getting a victim mentality if she only talks about bad things that happen to her. She may repeat stories over and over of when she was a victim of something. This can in part be due to the negativity bias, but it can also become a habit. Hearing about how the other person was wrong and she was right may make her feel good.

Hearing us criticise other people for being unkind to her may make our daughter feel *righteous*, even powerful. It can feel *good* for her to know that others have done wrong and that she was right.

We all enjoy telling friends about how awful our boss is, how bitchy a certain person is or how we were unfairly treated by an organisation. We get loads of sympathy and become the centre of other people's attention. They get angry on our behalf and may give us more support. It's really easy to see how this can become a habit.

A person with a victim mentality may not mention good things that happen to them at all. Even if something wonderful were to happen, they may twist the account so that they sound like victims. They may even want bad things to happen in order to have more negative material to talk about to others.

A victim mentality is dangerous for our child as it prevents him from doing things to improve his life. It prevents him from taking responsibility for what he *can* change in situations.

For our children to have happy and healthy lives, they need to feel empowered, and the victim mentality is the opposite of empowerment.

We can teach our children to recognise when they have been a victim, and we do need to support them when this happens.

To protect them from falling into a victim *mentality*, they will also need as much attention from us at times when they are *not* a victim and when things are going well. Due to the negativity bias, we probably need to give them *more* attention when they are not a victim as our child is more likely to forget positive experiences.

We can focus on what our child does during difficult situations, rather than only on things that are 'done to them' by others. We can say things like, 'Wow, that was tough but you really handled it well.' 'Looks like you took control of that situation. Well done.' Or 'Not much you could have done there. So you were so right to do nothing.'

BEING GRATEFUL

Gratitude is about appreciating everything in life and seeing the good as well as the bad. Research shows that people who are grateful for what is good in their lives are far less likely to suffer from depression and anxiety.[3]

If our child can get into the habit of looking for things to be grateful for, this can also protect them from falling into a victim mentality. It can also help to cheat the negativity bias. This is because we need to focus on five positive things to every negative thing to break even.

Just as victim mentality is a habit, so is gratitude. The difference is that gratitude is a good habit to cultivate. When we get used to focusing on and appreciating people and situations that are good, we gain control over our lives.

When we appreciate other people, they tend to be nicer to us. Gratitude seems to bring more of the good stuff into our lives.

We can teach our child the habit of gratitude by demonstrating it. We can tell them about all the things we are grateful for and how much we appreciate the kindness of a particular person. We can point out beautiful sunsets and listen to the singing of birds. We can tell our child how grateful we are for their smile and the helpful things they do.

Many religions include gratitude practices. We may give thanks before a meal or at harvest times. We may help other people who are less fortunate. These things humble us into not taking what we have for granted. Even if we do not practise a religion, we can make some of these practices part of our lives.

We can do this by making it a priority for our child to say please and thank you and make sure that we always do this ourselves. We can compliment others about things we genuinely like and encourage our child to do the same. We need to make sure that what we say is genuinely meant and not empty or meaningless words.

At mealtimes and at bedtime, we can share things that we are grateful for that happened that day. Even when unpleasant things have happened, we can ask our child to find something positive about them.

When we teach our children gratitude, we need to be careful not to go so far that we make them feel *guilty* for what they have. I remember as a child being told that if I did not finish my dinner, I should think of the starving millions in Africa. Being rather literal, I remember asking if we could send my dinner to Africa as they needed the food more than me.

There is a difference between appreciating having something and feeling guilty because others do not have it.

TAKING RESPONSIBILITY FOR THEMSELVES

Self-responsibility means recognising and being accountable for what we do or don't do and how we feel.

As they grow older, our children will need to take responsibility for figuring out what works and doesn't work for them. This includes remembering to take their treatments and go to appointments. They will need to commit to their self-care, including exercise, nature time and healthy eating. As they hit their teens, self-responsibility includes making decisions about their alcohol and drug use, relationships, the company they keep as well as their job and study choices. They will need to be able to acknowledge their own mistakes and be open to learning from them.

After a certain age, all of these things are down to them and not to us, no matter how much we nag or remind them.

There will be some things in life that our child cannot control. But there are many things that she can. Without self-responsibility, our child can check out of dealing with the things she *can* control and instead find other people or situations to blame.

This is why it is so important to cultivate an attitude of self-responsibility in our children. Children who do not take responsibility for their wellbeing are more likely to blame everyone else for how they are feeling or drift into a victim mentality.

One of the things that can prevent our children from taking on responsibility for themselves is the fear of being blamed. There is often confusion about these two words and some people use 'blame' and 'responsibility' to mean the same thing. There is a big difference. The word 'blame' suggests that something is someone's 'fault'.

Our children are not to blame for their symptoms and challenges. They are not to blame for being in protection mode. They are certainly not to blame for the unjust behaviour of others.

Being 'responsible' is about how they *handle* these things. The more our children are able to take responsibility for themselves, the more control they will feel over their lives. We already know that the need to feel control fuels a lot of our children's protection mode behaviours. This is why taking responsibility for themselves will help to both get and keep them out of protection mode.

We live in a blame culture where we often get what we want by blaming someone else. Much of our legal system is about pointing the finger of blame. It is not surprising that our child will want to avoid being blamed and possibly punished.

Fear of being blamed or shamed is one of the main things that stops a child taking responsibility for themselves. To help them learn self-responsibility, we need to make sure that they will not feel blamed or shamed when they do so. In fact, we need to do the opposite – praise and celebrate every attempt at self-responsibility, even if they get it wrong.

Being able to say, 'Dad, I'm really anxious today' is a sign of mature self-responsibility. The child is not blaming himself or anyone else. By taking this responsibility he is then open to thinking about what may help him.

If our child is able to say to us, 'I made a mistake today. I lost it and said a bad word to my teacher', this is a huge achievement. The achievement is the self-responsibility. If our child can do this, instead of saying that someone 'made him' say the bad word, it means that he can work out ways to deal with the situation.

The best way to teach self-responsibility is to make sure that we are practising it ourselves. Do we openly admit to our children when we have got something wrong? Or do we blame other people? Are we honest with our children about how we feel about things? When something bad happens, do we look for anything we can control in the situation, even if it is just our attitude?

If our children see us blaming others for things that we could have some control over, this is what they are likely to learn to do. If we are struggling with this, as I was, my companion book *How to Cope When Your Child Has a Hidden Disability: Self-Care for Parents* may help as it includes some techniques on this very issue.

The other main way to teach self-responsibility is to make sure that our child is not shamed when they take responsibility for a 'bad' thing that they have done. All acts of self-responsibility need to be celebrated and encouraged.

This can be difficult to manage if our child has done something that requires a punishment or consequence, like lying or stealing. If they have shown self-responsibility by telling us about it, it could look to them as though they are being punished or shamed for being *honest*, rather than for the 'bad' act itself.

This is a tricky one and there is no easy answer. Due to the power of the negativity bias, my own view would be to prioritise the praise for being accountable and to keep any necessary consequence clearly separate from it.

Instead of shame, it may be more useful for our child to recognise that the action was a *mistake* or not a good idea. Rather than being ashamed of the mistake, we can remember that mistakes are stepping stones to successes, as long as we learn from them.

Teaching self-responsibility takes time. It is very difficult for children who are deep in protection mode so we need to aim for it but not expect too much too soon. Once our children hit their teens, it becomes critical. This is the subject of the next chapter.

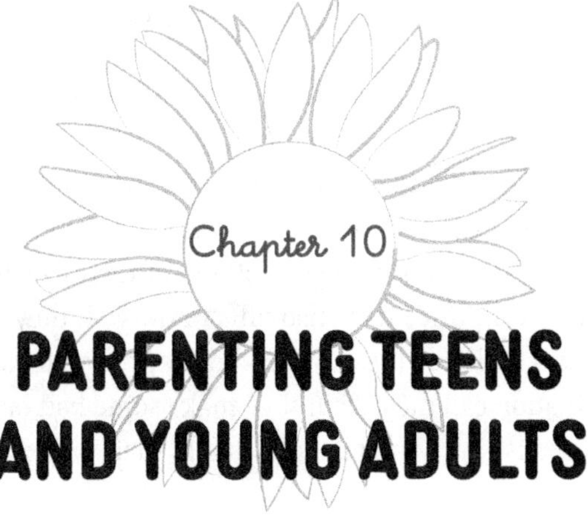

Chapter 10
PARENTING TEENS AND YOUNG ADULTS

Nowhere does personal responsibility and accountability become more important than when we are parenting teens and young adults. This is the time when we are literally handing them control over their treatments, their studies, their use of drugs and alcohol, their diet and wellbeing. As they get older we will have less and less control over these things. If and when they go away to college or leave home we may have no control at all.

After a certain age it is harder to impose a consequence if our loved one does something we do not approve of. We can no longer make sure that they take their medication or supplements or attend their medical or therapy appointments. We cannot stop them eating junk food every day or from doing reckless or dangerous things. This is a terrifying leap of faith for any parent of a teenager. If our child also has hidden disabilities it is much, much more complicated.

Unless they are able to take responsibility for their own behaviour, treatments, safety and feelings, they may have considerable difficulties transitioning to adult life. This is why teaching self-responsibility and accountability when they are still young children and under our domain is so important as it will hugely ease the handover of control later on.

For parents of children with hidden disabilities, it is not simply a matter of learning how to let go. Our children are far more vulnerable, and although they are in adult or teenage bodies, they may be much younger emotionally and socially than their chronological age and many of their peers.

Due to both their hidden disabilities and spending much of their childhood in protection mode, they may not have the experience or skills to assess situations as well as others of their age. In addition, their hidden disabilities may also affect how well they read social situations and pick up clues about who they can and cannot trust. This combination can mean that they make some bad or dangerous decisions or trust the wrong people, due to their lack of experience in life.

We can add to this the normal need for teenagers and young people to 'kick back' against parents to find their own path and to find out who they are independently of their parents' assessment of them. This is the time when many 'normal' teenagers develop mental health problems, often serious ones, due to the huge amount of extra pressures that they are under. Anxieties about exams and achievement, their looks and body, their popularity and abilities have been amplified beyond our imagination for the current generation by social media. Our children with hidden disabilities are at just as much risk of mental health problems as any other teenager, possibly greater risk, as they may have fewer coping skills in place.

With so many layers at play we can understand why so many parents fear and dread this 'transitioning' period of parenting so much.

And if this is not enough, how do we know what is normal, hormonal teenage behaviour and what is related to our child's hidden disability? Has my bipolar child's mood gone into mania or is this normal teenage 'high spirits'? Has my child gone into a shutdown depression from Asperger's or is it normal adolescent moodiness? Is he being rude to me because he's a defiant teenager or is this a cry for help from the emotional pain of his hidden disability? Is she in pain or is she just downright nasty? Is she stealing from me as a protection mode cry for help or is she just a difficult teenager who is defying my authority and values? Is my son with ADHD being a normal lazy, teenage slob in his bedroom or is he shut down due to being in protection mode?

If we are having problems answering these questions, we are not alone. There are no answers to these questions as no-one can know for sure what is due to 'normal' teenager-ness and what is due to our kids' hidden disabilities. Where does the teenager stop and the hidden disability begin? For our children, the two are likely to be enmeshed.

Some parents deal with challenging teenage behaviour using a *tough love* approach with strong consequences for violating rules about things like curfew hours, alcohol, respect and school performance. Some have great success with this and the children get through adolescence with the security of knowing clearly what is expected of them, what their key values are and what they can and cannot do to keep our much-wanted approval. Tough love can help children feel protected and although they may be kicking against authority, knowing the authority is there can help them feel safe and monitored.

The same parents may want to consider dealing with anything related to their child's hidden disability differently. Rather than tough love, they may prefer to address hidden disability behaviour with compassion and understanding and without judgement. When the child is suffering from protection mode or the symptoms of their hidden disability, strict rules may need to be softened or even done away with altogether as they may make things worse. If enforcing rigid rules adds heat to our child's pressure cooker, possibly causing it to explode, we may need to assess our tough love strategy carefully to make sure that it is actually achieving what we want to achieve.

If our loved one's hidden disability symptoms are mixed up with 'normal' teenage behaviour, knowing which parenting technique to use when can be exhausting and we are almost certain to get it wrong at least some of the time.

We may need to shift from one approach to another, depending on the situation and our child's needs at that moment. But this shifting can make it virtually impossible to be *consistent* in anything we do. As well as making us feel like failures, the lack of consistency can also make it hard for our children to take us seriously as parents. This problem is not unique to parents of teens with hidden disabilities. Most sensitive parents need to amend their parenting approach and rules according to their teenager's state of mind and by assessing how well their child is responding to whichever technique we are trying at a particular moment.

If we control too much, they may abandon us, thinking that we are not letting them be who they are. If we don't control enough, they may think that we have abandoned them by not trying to protect them. This is a complex dance for parents, and when we are exhausted it can feel overwhelming to navigate.

I have been through this and so have thousands of parents I know, either personally or through support groups and forums. Every time we open the newspaper, we are likely to read about things going wrong for children like ours. People are also more likely to share their bad experiences than their good ones. Because of the negativity bias, it is the bad experiences that we are likely to remember.

The reality is that many of our children get through their teens very well and go on to lead happy and productive adult lives. Some do startlingly well. We need to balance our fears for our teenagers with hope for a great outcome.

And most importantly, we have to remember that our children are separate people and how well they get through adolescence is not a reflection of our worth, either as a parent or as a person. If our child is struggling or failing it does not make us a bad parent or a failure ourselves.

Other than doing the best we can and accepting that we will often fail because we are human, we have to look after our own wellbeing as well as our child's. We can only do so much and have as much input into our teenagers' lives as they will let us have.

THE NO-SHAME SAFETY NET

Our teenager is likely to do some pretty stupid stuff. When we were teens we probably did too. I certainly did lots of things that I look back at now with a lot of embarrassment. Even if we were saintly teens, we probably had siblings or friends who were doing some crazy or irresponsible things.

Shame is a barrier to self-accountability and self-responsibility, which are essential things for our child to transition successfully into adulthood. For this reason, we need to find ways to deal with the stupid stuff that do not make our child feel ashamed.

In the last chapter it was suggested that instead of shaming a child for stupid behaviour, it can be more helpful to consider it to be a mistake that can be learned from. Many of our children's great successes as adults will be a direct result of learning from mistakes they made as teenagers and young adults.

This is obviously only the case if our children actually learn from their mistakes. As with everything else, they will not learn from them, or learn anything at all, if they are in protection mode, as neuroscience teaches us that the brain is largely shut down to learning at these times.

We also know that shame can prevent our child from learning from their mistakes. Shame produces such an overwhelming feeling of worthlessness that the only way to cope with it for many is to shut down from what happened, pretend it didn't happen or to blame someone or something else for it. We cannot learn when we shut down from the mistake.

So as parents of teenagers, we need to do what we can to get them out of protection mode and to keep the heat on their pressure cookers as low as possible. We can only have so much success with this because as they get older, there will be more and more influences that become out of our control. We can only do what we can. Even a small reduction in the heat of their pressure cooker can make the difference between learning from a mistake and not learning.

The no-shame safety net means that our child knows fully that they can call on us day or night if they need help of any type.

For our child to use this safety net, they will need to know that they can trust us not to judge them or shame them for the particular mess they are in at that moment. They will know they will be listened to with compassion and be offered any help that is needed, without being lectured at or judged.

They may test us on this by calling on us with minor problems to see how we react. How well we perform in response to these calls is likely to influence whether or not they call on us in a bigger or genuine emergency.

Caroline did a great job of this when her 14-year-old daughter with Asperger's took MDMA tablets at a party, a stimulant and hallucinogenic drug also known as Ecstasy. Caroline hadn't known about the party and thought that her daughter was playing video games with a friend. Bella called her mum to collect her:

> We'd had all the drug talks with Bella and she'd promised not to do it. But I also remember how desperately I had wanted to fit in with the crowd when I was her age and Bella already felt left out. I took her home and stayed with her all night to keep her safe. I resisted every urge to criticise, tell her the awful things that could have happened to her or to tell her off. I just kept telling her how loved she was and how proud I was with her for having the courage to call me. She told me that the drug made her feel great at first, invincible, but then she got super paranoid and that was when she had called.

Knowing that our child trusts us and will call if they need help is a huge relief. They may or may not have the 'what I learned from the mistake' conversation with us. If they do not want to talk to us about their experience directly, they may still be making the learning connections themselves or by talking to their friends.

Depending on the relationship with our child, sometimes it helps to tell them about what we learned from similar mistakes when we were their age. Our openness and humility may help our child to feel safe to be open with us. Openness builds trust on both sides, and trust can help both us and our children through these difficult years.

The no-shame safety net does not mean that there will be no consequences from breaking a rule we have imposed. Our child may feel safer knowing that there will be a consequence, as long as that consequence is not imposed with shame, humiliation or judgement.

TREATMENT REFUSAL

One of the biggest challenges for parents of teens and young adults is getting them to take responsibility for their hidden disability treatments. When they are children we are able to make sure that they take their medication, maybe giving them a reward every time they do so. If they haven't taken it for any reason, maybe because they refused or were sick, we are likely to know about it.

Then comes the age when they take the medication or supplements into their rooms along with a frantically written-out dosage schedule that we hope they will follow.

At this time our loved one is probably questioning everything. They may be questioning their diagnosis and whether they really need the treatments. With so much else on their mind, taking medication or supplements may seem like a low priority. They may resent our nagging on the matter. They may not be able to drink alcohol while on their medication and want to drink it, so stop the medication. Whatever is or is not happening with the medication in that room, we are unlikely to know the full truth of it.

A similar thing happens with appointments, be they with doctors, psychiatrists, psychologists, a communication therapist or anyone else our child may have previously benefited from. After a certain age, we need to trust them to attend these appointments and have little or no control over whether or not they do so. Privacy laws may even prevent us from speaking to the doctors or practitioners themselves if our child is no longer a minor.

Our child may prefer to self-medicate with alcohol, drugs, cake, sex or porn in order to dampen down their depressions, anxieties and other emotional pains. Unlike medical treatments, doing these things may even make them feel more 'normal', especially if their friends are sharing these experiences together. This is especially the case with alcohol or drugs. For a socially excluded kid with a hidden disability, this option can be intoxicating.

Others find that all the pressures of adolescence overheat their pressure cookers to the point that it is all far too much to deal with. Some may have outgrown meltdowns when their pressure cooker explodes and instead go into shutdowns, retreating into their rooms, not able or wanting to do anything. These teens may drop out of education and show little interest in engaging in life, other than perhaps the safety of a special interest or perhaps gaming, books or music.

If we are having trouble knowing where the boundary is between normal teenage behaviour, mental health problems and our child's hidden disability, we can be pretty sure that our children don't find this any easier than we do.

What can we do? We can try explaining why they need to comply with their treatment. They may or may not agree. Should we beg them to continue?

We can tell them that it is their life and that we respect their choices, but if they stop their treatment they will have to accept the consequences. It may be a relapse in their condition, possibly resulting in having to drop out of school or work. It may result in hospitalisation or institutional care. Stopping treatment may even involve dealing with the criminal justice system and in some cases prison.

At these times I believe the no-shame safety net is especially important. This involves being there, giving them time, listening with compassion, not judging, not lecturing, letting them learn from the mistake while keeping the door wide open to resume treatment right away, in whatever way they choose.

Many teens look back at when they were children and believe that they are now a completely different person. They may be disgusted with themselves as children and not like the way they used to look, their previous lack of 'coolness' or previous immaturity.

I can relate to this. For years I didn't want to look at photos of myself as a geeky, awkward pre-teen for this reason, not wanting to believe that the girl in the photos had anything to do with the me that I see in the mirror now.

Wanting to disassociate ourselves from a difficult or awkward childhood may be part of the reason why our teens may reject the treatments we arranged for them when they were younger. Just as they may have outgrown being children, they may feel that they have also outgrown the treatments. Anything associated with their childhood may just not feel relevant to them any more.

In this situation, allowing our teen to arrange a new treatment system of their choice can help. Maybe they do not want to take drug-based medication any more but they may be prepared to try nutritional supplements? Maybe it is the other way around and they are sick of taking all the supplements and prefer to take one pill prescribed by a doctor? Maybe they want to replace cognitive behavioural therapy (CBT) with a different form of counselling?

We may not agree with the treatment they choose. They may not have weighed up the risks and benefits as we did. We may know that their chosen treatments might not work.

What matters the most here is our teen's willingness to engage in thinking about and planning treatment, any treatment, regardless of how effective it is. Any engagement in their treatment, whether it is effective or not, is a sign of self-responsibility and self-accountability. The outlook if this is the case is excellent.

The alternative as far as I can see is no treatment at all, which as we know often means replacing treatment with alcohol, drugs and other addictions.

If our teen is very deep in protection mode, especially depression, or their hidden disability symptoms are too severe, they may not be able to engage in any treatment until their thinking brain is sufficiently online. If this is the case, the best we can probably do as a parent is to do what we can to help them out of protection mode.

There may be some cases where our child may be a danger to herself or others without treatment. In these cases emergency and involuntary treatment may be needed, at least for the short term, until they are able to make some decisions themselves. In some countries there are crisis psychiatric teams which are able to assist, and some of our loved ones may at times need hospital care.

SPEAKING UP FOR OUR ADULT CHILD

Part of the task of helping to lower the temperature in our teen's pressure cooker is to take on tasks that they may be able to do if they have the emotional resources but are unable to do if they are overwhelmed or stuck in protection mode.

As they grow up and transition to adulthood there will be more and more administration to do in life. As soon as they hit 18 it may be assumed that they can and 'should' do it all, with little concession to their inexperience, lack of maturity or the challenges of their hidden disabilities.

We are likely to have been fighting and advocating for our child's rights throughout their childhood, often to breaking point and desperation ourselves. We may have filled in hundreds of complicated forms, dealt with banks, insurance companies, benefits departments, lawyers, doctors and therapists, prepared appeals and argued and negotiated with educational and government institutions. We know how difficult it is, even for us as experienced and mature parents.

It may be clear to us that our child will simply not be able to take all this on, especially overnight, just because they are deemed by others to be able to on the basis of their chronological age.

If our child is struggling to stay in school and keep up, he may be very happy for us to continue to deal with these exhausting and time-consuming tasks. We would probably want to do so, preferring him to use what energy and emotional resources he has on studying and dealing with the ever more complex social demands of being a teenager.

If they go to university, the paperwork becomes immense and includes dealing with university administration, course tutors and housing providers, all with a long list of difficult requirements, deadlines, payment dates and tasks that challenge even the best-prepared teenager without a hidden disability.

One of my children was inundated with about 30 official emails a day when they started university. This was on top of starting a demanding course of study, figuring out how the faculty worked and adapting to life away from home, with new people, for the first time.

Something had to give if my child was to manage, and it was clear that this was the admin, which I could take on to free up my child's energy and resources to allow them to deal with the many other challenges.

I was aware that as soon as their pressure cooker was cool enough, my child would be able to take on some or all of this admin themself, and this has proved to be the case.

Children who are lucky enough to receive medical, psychological or educational help with their hidden disabilities often find that this support abruptly ends when they turn 18. They are likely to need our help to try to access adult services and may need us to fight hard for them to get them. Many organisations, however, have rules to prevent parents or carers from advocating for their children or completing their admin, even if our teens have given permission for us to do so.

I came up against this brick wall many times when my children were older teenagers. On each occasion, the organisations insisted that they knew best and that my children must fight for services and complete their administration themselves without help. I was even turned away during medical emergencies, when my child was begging them to speak to me. Rules often do not take into account our children's hidden disability needs or the need for common sense.

To ease this process, some sort of advocacy agreement may be needed with our child to clear the way for us to intervene when our child requests it or needs it. Some organisations accept a letter signed by our child requesting that they deal with us for administrative matters, and some may be prepared to take our child's verbal agreement to this. Others may accept a letter from a doctor or therapist that states that our child requires an advocate to help her with his or her affairs.

As the needs of students with hidden disabilities are often little understood by organisations, even disability departments, I strongly suggest taking any necessary steps to ensure that we can intervene in any matter that is requested or required by our child. This will give both of us peace of mind and help to keep our child safe.

In the UK at least, the most effective way seems to be to have power of attorney, which legally should be accepted by all organisations, regardless of any privacy or other policies they might have. If I had known this prior to my children starting college, we would have avoided a lot of problems and unnecessary stresses.

Having an advocacy agreement in place does not mean taking power away from our child. We can agree to use the power of attorney *only* in specific situations, which our child can define and control. As long as we both trust each other, having power of attorney actually gives our child *more power* as they will now be able to delegate all the tasks that stress them out unduly and therefore be able to control their own time and tasks more effectively.

RELATIONSHIPS AND DATING

The prospect of dealing with romantic and intimate relationships is an exciting and at the same time terrifying one for young people. It is a source of huge insecurity and anxiety for most people, especially when they compare themselves with others who may appear to sail through this with great success. There is nothing to beat a dating experience to bring up fears about ourselves. Am I enough? Am I too much? Am I weird? Am I boring? Am I too fat? Am I too thin? Are my clothes trendy enough?

And of course, there are additional challenges for our teens with hidden disabilities. The whole drama of flirting and dating involves a huge amount of nuanced verbal and non-verbal communication. Everyone struggles with it to some extent, even the most adept and savvy daters. How do we know if someone is interested in us? What does a particular 'look' mean? How do I show them I like them without embarrassing myself? What on earth do I say to someone I am interested in? Will I survive the humiliation of rejection? The list goes on.

Many people with hidden disabilities struggle with nuanced communication, where it is not completely clear what is being said and what is being intended by the person saying or doing something. This is particularly true for people on the autism spectrum. Many of our teens also have sensory issues and are very sensitive to touch and smell, again creating potential barriers to intimacy.

We can add to this how overwhelming the intense emotions involved in romantic relationships can be. Love and heartbreak challenge to the core even the most resilient of neurotypical teens – we just need to listen to any song lyrics to know this. Our children with hidden disabilities are often hypersensitive to emotions, as well as often confused by them. We know that feeling overwhelmed will often send our loved ones straight into shutdown and protection mode.

If we or our children have a hidden disability it can be particularly difficult to know how to behave appropriately in romantic and sexual situations. Our loved one may have similar difficulties in other social situations as well but getting it wrong on the relationship front is particularly unforgiving. If our daughter gets a social cue wrong at a job interview she may not get the job. If our son gets it wrong during a sexual or romantic advance, he faces humiliation and if he gets it *really* wrong, he may break the law and the police can become involved.

The problems are not only for the person making the advances, but for the person receiving the advances too. They may think someone is being very friendly when in fact they are being predatory. They may therefore be far more vulnerable to sexual and relationship abuse due to their inability to read the warning signs.

As we know, some teens with hidden disabilities have obsessive interests and can be hyper-focused on these pursuits. When they were children, these interests may be gaming, bird watching or science fiction. At puberty, the obsession can be directed onto a romantic interest, sometimes resulting in not wanting to let go if a relationship does not work out, or in extreme cases it can result in stalking.

For some with hidden disabilities, all of this is far too confusing and overwhelming, and many prefer not to have romantic or intimate relationships at all, at least until they are older, have more life experience and have less going on in their lives. Removing this pressure can be a relief and give them more energy and resources for other areas of their life! Instead of the angst about relationships, they can enjoy their interests, be it training their dogs, setting up a company, creating new algorithms or writing science fiction stories. For many, this is not a bad trade-off.

Others do choose to dive into the dating and romantic snake pit and manage to find compassionate and caring partners. They may then do really well with the love and extra support that these partners bring. Many people with hidden disabilities marry and have happy and healthy relationships.

People with hidden disabilities tend to be quirky, interesting, smart, trustworthy, honest and straight talking. These are very attractive traits indeed to the right partner, especially if they share the same passions and interests!

If an intimate relationship is what they want, how can we support our children and help them to stay safe and get it right?

Firstly, we cannot assume that our teens will know how to behave in relationships just by 'picking things up' as they go along, as may be the case for some neurotypical teens. Our children will likely need to be taught all the social and communication skills they will need for dating, relationships and intimacy step by step in a methodical way. They may need to engage their learning brain for this rather than rely on instinct or intuition, at least at the beginning.

Ideally our teen can be taught relationship skills by a professional such as a speech and communication or cognitive behavioural (CBT) therapist. However, I would not just assume and hope that our child's therapist will be dealing with dating and sexuality. This is far too important to leave to chance and I suggest asking them directly if they would be prepared to take this on. There are a lot of taboos about this area and some therapists may not feel comfortable about dealing with it.

If we do not have such a professional in our child's life, we will need to do relationship training ourselves. This will involve overcoming any embarrassment and awkwardness we or our teen feels about the subject.

We are parents and have personal experience of this that we can share with our child. No matter how upright or perhaps uptight we may be, we all have some experience in these areas.

I enjoyed sharing funny dating stories with my children, which were mainly about miscommunications and misunderstanding. It was also lovely to share heartwarming stories about when things go well and the happiness it can bring. The experiences we share need not be about us personally, although in my opinion it helps if they are. They could be about 'friends' or people we know. If the stories are funny or absurd, they may be more likely to grab our child's attention and bring us closer and increase their trust in us.

Our child may not want to listen to us and find it awkward and inappropriate, but I would suggest saying it all anyway in the hope that something sinks in. A friend's son would physically put his hands over his ears when his dad started talking about sex and relationships and tell him to shut up. But his father continued anyway and a number of years later the boy jokingly repeated everything back to his parents. He had taken it all in and applied it in his life too.

I found that TV soaps were a great help in this area too, especially if they were amusing. When one of my children was a young teen, we watched every episode of *Desperate Housewives* together. Doing this was really fun and we laughed our heads off as a lot of it was both entertaining and ridiculous. Just about every possible dating, intimate or relationship scenario occurred in one episode or other. We could talk about each mishap or misunderstanding, how the characters dealt with it and what we could have done in that situation. We talked about the motives of the people involved, who we would and would not trust, and tried to read between the lines. This allowed us to talk about everything we needed to talk about in a natural and non-threatening situation, as we were talking about fictional characters in a way that was funny and fun.

I learned as much as my child from that experience, especially from my child's ideas and insights. I was also single at the time and thoroughly enjoyed sharing this learning experience. I believe it brought us together and increased the trust and openness between us.

GETTING AND HOLDING ON TO A JOB

If we are to believe the very limited research statistics on hidden disabilities and employment, it is very depressing indeed. According to data from the Office for National Statistics in 2021, only 22 per cent of people on the autism spectrum are in any type of employment.[1] These figures are not much better for bipolar disorder with an employment rate of 40–60 per cent, with absenteeism being a particular problem for those in work. Things look a little more promising for ADHD with an employment rate of around 70 per cent. However, according to a study by the World Health Organization (WHO), adults with ADHD are 18 times more likely to be disciplined at work for 'behavioural problems' and 60 per cent more likely to lose their jobs.[2]

I would not be too disillusioned by this, especially if our child is on the autism spectrum. The quoted research had relatively small sample sizes and it is not clear where the people involved were on the autism spectrum. Many in the sample may have had low- rather than high-functioning autism as this was not stated. We obviously cannot compare someone who has non-verbal classic autism with someone with high- functioning Asperger's and a PhD in quantum physics.

With the other hidden disabilities, we do not know how many of the sample were receiving treatments that were helping them, how many actually had diagnoses or how many had multiple disabilities.

Rather than dwell on statistics, I would instead look at our individual teens, and help them to focus on their potential and what kind of career could work well with their interests and gifts as well as their challenges and needs.

Although not hugely helpful for us as parents, the statistics are useful as a campaigning tool to help overcome discrimination against people with hidden disabilities in the workplace and the obstacles they face in getting a job. Just like in every other area of life, including schools, many workplaces show a considerable lack of understanding of our children's needs and experiences. Government initiatives may help with this, along with companies such as Microsoft that specifically devise recruitment and work programmes for employees on the autism spectrum.

While we await a day of equality in this area, we still need to support our teens as best we can and give them hope that they can be productive, fulfilled and financially independent.

Apart from disability discrimination, many of our loved ones struggle at work with the complex social situations and multiple demands being made of them at the same time. Some find that their hidden disabilities make it impossible for them to be consistent at work as they may have good days and bad days. Others may become very resentful if they are asked to change tack when they are in a passionate flow with a task. Others become rebellious if they are bored or given a task that does not stimulate them enough. Rather than fight these needs and try to change our loved ones to fit in to the workplace, I believe it may be more productive to embrace and work with them, finding opportunities that are a good fit with how our child is best able to work.

Some of our children may be able to access occupational therapy assessments which allow workplaces to make reasonable adjustments to cater for their disability needs. This may include working from home sometimes, quieter work environments or a reduced working day.

Most of the adults I know with hidden disabilities are working and doing well. Saying that, this work is often not in traditional employment and many need or choose to work part time. What they have in common is that they find careers that work for them and the lifestyles they need.

Some of our loved ones will do great with regular, structured employment where it is clear what is expected and when. They will be happy and fulfilled knowing that they will clock in at the beginning of the day, do what is expected and then clock out, without too many surprises.

Although they may be over-skilled for the work, predictability may be what they need to keep the heat on their pressure cookers low. This can free up emotional resources and energy to spend on their interests and passions in their free time. I know a great many people who have chosen this path as being what works best for their welfare.

Others will not thrive in regular structured employment. Some hidden disabilities, such as bipolar disorder, result in 'good' days when our child can be productive and 'bad' days when they need to rest. For some this can be too unpredictable and hard for an employer to accommodate.

If this is the case for our child, traditional full-time work may well not suit them, as their productivity will by necessity be 'stop and start'. Some people who are wired this way can produce as much part time with rests in between as others produce when they work full time.

This is the case for me. I can produce what would be a number of days' work in only one good productive day, but then need a few days to recover. I have tried but have been unable to work at a steady pace full time. I get too exhausted by it. Working in short intensive bursts seems to be best for me. Recognising this, I have chosen to work for myself so that I can control my work flow, take breaks when I need them and organise my work so that it does not overwhelm or exhaust me.

If this is the case for your child, they may do best in freelance work or in running their own business, especially if it is connected with a strong interest they may have. Many successful entrepreneurs have hidden disabilities. Freelance work may also have the advantage of allowing our loved one to work from home and avoid much of the face-to-face interaction that can cause extra stress and exhaustion. To prevent too much isolation in these situations, I know of a number of people who share office space together and support each other, although they all have their own independent businesses.

Other young people with hidden disabilities thrive in a job that gives lots of stimulation, surprises and excitement. I am of course thinking of those on the ADHD spectrum. If their disability needs are not met, similar behaviour problems to school can reoccur in the workplace. Knowing this, our child will need to find a career that they are passionate about and that has real meaning for them. To keep their work stimulating, they may be happier being the boss or running their own show. Others enjoy the edginess and danger of being in the military or a crisis paramedic. Understanding their stimulation needs can help our children to make career choices that work for them.

ADD expert Lara Honos-Webb gives a lovely example of this with firefighters:

> How could a person take such incredible risks, deal with so many unknowns, be able to make decisions without reams of data, and yet get a kick out of standing on the roof of a burning house in an icy rainstorm unless he was impulsive, creative, and ready to take risks, and had lots of physical and mental energy to spare?[3]

So, in this example, the same impulsivity and energy that may have got our ADHD kids into trouble at school can be perfect and valued qualities in the right job. For our frontline workers, the ability to think and act fast is critical, and Honos-Webb reminds us that we all have the gifts of ADHD and ADD to thank for our very safety and protection.

While some of our loved ones do better in work with limited social interaction, others thrive on social interaction that they can *control* and enjoy performing as part of their job. We may be surprised how many gifted public speakers, actors, teachers and other performers have hidden disabilities. Many comedians have hidden disabilities, some openly so. Sometimes 'performing' can be easier than dealing with day-to-day communication, as they can 'hide' behind the mask of the personality they create.

Some of our children with hidden disabilities will not be able to do any paid work at all. This can be fine too, and as long as they amend their expectations they can be very happy and fulfilled doing voluntary work at a pace that works for them or spending their life following their interests and passions.

Although workplace discrimination is still a very big issue, changes in working practices due to new technologies can bring many new opportunities for our loved ones. More and more workplaces are now happy for employees to work from home at least some of the time, and internet working from any location is becoming more and more commonplace. So as society as a whole becomes more flexible about how people are expected to work, the knock-on effect for our children can be positive.

Chapter 11
PARENTING SIBLINGS

No matter how mindful and careful a parent we are, there may be times when our home is like a combat zone. This is no-one's fault. The symptoms of our child with a hidden disability may be out of control. We may be dealing with hostility from family members or organisations that are supposed to support us. We may be fighting many battles at the same time.

When our home is a combat zone, everyone in it can feel insecure and under threat. This can affect all of our children, not least those without the hidden disability. Many parents feel guilty when we see our other children suffering as a result of living in a combat zone. We can be frustrated that we cannot fix this situation to provide the calm and loving environment that all of our children need to grow and thrive.

The brothers and sisters of children with hidden disabilities have a lot of challenges of their own that are rarely recognised. It is not uncommon for the sibling to be sent out of the house for their own safety during rages and meltdowns. They may witness aggression and even violence that we would never dream of wanting them to see. They may be hit or punched when their sibling is unstable or have their possessions or work destroyed. They may be living with a parent who is seriously sick with stress, anxiety and depression, making them unable to get all the attention and reassurance they need from us. They may be unable to go to parties or take part in activities as a result of their sibling's needs. Dinner choices may be affected by their sibling's food preferences. They may not be able to invite friends home in case it unsettles their sibling with a hidden disability. Family outings may be restricted to what the sibling can cope with. The sibling with the hidden disability may need to receive nearly all the attention of the parents, leaving the non-disabled one feeling overlooked and resentful.

And what can make this feel even more unfair is that there may be different expectations of behaviour for the sibling. So, while the child with the hidden disability may need to be excused from homework or household chores, our other children may be expected do these things. They may be disciplined for things that their sibling with a hidden disability may not be disciplined for. If the parents are under a lot of strain, the sibling may be called upon as an extra carer. They may be offering practical and emotional support to both the child with a hidden disability and to the parents.

The siblings may experience challenges and needs that are unimaginable to their friends who may be able to get on with the job of being a child.

And to make things even more complicated, one or more of the siblings may have a hidden disability of their own, creating different and possibly clashing parenting needs.

HOW CAN WE BE FAIR?

Whatever parenting style works for us, we face a dilemma if we have more than one child. How do we make things fair for the brothers and sisters of our child with a hidden disability? Is it possible to make things fair? Are the siblings being damaged, and what can we do about it?

We may have one child with ASD who needs quiet time. Another with ADHD who needs action and stimulation. One may need firm boundaries and respond well to discipline. Another may react terribly to these things and need a different approach. If we are managing this single-handedly, which most of us are doing at least during the day, we can end up feeling torn in every direction. It can look like we are not addressing anyone's needs properly, least of all our own.

This can leave us feeling guilty and like a terrible parent. How do we juggle this?

In my experience it is by being clear that we parent *by need* rather than by inflexible rules. Just as our child with a hidden disability will need to be treated differently depending on how hot their pressure cooker is, each sibling will have their own set of needs at different times.

When our son tells us that we are being unfair, we can remind him that we have different expectations depending on what each child is able to do. If we are asking one sibling to do chores and the other not, we can explain that this is because we trust that he is able to do it and that their sibling is currently unable to or doesn't yet have the skills to do it.

Parenting by need makes it *fair* to treat our children differently.

There will be times when the sibling will be really fed up and resentful of the situation. This is normal and understandable. They may also feel guilty about feeling these things.

According to Shennah, whose brother has OCD (obsessive compulsive disorder):

> The situation at home makes me feel so angry inside. And then I feel bad because I know it's not my brother's fault. But still it feels so unfair. I know it's bad to think this so I don't say anything and just keep away from it all.

We also need to bear in mind that most siblings struggle with feeling compared with each other, even if we do all we can to treat them as individuals. When we add a hidden disability or two to the mix, it can become more complicated.

Carole had to deal with this with twins:

> My Aspie is a twin. It was very frustrating for him to be compared to his 'normal' sister. He'd grab her school report and run away crying. This is why I changed him to another school, which had a different curriculum so that he wouldn't compare himself or have others compare him to his sister.

So, how do we help the brothers and sisters of our children with hidden disabilities? Firstly, the good news. Without downplaying how difficult it is for them, science seems to show that siblings of children with additional needs can become more rounded, more resilient and multi-dimensional than other children. They can be beacons of light for compassion, acceptance and unconditional love.[1]

The key word here is *can*. We cannot assume that this will happen automatically. The research suggests that the most important thing for them is facing with honesty the mixture of emotions that they are likely to be feeling. For many of the siblings, this could be a cocktail of love, fear, jealousy, protectiveness and resentment.

SUPPORTING OUR OTHER CHILDREN

Here are some ideas on how we can help the siblings to thrive. They are likely to sound familiar as we use similar techniques to help our child with a hidden disability out of protection mode:

- 'listening to the music not the words' with our child
- educating them about their sibling's hidden disability
- reassuring them of our unconditional love
- spending special alone time with them
- listening to them fully by 'holding space' for them
- teaching them to 'invite their feelings to tea'
- teach them self-acceptance
- encouraging contact with siblings in a similar situation.

As with our child with a hidden disability, our starting point is to learn to *decode* the sibling's clues from their behaviour. It is likely that the sibling will not be able to tell us what they are feeling or experiencing. If we ask them, 'What's the matter?' they may be too overwhelmed or confused to know the answer. They may not have the vocabulary or experience to find the words to let us know. They may be too ashamed to tell us if they are feeling resentful and not want to be an extra burden on us.

As they might not have the words, they may need to communicate with us with their behaviour. They may go into protection mode to protect themselves from the threat of uncertainty and fear in the home.

This is why we need to 'listen to the music not the words' when we watch the sibling's behaviour. We need to become expert code breakers and try our best to figure out what their behaviour is actually telling us.

We can watch out for any of the protection mode behaviours discussed in Chapters 4 and 5. One that comes up quite commonly is for siblings to withdraw into a type of shutdown state. They may absent themselves physically or emotionally from the family by spending all their time in their room or only want to be with their friends. They may shut down from sharing with us and avoid contact with their sibling.

Due to the intensity of the emotion in the home, they may shut down to *all feelings* as they may not yet have the tools to know how to deal with intense emotions.

Benjamin, whose sister has multiple hidden disabilities experienced this:

> So many people have said to me that I don't seem to have any emotions, or at least to show them. I think that things were so extreme at home that I just shut down feeling anything. That made me feel safer as I could put it all out of my mind. Maybe it became a habit. Talking about this now that I'm older really helps, but I don't think I would have been able to talk about it then, it was too raw.

Some siblings feel that they can never be naughty or assert themselves, as they can see that their parents are at the limit of coping and do not want to push them over the edge with their own needs. These kids can be 'too good to be true' and are often wonderfully caring advocates for their sibling with a hidden disability. 'Too good to be true' is often accurate. By putting their sibling's needs before their own they are often not truly being themselves and may not be honouring their own emotions, needs and contradictions. It is the not being 'true to themselves' that makes them 'too good to be true'.

Second on the list is to help the sibling understand as much as possible about their brother or sister's hidden disability. This is not just about data about the condition but also helping them to feel empathy for their sibling's feelings and experiences, helping them to understand *why* their sibling is acting and reacting the way they do.

It helps for them to understand that their sibling is struggling with challenges that they, luckily, do not have and that there are things that we simply do not yet understand. This gives them a context to understand why their sibling sometimes will not play with them or may be aggressive, why they often cannot have friends over. When they are able to understand, they may take things less personally and this may help them develop compassion for their sibling and make it easier for them to love him or her.

To educate our child about their sibling's hidden disability, there are books, TV shows and resources designed for siblings of different ages.

It is helpful to keep reminding them that the sibling has *not chosen* to have this condition and that it is no-one's fault. Although what they are seeing may look like bad behaviour that they are getting away with, we can explain that the behaviour is often a reaction to their hidden disabilities.

Depending on their age, we can also explain to the sibling about what happens when a pressure cooker explodes and why we need to keep the heat down for the child with the hidden disability. Reminding our child that they too have a pressure cooker can help, pointing out that the sibling has a lot more heat under it due to his or her additional challenges.

We can reassure our child over and over that although we cannot spend as much time with them as we do with their sibling, we love them just as much and are proud of how well they are dealing with the challenging situation. We can remind them often about how well they are doing, such as the times when they are patient, forgiving and kind.

We can do whatever we can to have time alone with the siblings of our child with a hidden disability. This can be quiet time before bed or day trips away, just with them, totally dedicated to their needs and preferences and celebrating the bond and love between us. They may get to spend less time with us than their sibling, but we can do our best to make sure that this time is really fun or really special.

We can reassure the sibling that it is perfectly normal to feel all sorts of emotions in challenging situations. It is fine sometimes to feel angry, upset and jealous, especially if something appears unfair or is upsetting. It doesn't mean they don't love their sibling, it is just a normal part of being human.

When our child is upset or needs to be heard, we can practise 'holding space' for them in exactly the same way as we would for our child with a hidden disability. How to do this is described in Chapter 8. One of the most caring and supportive things we can do for the sibling is to give our full attention and listen to them without judgement.

Just as with our child with a hidden disability, we can teach the sibling to 'invite their feelings to tea' and let themselves fully feel whatever they are feeling until the emotions change or fade away. We can teach them this in exactly the same way that we teach this to our child with the hidden disability. How to do this is explained in Chapter 8. Our child can learn to accept that she is angry, that he is scared, that she is confused. Facing emotions without feeling ashamed of them will help our child feel lighter and freer. This can help to improve the relationship between the siblings, as resentments will no longer be being held in and left to fester.

Probably most importantly we can teach the sibling *self-acceptance* to give them resilience in the face of all the challenges they will face, including those that come from being the sibling of a child with a hidden disability. The attitudes to life described in Chapter 9 are equally relevant for all of our children, regardless of whether or not they have a hidden disability.

Knowing that we are not alone is very supportive, so it may be good to encourage our child to spend time with other siblings of children with hidden disabilities. Knowing that many experiences will be shared also helps our child feel less different and makes the experience feel more normal. Contacts could be made through support groups. There are also activity clubs in some areas for whole families of children with hidden disabilities to get together to have fun.

This can be an opportunity for siblings to meet each other. For older children or teens, there are also support forums online specifically for the siblings of children with hidden disabilities.

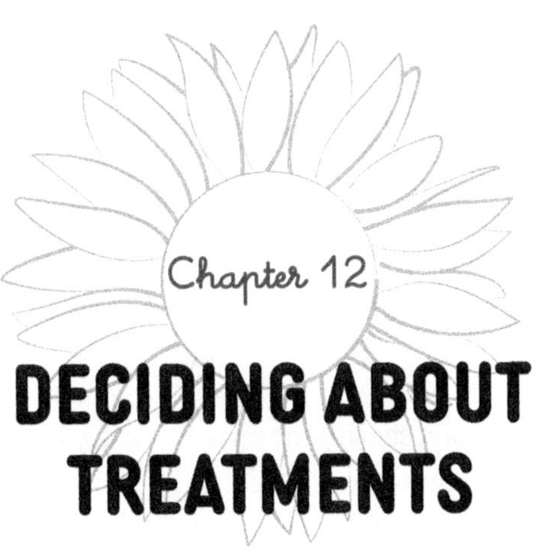

Chapter 12
DECIDING ABOUT TREATMENTS

Protection mode is only part of the story for children with hidden disabilities. It is a large part but even when we have done everything we can to get them out of protection mode, some are still left with debilitating symptoms from their hidden disability. Getting our child out of protection mode will help them grow and thrive, but they will still have ASD, ADHD, OCD, bipolar disorder or clinical anxiety.

Many of our children's difficulties are biological and genetic. Getting them out of protection mode can make it clearer to see what problems remain that may need additional help or treatment. This is because getting them out of protection mode removes the 'fog' around our child. When the 'fog' is removed, we can see what is left and what problems persist.

For some of our children, helping them get and stay out of protection mode will be the *only* treatment they will need. Free from protection mode, with reasonable adjustments in place at school and with an understanding of their strengths, challenges and needs, they can simply accept themselves as a little quirky and get on with their lives.

This is not the case for all of our loved ones. Some will still suffer from psychosis, delusions, clinical depression, phobias, mania or crippling anxiety or from obsessions and rituals that prevent them from participating in a productive life. Others may still be suffering crippling fatigue, muscle pain or disabling digestive problems.

Although getting and staying out of protection mode is likely to improve all of these symptoms, many of our children still benefit from additional treatment. Finding the right treatment can free our children from suffering and control their symptoms enough to give them a chance of a fulfilling life.

> In this section, I am sharing my understanding of the risks and benefits of different types of treatment, to help parents with the informed choices we all need to make. This is not intended to replace the services of trained medical professionals or be a substitute for medical advice. You should always consult a doctor on any matters relating to your child's health, in particular any matter that may require diagnosis, medical attention or prescription.

Treatment can also work *alongside* getting our child out of protection mode. For example, if they are deep in depression, antidepressant medication may lift them enough to enable other strategies to help them out of protection mode to work.

Sometimes treatments need only be short term, until strategic, attitude and lifestyle changes remove the need for them. Others may need to be longer term, possibly lifelong, depending on our child's needs and circumstances.

For many people, the word 'treatment' simply means drugs, medication that is prescribed by a doctor. For some this may be the right way to go for their child. Others use treatments that do not involve medication. Non-drug treatments include dietary supplements, cognitive behavioural therapies, gut healing, and energy and other types of healing.

Rejecting medical drugs for whatever reason does not mean that we have to reject treatment. What we need to do is to weigh up the pros and cons of all the options available to us and expect a fair bit of trial and error.

Some will need treatment throughout their lives in order to live fully and others may only need it for certain periods, depending on the many factors that affect their conditions.

Denys Reid Margolin talks about the benefits of treatment for her son who has childhood bipolar disorder. She is referring to nutritional therapy, but the point she makes is valid for other treatments, including medical drugs:

> Ben's symptoms weren't willful – they weren't a sign of weak character, immaturity, or unwillingness to change. They were due to severe biochemical imbalances causing body processes to function improperly. While he was sick, he wasn't capable of searching for solutions or self-motivating to navigate through challenges and setbacks. He didn't need to reach a low point to finally 'get it' and get himself well. He needed nutrient therapy and advocates to assist along the way. I wish I'd known this 25 years ago, but I am grateful to have Ben back.[1]

Hidden disabilities do not have a cure. If they did, they would be illnesses rather than disabilities. Like any any other chronic ongoing health condition, what we are generally looking for with treatment is a way to control symptoms and pain (including emotional pain), to enable the person to live as normal a life as possible, free from unnecessary suffering.

Some parents and people with hidden disabilities fear or wish to avoid treatment. We may think that treatment can only mean one thing, medication. We may worry that any form of treatment could change our child's personality and mean that we don't accept them fully for who they are.

We may fear that treatment will make our child worse or cause extra suffering from side effects. We may dread other people's judgements about choosing treatment for our child. I have even heard quite a few parents want to avoid treatment as they believe it shows that they have *failed* in their parenting skills, that if they were more effective parents, treatment would not be necessary.

Added to this are people who are strongly *against all treatments* for hidden disabilities regardless of how much our child is suffering. This point of view may come from people whose children do not need any additional treatment after protection mode is dealt with and reasonable adjustments are in place. As their children are lucky enough not to need extra treatment, they may be judgemental about those who do. I have also heard this view from adults with hidden disabilities who do not choose or need extra treatment. Others may insist that our child does not need treatment due to their ignorance of their needs, perhaps because they judge our parenting or for any number of reasons.

Some people compare our children's challenges and needs to those of minority groups who are subject to discrimination. They may argue that just as gay people or people from ethnic minorities do not need treatment, neither do children with hidden disabilities.

While we need to tackle all discrimination and ignorance, this does not take away the need for children suffering debilitating symptoms from their hidden disability to have access to treatment.

While we campaign against discrimination against people with physical disabilities that we can see, we would not deny people wheelchairs, painkillers or other medical help. Why should this be any different if our child's disability is hidden?

There is a big difference between a treatment and a cure. A treatment recognises our child for who she is and aims to improve her life and reduce her suffering. A 'cure' suggests that the hidden disability can be removed completely, changing our child into a neurotypical child.

For our children, their hidden disability is a part of who they are, often a positive part. For this reason, I would personally be very cautious about anything that claims to be a 'cure', even assuming that such a thing would ever be possible given that our children have disabilities rather than illnesses.

A good treatment will not change who we are or who our children are. It will not change how our child is wired neurologically, and neither should it. How their brain is wired and their hidden disability bring both strengths and challenges. The aim of treatment, in my opinion, is to help our child overcome their biological challenges to enable their natural strengths to shine.

A great treatment can help our children better express who they really are.

Choosing a treatment or whether or not to treat is a really difficult issue. As with any parenting decision, many people have very strong opinions on what treatment choices we *should* be making, and we are likely to be inundated with contradictory advice.

When we are faced with our child's suffering, the responsibility to get the treatment choice right can feel both overwhelming and terrifying. We may hear horror stories about treatments going wrong and others about crazy-sounding 'miracle' treatments or 'cures' and wonder if we should try them. Everyone and their dog will tell us about a friend of a neighbour who tried a particular thing and that we absolutely 'must' try it.

When faced with this pressure, we need to remember that all types of treatment are very individual. Everyone's body chemistry is slightly different, and children can respond in different ways to the same medication, supplements or therapies. Some options just don't make sense when we look at them. Just because a particular treatment choice helped a friend's child with a similar diagnosis, it does not mean that it will be right for our child.

To confuse things further, in these days of internet research, any basic search for hidden disability treatments will bring up a huge number of options, some of which may be bogus attempts to make money from our desperate desire to help our child. The websites that offer these treatments typically include lots of glowing testimonials from people who are apparently completely 'cured' as a result of what is being offered.

Common sense tells us that if a website or practitioner is offering something too good to be true, it probably *is* too good to be true and is in fact *not true*. We should look at the credibility of the website and look for independent reviews in other places, especially organisations and people we already trust.

We have to be prepared to make the best decision we can with the information available to us at that time. This means being prepared to risk getting it wrong. As we already know, getting it wrong is a stepping stone to getting things right if we are prepared to learn from our mistakes.

CHOOSING A TREATMENT

The best advice I received on choosing a treatment was to consider the following questions:

- Does the risk outweigh the benefit?
- Does the benefit outweigh the risk?
- Does it help?

When we look at treatment options, we need to keep in mind that there needs to be a balance between the *risks* to the child of the treatment and how much the treatment may *help* them. This weighing-up of risks and benefits needs to be part of an ongoing assessment of the treatment.

If the benefits are great and our child is responding really well, this will naturally offset some of our fears about the risks. If the risks are assessed to be too high, too dangerous, then we may prefer to sacrifice any benefits in order to avoid the risks altogether. Or if our child is having *some* benefit and also having *some* side effects, we will need to see if the benefits are strong enough to offset the negatives.

Weighing up risks versus benefits sounds really obvious, but when we are stressed and overwhelmed with the decisions we need to make, we may need to have it spelled out to us. Nothing is obvious when we are stressed, and I am still grateful to the person who explained it to me.

The 'risks versus benefits' questions really helped me to find a foothold through the treatment maze. I would visualise old-fashioned kitchen weighing scales to help me see what I was dealing with. Benefits would be on one side of the scales, risk and side effects on the other. I would see which way the scales would tip and have my answer.

To help figure out how a treatment is affecting the weighing scales, we need to keep an eye on how much the treatment is helping, if at all, and if so, in what ways. Some treatments, whether drug or non-drug, simply will not work for our child. Or they may work for a while and then stop working. Or they may work a little but not enough to outweigh the side effects.

In order to assess the risks and benefits we need to look at them separately. With benefits we need to find the answers to questions like, 'Is this working?' and if so, 'How much is this helping?' For risks, we need to think, 'Are these symptoms side effects from the treatment or are they unrelated?', 'Is this making things worse?', 'Is this having any effect at all?', 'Is this treatment causing too much additional stress and overwhelming my child?' These are not easy questions.

ASSESSING THE BENEFITS

When doctors or practitioners ask, 'How are things going?' it can be very difficult to answer, both for us and for our child. Things may seem a bit better or worse, anxiety or depression may seem to have improved or worsened, but have they really? There are so many factors involved in addition to the treatment. How can we know if it is the treatment that has helped the depression or if the improvement is due to something else, like a new friend, a change in the weather or a more understanding teacher?

It is normal to have good days and bad days, and if our child is feeling particularly good on the day of the consultation, they may naturally answer that things are going great, even if for the months before the consultation things were generally worse.

Or the opposite may happen, a treatment seems to be working well, but the child is feeling bad at the consultation due to it being a scary environment or because we had a difficult train journey to get there. She may then tell the doctor or practitioner that everything is terrible.

Even if we are answering on our child's behalf, because they are too young or unable to answer for themselves, without keeping clear records our judgement can easily be as unreliable in that moment as our child's.

This is why using a good treatment and symptom tracker can really help, ideally one that also tracks environmental, diet and lifestyle factors. We can also use it to track any side effects, allowing us clear evidence of how the treatment is performing on the risk–benefit scales. Treatment tracking tools are available online as well as through organisations that support the different hidden disabilities.

ASSESSING THE RISKS

As well as assessing benefits it is equally important to assess risks. Some treatments involve a higher level of risk than others. The doctors or people who argue for a particular treatment may minimise these risks or not mention them at all. We also need to remember that those recommending a particular treatment may have a commercial or other interest in doing so. Their livelihood may depend on people like us choosing what they have to offer. Regardless of whether the treatment is drug or non-drug, it is important to consider possible short-term side effects as well as the risks of longer-term dangers.

Information on this is very difficult to come by and it is very hard to assess the level of risk for our individual child. The information leaflets that accompany drug medications list every possible side effect and risk and help to protect the manufacturer from legal action if things go wrong.

Even the most 'mild' of medications, that most of us would not hesitate to take, contain these information leaflets and if we really took notice of them then we probably wouldn't even take a tablet to relieve a headache.

While possible side effects can be listed, the long-term effects of these medications are often not well known or understood, especially on the developing brains of children, and we know that medications are very rarely tested on children.

The US Food and Drug Administration states:

> Most drugs prescribed for children have not been tested in children. Before the Food and Drug Administration initiated a pediatric program, only about 20 percent of drugs approved by the FDA were labeled for pediatric use. By necessity, doctors have routinely given drugs to children 'off label,' which means the drug has not been approved

> for use in children based on the demonstration of safety and efficacy in adequate, well-controlled clinical trials.[2]

Many medications, not only ones for mental health, include 'death' as a possible side effect in the small print of the information leaflet. Without a lot more context to understand drug risks, sample sizes and percentages, this information is pretty meaningless. This may encourage us to either have blind faith in our clinician or to be too overwhelmed by the unknown risks to want to chance the treatment for our child.

As doctors will tell us, not everyone has side effects as everyone's body chemistry is different. While this is reassuring, there are still so many unknowns that treatment choices can still feel like Russian roulette.

Assessing risk and benefit does not get a whole lot easier with non-drug treatments. If we are planning to use dietary supplements or physical therapies, for example, there may be a lack of research to demonstrate both risk and benefit. In fact, the medical profession often dismisses the non-drug treatments precisely due to this lack of evidence.

However, a lack of evidence does not mean that there are no risks or no benefits, simply that they have not been substantially studied. For benefits, there is a big difference between there not being evidence for something working and there being actual evidence that something does not work. For example, honey was used to treat and prevent wound infection for thousands of years until the development of antibiotics. Despite there not being any large-scale studies to show the benefit of honey, the evidence came from doctors' own eyes as they saw how effective it was in the field. The research evidence of the benefits has come more recently, and honey is again being increasingly used in wound dressings to prevent the unnecessary use of antibiotics.

The point I am making is that the treatment worked *prior to* the research evidence. In the same way, non-drug treatments for our children *may* also work, and we may, just like for honey in the past, need to rely on the evidence of our own eyes to see if it is helping or not.

The same applies with risk with the non-drug treatments. In the absence of big trials and a leaflet listing all the possible side effects, we may also need to use the evidence of our own observations, research among others who have tried the treatment, and the experience and expertise of the practitioner.

Just because something is 'natural' we cannot automatically assume that it is safe. There are many poisons in nature. But common sense may tell us that a remedy that has been used without substantial problems for thousands of years and is highly recommended by people who are using it but not selling it *may* be worth considering.

When considering risk, we also need to consider the risk to our bank balance if a treatment does not help. As well as the financial cost, another risk is the emotional and social cost of the exhaustion of dragging our child to endless appointments and the upheaval of time off school and work in order to do so.

Everyone responds differently to treatment and whatever we do will have an element of risk. There is also a risk in *not doing anything*. Leaving our child untreated may risk them leading unhappy, unfulfilled and unproductive lives.

In fact, not offering treatment at all can result in our loved ones self-medicating with alcohol, drugs and reckless behaviour to try to relieve their suffering and feel some control over their lives. Prisons seem to be full of people with untreated and undiagnosed hidden disabilities or mental illnesses. Sadly, we cannot know the full extent of this, but, as many as 90 per cent was estimated in a now outdated UK government report.[3]

With my family, we had bad experiences with medication and very good experiences with some of the non-drug options. At the time, although I didn't have the facts and figures to back me up (because they did not exist), I wanted to try what I believed to be safer options first, and my child's bipolar was stabilised with a combination of nutritional supplements and an amended form of cognitive behavioural therapy. Saying this, I respect parents who make other decisions as there really is no right or wrong, only what looks right on the risks versus benefits scale and what actually works for and helps our child.

Whatever treatment we choose, there is a very good chance that it will bring us into contact with 'experts'.

But the reality for most of us is that very few 'experts' have specialist training or experience in treating children with hidden disabilities. There is considerable misinformation, misdiagnosis, ignorance and at times arrogance among some professionals in the area of hidden disabilities. It is therefore possible that we may be the ones who are educating the 'experts' about our child's hidden disability. Some practitioners will be prepared to acknowledge their lack of knowledge in this area and work with us and our expertise to support our child.

This is often a reason why no intervention may sometimes be better than a bad intervention. A poor therapist or practitioner is like putting another big weight onto the 'risk' side of the weighing scales.

When my children were young, finding professionals who were knowledgeable and experienced with hidden disabilities was virtually impossible. After some very bad experiences, I lost a fair bit of trust in 'experts' and it felt safer to learn as much as I could to help my children myself. Nowadays, even if there is not a suitably qualified or experienced professional in our area, many fantastic doctors and practitioners offer their full services online through video consultations. This is a wonderfully helpful development.

Also, the growth of social media allows us more easily to tap into the networks of support groups and knowledge worldwide to help us make more informed decisions.

DRUG TREATMENTS

For many of our medical advisors and doctors, drug treatments in the form of pharmaceutical medication are the first point of call. For many it is the only point of call. This may be for good reason if they believe that there is insufficient evidence about alternatives. Or it could be that the doctor does not have personal experience or knowledge about alternatives.

Drug treatments may be the best way forward for our child, at least for a period of time. This is why it is worth understanding a little about the different types of drugs and their risks and benefits.

> In this section, I am sharing my understanding of the risks and benefits of different types of medication, to help parents with the informed choices we all need to make. This is not intended to replace the services of trained medical professionals or be a substitute for medical advice. You should always consult a doctor on any matters relating to your child's health, in particular any matter that may require diagnosis, medical attention or prescription.

Books about treatments for hidden disabilities talk about the importance of choosing a great doctor or psychiatrist, often by interviewing them about their experience and approach before they treat our child. For this to happen, we need to know a certain amount ourselves, so that we know what to ask and how to respond to what we hear. Interviewing potential doctors is great if we are in a position to do it. Many of us do not have this choice and instead spend long periods on waiting lists and are then allocated a doctor without having any control over who we see.

Others struggle to access any suitably qualified doctor at all, either because of shortages where we live or because they are prohibitively expensive. We may therefore be forced to deal with doctors we know little about and who we may not have chosen for our child. This is another good reason for us to empower ourselves and learn what we can about the medications our children are being offered.

Although there is no magic pill that will 'cure' or relieve the suffering of our child, drug treatments are often prescribed to help them with *specific symptoms* of their hidden disabilities, such as anxiety, depression or restlessness. Some medications can be prescribed by our child's GP and others can only be prescribed by a specialist or psychiatrist.

Choosing between medications and non-drug treatments does not need to be an 'either–or' decision. Many doctors offer both and it is very common for talking therapies such as cognitive behavioural therapy (CBT) to be offered alongside drug treatment.

Saying that, some of the non-drug treatments should not be used alongside drug medication and this is talked about in the next chapter.

ANTIDEPRESSANTS

Antidepressants are often offered to combat low mood and anxiety, very common problems for many of our loved ones with hidden disabilities, especially those with autism spectrum disorders, OCD and chronic depression or anxiety.

Many families have told me that antidepressants like Prozac (fluoxetine) or Zoloft (sertraline hydrochloride) have had a really good effect. They may help to lift our child above their depression and anxiety enough for them to then respond to non-drug treatments, as well as all the things we are doing to help them out of protection mode.

Others have found that a low-dose antidepressant can lift their child out of being stuck in the blues and may be all that they need to transform their experience, perhaps getting them back into school or able to participate in life. This is a potentially big benefit that should not be dismissed, obviously through discussion with your doctor.

On the other hand, a number of families I have spoken to have found that antidepressants simply do not work or have even made their child's depression or anxiety worse. Some found that the side effects were actually worse than the symptoms that these medications were trying to address. This is why careful monitoring is so important and why a doctor may wish our child to try out a number of options.

A potential danger of antidepressant use in people under the age of 25 is an increase in suicidal thoughts or behaviour. While this side effect is uncommon, it was significant enough that the US Drug Administration Agency (FDA) has put a black box warning on all prescription antidepressants.

It is my understanding that it may be difficult to get a child off an antidepressant after they have been on it for some time. Even tapering off the medication slowly can cause pretty debilitating withdrawal symptoms and Mind UK lists what your child may experience when coming off these medications.[1] I have come across people who are stuck on medication for years, which although not helping with their symptoms they are unable to stop taking due to the severity of the withdrawal symptoms.

While withdrawal symptoms are a real concern, we need to balance this by remembering that some people may not have a problem with this. For example, Rachel points out:

> I was on Zoloft [sertraline hydrochloride] for years and with the doctor's help I successfully withdrew over several months once I felt strong enough, while at the same time looking after my gut with probiotics. This worked for me and I do not regret taking the drug at a time I needed it.

From personal experience, I suggest bearing withdrawal in mind if we decide to try antidepressants for our child, as this is something doctors do not always tell us about. We could discuss with our doctor the possibility of a trial of the medication for a short period, enabling us to be able to get our child off it relatively easily if it is not a good fit for him or her.

> These are just personal thoughts, experiences and reflections. Speak to your doctor for advice on this and any other area of prescribing.

ANTIPSYCHOTICS AND ANTICONVULSANTS

Our loved ones with psychotic or more complex mood disorders are commonly prescribed antipsychotics or anticonvulsant medications, sometimes in combination with antidepressants. It is my understanding that antidepressants alone can push a person into mania if they have this predisposition.[2]

This is a complex area of prescribing. Whereas an antidepressant is often prescribed by a GP, antipsychotics and anticonvulsants are generally prescribed and monitored by consultant psychiatrists as they are considered to have stronger risks attached to them. The National Institute for Mental Health (NIMH) reports that the side effects can include weight gain, low blood pressure, tics and tremors, seizures and low white blood cells which fight infection.[3]

To stabilise someone with these medications, a lot of trial and error may be needed as what helps one child will not help another and can cause more problems than benefits. Over a number of years I have talked to hundreds of parents in the Balanced Mind Parent Network groups whose children had mood disorders, especially bipolar. Many told me that it took about two years to find the right combination of medications to stabilise their child along with an acceptable number of side effects.[4]

When my child was trying these medications, being aware of this was very helpful so that I could manage my expectations about the benefits of the drugs and know that they were unlikely to provide an immediate fix and that time and patience would be required. As my child's exams were looming, we did of course hope and pray that we would get the medication right first time.

I have been told of many children who have done really well with these treatments, and despite often quite severe side effects, credit their medication cocktail with giving them back a meaningful life.

I have also heard of others who do less well. My family were in this latter category, which is why we were lucky and happy to find non-drug alternatives that worked better for us.

If a doctor suggests antipsychotics or anticonvulsants for our child, be aware that it can be difficult to get a child off these medications if they are not working for them, or if they are causing side effects that outweigh the benefits.[5] Obviously this is something to weigh up with the advice and support of our child's doctor.

In my experience, psychiatrists suggest coming off the medications by slowly reducing the dose over time as coming off medications 'cold turkey' can be dangerous. But even when slowly reducing the dose, some people find that the drug withdrawal symptoms are overwhelming and may even compare them to the symptoms of coming off heroin or cocaine. The sheer number of antipsychotic withdrawal support groups online gives some indication about the extent of this problem. We were not aware of this when my child tried antipsychotic medication. Knowing the risk of withdrawal problems might have affected our decision to try it.

ADHD MEDICATION

Another very common area of prescribing is for stimulants and non-stimulant drugs to treat hyperactivity, impulsivity and focus issues of children with ADHD. Examples are drugs such as Ritalin (methylphenidate hydrochloride) and Concerta XL (methylphenidate extended-release tablets).

Parents are often very torn on whether to accept them for their children. The good news is that these medications appear to have a pretty good success rate in reducing symptoms, 80 per cent by some studies.[6] In fact, for some of our children the results can be life changing. This suggests a good weighting in the area of benefits.

In the area of risks, the picture is more uncertain with a range of possible side effects and possible long-term health considerations. These can include sleep problems, brain fog, mood and growth concerns as well as stomach- and headaches. There is also evidence that stimulant drugs can affect the development of the brain and nervous system.[7]

Another consideration is that people with unmedicated ADHD are thought to be at higher risk of addictions and self-medicating behaviours like drug and alcohol abuse. Evidence shows that people with ADHD who take these medications as prescribed are significantly less likely to abuse other substances.[8]

Some argue that if a child with ADHD benefits from stimulant drugs, an alternative may be to give them more stimulation in life instead, by fanning their passions and interests and protecting them from the boredom triggers at school. However, as most children with ADHD are in mainstream schools with a limited understanding of our children's needs, medication may be the only viable way of getting them through school.

A paediatrician also explained to me that there may be options for compromise and choice in how to take these medications, to reduce the impact of side effects. She told me that some of her patients only take the drugs during the school week, while others take breaks from their medication when life circumstances permit. She also reminded me that some children have mild or no problems with side effects, so fear of these things should not necessarily put us off trying medication if it may help our child.

It is reassuring to be aware of this, although everyone's experience will be different and our child's doctor will be able to guide us through this.

ANTI-ANXIETY MEDICATION

As severe anxiety is a very common symptom of many hidden disabilities, especially anxiety disorder itself, anti-anxiety medications are also often prescribed. If our child is on an antidepressant, this may already help with anxiety and it is my understanding that antidepressants are often the medication of choice for anxiety.[9] If antidepressants are not chosen, our child may be prescribed a beta blocker (like propranolol) to be taken at times of anxiety to slow the heart rate down. Some people find these to be very effective for mild anxiety. In my personal experience they are pretty ineffective for severe anxiety and for panic attacks.

As with all medications, there is a risk of side effects.[10] But as beta blockers are generally only taken when needed, rather than all the time, it is my understanding that they are less likely to cause dependence or too many side effects.

For more severe anxiety, doctors may consider prescribing stronger drugs such as tranquilisers (like Xanax [alprazolam] and Valium [diazepam]). These medications can be very effective in the short term for panic attacks but come with quite considerable risks of addiction, side effects and longer-term dangers.[11] Again, these risks will need to be weighed up against the benefits. There may be times when they can be useful for a very short period during a specific crisis. In my experience, doctors are very reluctant to prescribe tranquilisers to children and young people, in the UK at least, although I believe their use is more common in the US and some other countries.

YES OR NO TO DRUG TREATMENTS?

Some people argue strongly that too many children are on medications. This may or may not be the case, but what really matters is what we decide for *our* child and whether trying drug treatments is the right thing to do for them. Obviously, any decision made will be in conjunction with our child's doctor or medical professional.

When our doctor offers a range of drugs for our child, including perhaps antipsychotics, anticonvulsants, antidepressants or stimulant drugs, we may feel very apprehensive about what to do. Our doctor may advise us to take them, but as parents, it is usually we who need to make the actual decision and I know from experience what a frightening decision this is.

When we ask if they are safe, our doctor may reassure us that *all medications* have risks and can cause side effects, and that giving these to our child is no different from treating any other chronic illness with drugs. This is absolutely true in a literal sense.

One way of looking at it is if our child's disability was visible and not hidden, for example, if she had epilepsy or diabetes, how would we feel then about using medications to control it? If the answer to this question is 'yes of course, bring on the meds', then why would this be any different if our child's condition is a hidden disability? Why would we be happy to accept the risks of medication for one and not for the other? Why is it OK to treat asthma and epilepsy but not ADHD and bipolar disorder? What is the difference?

Alternatively, we may prefer to avoid medication for *any* of our children's chronic health conditions, especially where there are concerns over safety and whether the benefits outweigh the risks. If this is the case, it would make sense to look at non-drug alternative treatments and possibly try them first. If we like to use holistic treatments where possible, we probably wouldn't distinguish between hidden and visible disabilities and chronic health conditions and treat them all with the same approach.

The choice I made for my family was, where possible, to try natural or non-drug options first as I believe, although I cannot prove it, that there may be fewer risks associated with them. If I cannot get enough benefits from the non-drug treatments, then I will consider pharmaceutical medications. I would then feel more comfortable about the risks of drugs in the knowledge that I have exhausted the alternatives.

This was my choice but it is not right for everyone. With non-drug treatments, we are often required to pay for them up front as they are rarely included within private health insurance or government healthcare programmes such as the NHS. This is a big consideration if money is tight, especially if we are able to get pharmaceutical drugs free of charge or at a very subsidised rate.

Another reason to go with the drugs option may be that we have tried various non-drug options and they have not helped. We love and want to support our child so may wish to try anything that might help them, having weighed up the risks and benefits.

It can also be harder to get our loved ones on board with non-drug treatments, which may involve making lifestyle changes that our children are not prepared to make or require them to take many supplements a number of times a day. Getting our child to follow these protocols can add extra stress to our home, stoking up the heat on both their pressure cookers and ours. There may be a whole range of things our child would need to do for their care which seem overwhelming compared with the ease of simply popping one small medication pill every morning.

Figuring out what non-drug treatment to try can also be overwhelming when we and our children are at breaking point. When we are exhausted, letting the experts choose can be a very attractive option.

This can be a logical thing to do and the decision can always be revised and reversed at a time in the future when we have more time, energy and resources to look at alternatives if we so wish.

With my family, I did make the decision to try medications at a particularly stressful time in my child's life and it would probably have been the right decision if the medication (an antipsychotic) had actually helped. In fact, it made things worse and it took a year for my child to recover from the withdrawal symptoms when they came off the drug. Saying that, many others make the same decision and it goes very well for them.

There is no right or wrong!

Here are some contrasting views of parents who were asked why they chose to medicate:

> When I was a kid, aged around nine I started medication for my ADHD. It did not have any negative effects on me and helped me tremendously in school and life in general. That's why I wanted the same benefit for my son when he was diagnosed with the same thing and did not hesitate to get him onto medication.

> I truly believe my daughter would not be alive right now if not for her medication.

> I chose medication because at the age of seven my son had no control over his emotions or behaviour and did not sleep. Also he was a risk to himself and others and I tried all the alternatives without any success so medication was the last step and the best one for him.

> I use drugs to cure ear infections, to aid in teething and so my middle child doesn't die of asthma. I give medication to my children for their welfare, same as I take my medications for my welfare. This is the same reason my ADHD, ASD, GAD, OCD, SPD son takes medication for his welfare.

> I was really scared about giving my son medication and cried the first day he took it, thinking I was a terrible mum. Then I saw him smile for the first time in years and I knew I had done the right thing.

And here are some who chose not to use medications:

> Many drugs are not clinically tested on children even though they are prescribed to them. This bothered me. My son is not a lab rat, and I didn't feel safe giving him medication that could potentially harm his developing brain because it was clinically tested on only adults.[12]

> We decided to only put my daughter on medication if the nutritional therapy and occupational therapy didn't help her. But they helped so much that we never had to try the meds. Everyone is different though.

> The school was pressuring me to put my son on Ritalin [methylphenidate hydrochloride] as he wasn't concentrating and wouldn't keep still. In my opinion this is the school's problem, not my son's. I wasn't going to drug my child to make life easier for teachers.

> Deciding on drugs is a big decision so we decided to wait until our son was old enough to make the decision himself.

Chapter 14

NON-DRUG TREATMENTS

My choice to go for non-drug treatment for my children had nothing to do with weighing up risks and benefits. I had a child who needed urgent help but I was unable to access any medical psychiatric services. At the time in the UK, there were very few child psychiatrists, and mood disorders among children were little known, recognised or understood.

After seven years of waiting and fighting we eventually got medical help from a consultant neuropsychiatrist at Great Ormond Street Hospital in London. This resulted in multiple diagnoses and the offer of pharmaceutical drug treatment.

But during the seven-year wait, I could not leave my child without any form of treatment as the risks of doing so were too great. So, to support my child I felt compelled to research and try alternatives myself. As we had no access to drug treatment in the form of medication, I had to find things I did have access to and my child was so in need of help that we had nothing to lose.

By the time we were offered pharmaceutical drugs we no longer needed them as my child was now stable and had resumed a relatively normal life. Had my child not been stable, we would probably have chosen to try the medications at that time.

There are an endless number of non-drug treatments; some may help and some will not. Although far from complete, I will only refer here to treatments that I have personal experience of, either for my own children or for a significant number of families I am in contact with.

I am in no way endorsing these treatments and they may or may not help your child. I have no vested interest in promoting any form of treatment. What works for one child may not for another and ultimately the judgement will come down to you, the real expert on your child. Do your research, take advice only from people you trust and weigh up the risks and benefits.

WORKING WITH NUTRITION

DIET TREATMENTS

Some of our children find that a change of diet works either alone or in combination with other methods as an effective treatment.

While all children benefit from healthy eating and being encouraged to eat up their greens, for children with hidden disabilities this can have another dimension to it. Many of our children have gut problems that can make their symptoms worse, and in some cases even cause their symptoms in the first place.

You may have heard about the gut–brain connection that is making a lot of headlines at the time of writing. The nutrients in the food we eat are absorbed in the stomach and gut. If our guts are inflamed and we are not able to absorb our food well, vital nutrients needed to nourish the brain may be lacking. This can cause our brain to lack or have an imbalance of the chemicals it needs to in order to maintain healthy moods, anxiety levels and focus. This is often referred to as the gut–brain axis or GBA.

Research has shown that up to 90 per cent of people on the autism spectrum suffer from gut problems and it is believed that the same gene mutations that are found both in the brain and in the gut could be the cause.[1]

There is similar evidence on the gut–brain connection with other hidden disabilities, including bipolar disorder and ADHD. Some of this research has focused on the importance of *gut bacteria* (the microbiome) and how taking the right probiotic supplements can help to improve our children's symptoms.

According to a study discussed in the Harvard Medical School Health Blog, the data suggests that gut flora does have an effect on psychiatric diseases:

> The evidence of a 'gut–brain axis principle' is more robust, especially after some studies showing that the type of bacteria that live in our bowels could cause brain inflammation. This most recent research indicates that we could potentially manage the symptoms of severe cases of bipolar disorder merely by changing the makeup of our microbiome.[2]

If our child has food allergies or intolerances, this can cause yet more gut inflammation and makes it even harder for the necessary nutrients to be absorbed, possibly causing even greater brain chemistry imbalances.

Despite this research, not all doctors accept this idea and some feel that there is insufficient evidence that changing the diet or sorting out gut flora can help. This is something to weigh up when we visualise the weighing scales of risks and benefits.

I am not a medical expert or a nutritional therapist, so if dietary treatment interests you I would suggest reading more on this subject and finding a nutritional therapist with experience of your child's hidden disability to assist you.

Commonly, elimination diets are recommended to find foods that are causing difficulties for our child, especially gut inflammation that can affect the brain. Many people find that eliminating gluten, dairy, sugar and junk food makes a big difference to their child's hidden disability symptoms and testing may identify other specific dietary triggers that affect our child's gut.

Nutritional therapists will then generally suggest foods or supplements to rebuild healthy gut bacteria, such as live yoghurt or probiotics.

I have personally seen families who have religiously stuck to dietary treatments obtain staggeringly successful results, both for the symptoms of the hidden disability and also for their family's general health. There is much to favour this approach, if you are able to commit to it and it feels right to do so.

My personal experience of dietary treatment was not quite so positive. I found it very, very difficult to implement the dietary recommendations much of the time and sometimes I felt that trying to do so would be counterproductive for my children.

Due to their hidden disabilities, my children already felt apart, different and often excluded socially from their classmates. They were desperate to fit in, feel part of the gang and feel as normal as possible, and this is something I supported them with to the best of my ability.

Andrew found this for his daughter Paige:

> To exclude her from a pizza party because she couldn't eat pizza along with others, or send her with a 'special food box' would, I felt, mark her out as different even more, something I did not have the heart to do.

Additionally, many of our children have eating disorders or perhaps will only eat one or two 'safe' foods, as is often the case for children on the autism spectrum or those in protection mode. If this is the case, imposing a lot of *additional* dietary restrictions could make things worse as by making certain foods forbidden (gluten, sugar, etc.) it adds to the impression of food being *unsafe* and thereby increases anxiety around food in general.

Another problem with this approach is for it to work, we have to get our children on board to cooperate with it. This can be very difficult if our child cannot directly see the effect of cutting out the foods in question. With severe allergies that cause a histamine reaction, this is more straightforward, as some children cannot breathe, develop rashes or get severe stomach pain when they eat a certain food. With intolerances the effects are more subtle, so harder for the child to see or understand.

NUTRITIONAL SUPPLEMENT THERAPY

Nutritional supplement therapy is one of the treatments that most helped my child with bipolar disorder find stability and regain as normal a childhood as possible. There is contradictory data on this and the evidence is mixed. Saying this, it appears to have had a good effect on many children and adults with psychosis, depression, anxiety and hyperactivity as well as chronic conditions such as chronic fatigue. Do not take my word for it. I am not an expert and I urge you to do your own research and speak to experts who you trust. I am not advocating or recommending this approach, I am simply sharing my experience of it.

Speak to your doctor before embarking on any type of supplement treatment. Please be aware that some supplements can not be taken alongside pharmaceutical drugs without medical advice.

Nutritional supplement therapy uses the same starting point as dietary treatment. It recognises that many children with hidden disabilities have a reduced capacity to absorb the nutrients they need for brain health from a normal diet. This could be due to inflammation in the gut as well as a whole range of other reasons, many of which are poorly understood. For example, although our child may eat plenty of vitamin B in her diet, it may not be absorbed properly, and we know that the lack of particular forms of vitamin B in the body might trigger psychiatric illness or make the symptoms worse.

According to one report:

> B12 deficiency can cause almost any psychiatric symptom, from anxiety, and panic to depression and hallucinations. This is because B12 deficiencies trigger symptoms in the nervous system and red blood cells.[3]

As with the diet approaches, this kind of nutritional therapy (sometimes called ortho-molecular therapy) also works on healing the gut–brain axis, the two way communication between the gut and the brain.

However, with this approach, diet is only a part of the treatment. This approach targets the *specific* nutrients that may be affecting our child's brain chemistry and finds ways to get them into their body in a form that may help them find stability.

There seem to be three approaches to nutritional supplement therapy. The first is an individual range of supplements, tailor-made for our child. The second is a general 'off-the-shelf' approach. The third is to treat each symptom individually with specific supplements. All or none of these may be right for our child and the research evidence is conflicting. We have tried all three approaches and had good results with each, depending on my children's needs at the time.

Individualised approach

The first approach is to work with a nutritional therapist who specialises in this area. For example, practitioners who use the Walsh Protocol will firstly test our child with blood and other tests to see which nutrients are not being adequately absorbed or are out of balance. They will then prescribe specific nutritional supplements based on our child's individual needs to address this. It is felt that this will level out our child's brain chemistry, heal the gut–brain connection and improve their symptoms.[4]

The prescription of supplements may change after each round of testing as our child's nutrient levels improve. With time, they will only need a minimum number of supplements for maintenance if or when our child is symptom free and everything is in balance.

If you decide to try this approach, be prepared for a cupboard full of supplements as your child may need to take many different vitamin pills a number of times a day and there will be a dent in your bank balance. You will also need pill organisers and to find a way to get your child to take the supplements! This can be a challenge.

What helps is that our child will be present at the consultations with the nutritional therapist, so it will be an 'expert' rather than us asking them to take the pills. The nutritional therapist will also be able to show our child the result of the blood tests so that he can see and understand why he is being asked to take the supplements. If we also use mood and symptom charts or trackers, our child will also be able to see evidence of a decrease in his anxiety and other symptoms, increasing his motivation to comply with the treatment.

In some parts of the world, especially the US and Canada, there are compounding pharmacies that will mix the supplements into single capsules, making the whole process much easier. It may also be possible to blend them into a form that can be added to milk shakes or smoothies for younger children or those who cannot or will not take tablets.

Our child will also need to be prepared for regular blood testing. We found that this was pretty tolerable for my child if we used a skin-numbing cream first such as EMLA™ cream (which contains lidocaine and prilocaine).

The 'off-the-shelf' method

If you cannot or do not wish to see a nutritional therapist for an individualised supplement programme based on testing, there are a number of 'off-the-shelf' alternatives. These are supplements that blend a range of nutrients that are most commonly deficient, for whatever reason, in adults and children with brain chemistry conditions such as ASD, ADHD, and mood and anxiety disorders. As the supplements will not be tailor made, they may or may not address your child's individual biochemistry needs and it may be rather hit and miss.

Saying that, we personally had great success with such supplements when one of my children was particularly unstable. Within six weeks of taking them, moods were balanced, my child was back at school, had an active social life and became one of the highest academic achievers in the school year.

This sounds wonderful, but it isn't always easy to get a child to take a great many capsules a day, especially if some need to be taken at school. We were very lucky to have a member of staff who my child trusted to supervise this at lunch breaks.

An advantage of this approach over the individualised methods is that there is only one bottle of supplements, rather than multiple pills in a pill organiser. This makes it much easier for our child to manage his own treatment. Also there are no blood tests or appointments with nutritional therapists to attend. It is also possible to buy the supplements in the form of smoothie shakes for children who are not able or willing to take capsules.

Most of the better providers of this type of supplement offer regular telephone support to help track our child's progress and to give individual advice on dosage and any additional supplements that would be recommended.

> Please note that I am sharing my understanding and experience with these treatments, but am not endorsing or recommending them in any way. Always seek medical advice.

Supplements for symptoms

While the first two approaches aim to bring the whole brain chemistry into balance, another approach is to use supplements to target specific symptoms with specific supplements.

Many families swear by the use of CBD (cannabidiol) supplements to control both anxiety and hyperactivity and to help their child to sleep. CBD is produced from the hemp plant and is a legal form of medical cannabis that does not make a person high. We tried it and found it of limited help, but everyone is different and I have heard many reported successes with it.

Another popular supplement to help to calm an anxious or irritable child is magnesium, especially in the form of magnesium citrate, which is a muscle relaxant. It can be bought in the form of a drink and can also help our child to sleep. I have probably had more success with this than my child and it certainly helps me to stay calm and improves my sleep. For moments of extreme anxiety, I also have found inositol supplements to be very helpful, both for me and for my child.

For focus, there seems to be quite a bit of evidence that omega 3 oil can help. Research seems to suggest that children with ADHD have naturally lower levels of this brain-protecting oil, which can be addressed by eating lots of oily fish, or by taking supplements.[5]

For sleep, probably the most popular supplement is melatonin, a naturally occurring hormone that helps to reset an unbalanced body clock and is often used as a remedy for jet lag. In many countries it is available over the counter in health food stores. In the UK it requires a prescription from a doctor. Such prescriptions are easiest to obtain if our child has a diagnosis of an autism spectrum disorder. Melatonin for sleep has transformed the life of many families.

Families have also reported good results from the use of herbal supplements, especially relaxing herbs such as lavender and ones that promote sleep such as valerian and lemon balm. For many years, we found it helpful to add camomile tea bags to my child's bath at night as it helped with relaxation and soothed itchy hypersensitive skin.

If you are interested in herbal medicine, it is worth consulting a qualified herbal medical practitioner who would be aware of safety concerns around different herbs and be able to prescribe an individualised blend for your child. Other families have had very good results with Chinese herbal medicine and acupuncture, especially for easing digestive problems and helping with sleep, anxiety and depression. I know of a number of families who have had similar success with homeopathy.

TALKING THERAPIES

Many loving parents of children with hidden disabilities regularly ask ourselves, 'Am I doing enough to help my child?' With so many different therapies out there, especially if we are able and prepared to pay for them, it can be overwhelming to know where to start. As with other forms of treatment, the same questions also apply to talking therapies. Does it help? Do the benefits outweigh the risks?

These therapies seem to fall loosely into three categories:

- therapies to prevent negative thinking patterns and unhelpful behaviour
- therapies to teach social, communication and life skills
- psychological therapies to explore feelings and relationships.

Many of these therapies promise a lot, but in my experience, very few therapists have received detailed training on hidden disabilities and how they affect the therapies they are offering.

Many of the therapies seem to be designed for the needs of

neurotypical children and adults, who may have psychological problems as a result of difficult life experiences.

I must have contacted hundreds of therapists who told me that they were unable to help children with hidden disabilities and I am very grateful that they recognised their limitations. As some talking therapies involve playing with our precious child's mind, I would be very careful indeed about who you entrust this side of their care to.

However, if we are able to find a caring, empathetic therapist who is fully trained and experienced in treating children with our child's hidden disabilities, the support and help for both us and our child can be life changing.

On the risk side of the balance, one bad experience with a misinformed therapist can set our child back for years and perhaps make them resistant to seeking help in the future when they really need it.

Another risk of choosing therapies, one of the biggest, will be to our wallets as therapy is not cheap and some practitioners want it to go on and on. Another factor for the 'risk' side of the scales is the additional stress of travelling around to extra appointments and motivating our child to comply with any requests made of him by the therapists.

Some of the therapies, such as cognitive behavioural therapy (CBT), speech and language therapy and occupational therapy, may be available under the NHS, government medical care or private insurance. These may be worth trying as long as the therapists you are allocated truly understand our child's disability. Experience shows that we cannot assume that this will be the case.

COGNITIVE BEHAVIOURAL THERAPY (CBT)

For many of our children, the starting point is cognitive behavioural therapy (CBT), which is considered often to be effective for treating anxiety and depression. This is a talking therapy where our child learns to identify the triggers to particular behaviours and find alternative ways to react to them. For example, they may learn to recognise when a meltdown is imminent and immediately do a calming activity to try to prevent it from happening. They may realise that transitions and changes during the school day ramp up their anxiety, so prepare for this with their therapist by perhaps learning some breathing exercises that they can do just before the lunch bell rings.

CBT is very different from general counselling, psychotherapy or psychoanalysis. It does not involve delving deep into our child's psyche and is instead concerned with finding *practical* ways of changing thoughts and behaviours to improve our child's mood and relieve anxiety. This makes if far less threatening to children and potentially very helpful.

In CBT sessions, our child may also learn to recognise negative and unhelpful thought patterns that can add to anxiety and depression. They may be encouraged to look at the evidence and to counter the thoughts with new ones that are more accurate and more self-supporting.

For example, if our child is thinking, 'I am useless. I can't do anything', by focusing on the evidence of all the things she *can* do, how she is far from useless, she can reframe the thought as, 'I am very able. I can do many things well.' If he is thinking, 'I have no friends. No-one likes me', he can be encouraged to remember all the friends he does have and the people who do like him, to reframe the thought as, 'I have a small number of good friends and many people like me.'

CBT also challenges the tendency we all have, including our child, to catastrophise things in our mind and believe that every setback is the end of the world, or far worse than it actually is. For example, our child may fail a test at school, maybe due to anxiety, and think, 'This means I am a failure and my whole life will be a ruined as a result.' This can be reframed to, 'Yes I failed that test and it is a setback, but I will not let it stop me in my ambitions to succeed. I will find another way.'

I have also heard good reports of a slightly more developed approach called dialectical behavioural therapy (DBT). This has similar aims to CBT but adds more weight to behaviours in relationships with others.

In order for CBT or DBT to help our child, finding a practitioner who really 'gets' our child and understands their hidden disability is critically important. If the rapport, trust and understanding is not there, our child is unlikely to engage with the therapy and it may even be counterproductive and turn them off from trying again with someone else.

After one bad experience where one of my children felt patronised, put down and demeaned by the therapist, we were then lucky to strike gold with another who specialised in treating children with neurological hidden disabilities. My child was treated with so much respect for their intelligence and abilities and made amazing progress. So much trust was formed that the relationship with this lady endures to this day.

Be aware though that CBT is most effective when symptoms of anxiety and depression are mild to moderate. If anxiety attacks are very severe or if our child is in a very deep depression, it may be impossible for them to think beyond how they are feeling at the time. A panic attack may be too severe for our child to breathe through, or the meltdown may come on too quickly for them to distract themselves in time. If this happens, they are not failing, it just means that other treatments may be needed first to get their symptoms into the range whereby the CBT skills can be effective.

Using the idea of the traffic light, a child may need to be in code orange or code green for CBT to help, so my suggestion would be to give priority to getting your child out of protection mode and perhaps adding CBT only when your child is ready to engage with it.

Finding a CBT therapist with an understanding and experience of hidden disabilities is very difficult and may be impossible, depending on where we live. It may, however, be easier to find a suitable person able to offer online consultations.

If we do not have access to a therapist, or cannot afford one, there are a range of online CBT courses that our child could benefit from. There are also a lot of books on the subject, which could help us to teach these thinking skills to our child ourself. It is better if this can come from someone other than the parent if possible, but we have to be realistic and make use of whatever resources we have.

SOCIAL, BEHAVIOURAL AND LANGUAGE THERAPIES

Due to their hidden disabilities, many of our children have difficulties with their relationships, with effective communication (verbal and non-verbal) and with controlling their behaviour. They may also have problems with life skills such as doing certain things for themselves or getting themselves organised. This is where social, behavioural and language therapies can potentially help.

I have no personal experience of this directly, but according to a survey conducted by MyAutismTeam among its social network of 28,000 parents, the two social, behavioural and language therapies found most helpful for their children were occupational therapy (38%) and speech and language therapy (27%).[6]

Clearly our children's needs in this area will vary hugely and the needs of a child with classic autism, which is rarely a 'hidden' disability, are very different from a child with Asperger's, OCD or ADHD. However, if we have limited resources and time, this survey can assist us in prioritising what may help most.

Looking around at these therapy options it seems that there is some overlap, meaning that if we are lucky we may not need more than one therapist, as long as we are clear what we are trying to achieve.

For example, an occupational therapist may be able help our child to develop social and self-care skills. They may also help our child with sensory problems and to develop their fine motor skills, bearing in mind that some of our loved ones may be somewhat clumsy.

A speech and language therapist may help our child rehearse and address all the communication challenges they have, learning how to respond to particular situations, what to say if someone compliments them, where to look, where to put their hands, etc.

These therapies can also help our children with the executive function difficulties that so many of our children have, problems with organising themselves and their work.

We were extremely fortunate that our CBT therapist covered social and communication skills as part of her CBT therapy, along with techniques for dealing with getting organised (executive functioning).

Again, it may be frustrating to recognise that our child would benefit from social, communication and behavioural therapies but not have access to a therapist who can help. Many families do not have the resources for this, or suitable practitioners may not be available. Sometimes this support is available on the NHS although we may need to wait and be prepared to fight for it. We are not failing in any way as a parent if we are not able to access this help.

In my experience, many families find that if they are able to get their children out of protection mode, their child's thinking brain will be online and they will be able to learn much of the social and communications skills themselves without the need for a lot of extra help.

There are also a lot of resources available to help our child at home. There are computer games that our child can use to teach them organising and social skills. There are books and online learning programmes to help us to support our child ourselves.

Although not ideal, doing this work ourselves does have some advantages. Appointments to see too many therapists and doctors can add heat to our child's pressure cooker and keep them in protection mode. Treating them ourselves allows us to make sure that our child is not overwhelmed by the therapies they are receiving.

We can make judgements ourselves about whether our child is too tired or too stressed to do the training at any particular moment. For our children, there are many times when doing nothing is the best therapy, enabling them to rest, recover and replenish their emotional resources. Doing the therapy with our child ourselves allows us to assess what is helping and what is not and choose exactly the right timings for our child.

PSYCHOTHERAPY AND COUNSELLING

Unlike behavioural therapies which focus on actions and ways of thinking about things, psychotherapy and counselling take our child into a deeper exploration of their mind and past experiences. There are many types of counselling and psychotherapy and many types of therapist. Some are excellent are some are less so. As our child will be opening up and possibly making themselves very vulnerable to this person, finding a therapist that both we and our child trust can be a challenge and is a very big responsibility. If we find the right person, a good counsellor can be an amazing resource for our child and the whole family. Get it wrong and the therapist can quite literally mess with our child's head, causing problems that could take years to unravel.

As with all treatments, we need to visualise the risks and benefits weighing scales. If we find the right therapist, the potential benefits are many:

- Our child will have someone who will listen to her fully and allow her to express everything she wants and needs to say. Some of these things may be difficult for the parent to hear, which is why it is important that this is someone confidential outside of the family.
- We can relieve ourselves of some of the burden of our child's emotional needs. It is very supportive for us to know that if he is worried about something, there is someone else to deal with it with him. We cannot do everything so having a trusted person on board who our child trusts really helps.
- Most therapists and counsellors will help our child to connect to his emotions and learn healthy ways to express them. This is a big part of getting out of protection mode.
- A good therapist will help our child accept and be at peace with their hidden disability, value their strengths and gifts while acknowledging fully the challenges it brings.
- A counsellor can help our child develop coping strategies and relaxation techniques and deal with relationship issues and problems such as bullying.

There are also risks, which can be substantial.

It is extremely difficult to find a therapist or counsellor who has knowledge, understanding or experience of hidden disabilities. Most appear to be trained to offer psychological support to neurotypical children who are having emotional difficulties for a wide range of problems. For this reason, many may be reluctant to take on our child.

Although hidden disabilities are caused by a mixture of genetic, chemical, hormonal and environmental factors, less enlightened therapists may still hold the outdated belief that our child's difficulties are caused by poor parenting or trauma. Some, who take this view, may choose to reject our child's diagnosis, believing that it is a label that can be disregarded and that there will be deeper psychological causes of our child's condition.

Our child may well have experienced trauma or negative life situations that have affected her mental health and it is perfectly possible that a therapist can help with this. However, I would be very cautious if a therapist seems to dismiss our child's hidden disability or plays down the effect it has on our child's life.

On a personal level, when I requested an assessment for hidden disabilities under the NHS, we were instead referred straight to a therapist who, without asking any questions about our home life, told my children and me that hidden disabilities did not exist, only problem families. I do not claim to be a particularly good mother but telling my child that her problems were caused by her family challenged her trust in me, trust that was needed for me to care and advocate for her and that was an important part of her security. If the therapist had believed there was a problem with my parenting, this could have been addressed with me directly.

The therapist in question later told me that she knew nothing about hidden disabilities and that her training was exclusively in the dynamics of relationships.

My child may or may not have needed to address family issues with a therapist, but at that time we were seeking a diagnostic assessment for their hidden disabilities, something that this therapist was unable to offer us.

PHYSICAL AND ENERGY THERAPIES

There are a range of other treatments that I have not had experience of personally for treating hidden disabilities but I have had enough feedback about the benefits from other parents to consider them worthy of mention. These tend to work by correcting imbalances in the physical body or in correcting imbalances with bodily energy, vibration or other frequencies.

I am not endorsing them, simply reporting back. If anything here resonates with you as potentially helpful, you will obviously need to do your homework.

CRANIOSACRAL THERAPY OR OSTEOPATHY

Craniosacral therapy is a hands-on therapy that is carried out through very gentle touch to the head, neck and spine. The practitioner tunes in to the craniosacral rhythm of the body to bring bones and muscles into rhythm with it. This treatment is designed to relieve restrictions and increase the activity of the parasympathetic nervous system.

Craniosacral therapy was first tested on people on the autism spectrum, apparently with good results. Although I have not tried it to deal with hidden disability symptoms, I have used it personally to help my breathing and sinus problems with great success.

Some parents I have spoken to report staggering improvements in their children while others report that the main benefit was in helping their child to relax, reach a meditative state and learn to trust the healing nature of touch.

Scientific evidence is patchy, but a 2017 study of the use of craniosacral therapy for people with ASD did conclude:

> The results of the survey suggest that craniosacral therapy is already being professionally recommended as a treatment. This study found that there were positive responses observed by all three targeted groups leading to the authors concluding that there is worthy cause to further investigate how craniosacral therapy benefits autism spectrum disorders (ASD).[7]

So although evidence may be promising but inconclusive, to me at least the risks seem minimal or non- existent. If nothing else, the therapy is likely to help our child to relax and release pressure from their pressure cooker.

Another advantage is that craniosacral therapists tend to have knowledge and experience of treating children with hidden disabilities, and in fact many specialise in this area, especially autism spectrum disorders. As practitioners with this knowledge and understanding are so rare, this if nothing else makes them potentially really helpful both to us and to our child, as an ally, a resource and a person that both we and most importantly our child could potentially trust.

REFLEX THERAPY

A physical therapy I am hearing more and more about from parents, pretty positively, is reflex therapy. This therapy is based on the observation that some children (and adults) have retained their primitive reflexes. The claim is that this can cause some of the symptoms associated with hidden disabilities, especially anxiety and other issues that hold our children in a state of fight or flight or protection mode.[8]

Primitive reflexes are automatic, involuntary responses which develop when we are in the womb and are essential for the birthing process as well as our survival and development in the first year of life. These include the instinctive abilities to latch on to feed, to grasp, to learn to roll over and sit up.

According to Access Potential:

> The primitive reflexes should inhibit ('switch off') by the time we are 12 months old. If they remain active beyond this time, they can act as a barrier to normal development of the central nervous system and this can result in a host of behavioural, emotional, learning and physiological issues.[9]

The therapy itself combines special skin stimulation and physical exercises designed to inhibit the primitive reflexes.

Again, research evidence on this is patchy, although an increasing number of occupational therapists are becoming interested in this area and are recommending treatment for retained reflexes. One piece of research conducted by specialist occupational therapists concluded:

> The current study offers an evidenced-based rationale for one element of current occupational therapy paediatric practice, the assessment and integration of primitive reflexes in children with concurrent diagnoses of ADHD or ASD. Data collected in this proposal can encourage OTs [occupational therapists] to focus more closely on this area in assessment, as well as to recommend more specific interventions to

address reflex integration, in order to facilitate improved functional cognition.[10]

If reflex therapy interests you, there is an interesting short film about the topic, usually available online, called *Attention Please*.[11] Many of the therapists who specialise in this area are highly knowledgeable and experienced in treating children with hidden disabilities and this alone can be very supportive to both us and our child.

BIOFEEDBACK

Biofeedback therapy is one of the most researched non-drug treatments for anxiety, including the clinical anxiety so associated with hidden disabilities.[12] As we know, anxiety can manifest in many ways for our loved ones and is a key component of what keeps our children in protection mode. Cracking the anxiety issue is a big part of helping our loved ones to re-engage with life and with learning and to find happiness, fulfilment and productivity.

When we become stressed and anxious, there are physical changes in the body. Our heart rate increases, our hands become cold and clammy, our breathing becomes rapid or shallow, our temperature and muscle tension change. There are brain changes too, higher activity for high beta waves and less activity in the frontal lobe.

Biofeedback therapy teaches our child to identify these changes with the help of sensors attached to the skin. Seeing physical evidence of the anxiety on the screen can be empowering and motivating, helping our loved ones to 'get it'.

Biofeedback is often used alongside cognitive behavioural therapy (CBT) as it allows our loved ones to compare their readings when they are having fearful and negative thoughts with their readings when they have changed their thoughts to more empowering ones. They can also compare their readings before and after exercise, meditation or in fact any other of the suggested treatments or changes.

There are a number of controlled studies that show the effectiveness of biofeedback to reduce anxiety in children. A 1996 study of seventh and eighth graders found that after six sessions, the children had significantly lower post-test states of anxiety.[13]

In my humble opinion, I feel that this is unnecessarily technical, but we are all different and some children will respond well to seeing hard data evidence of changes to their stress and anxiety levels.

As medical technology is moving fast, the principles of biofeedback can be, and perhaps already are, available through smart phones or fitness watches, allowing real-time monitoring of states of mind and how well different interventions are working.

OTHERS

There are many other bodywork and energy therapies – acupuncture, shiatsu, bioresonance, brain gym to name but a few, which are probably as worthy of consideration and need to be approached with the same openness and caution as the other therapies discussed.

I have not discussed these, not because they will not help our child, they may, but because I have not had enough feedback on them. This is why it is important to share our experiences so that we can learn and support each other.

Chapter 15

FINAL THOUGHTS

One word sums up everything I learnt from my many mistakes raising my children with hidden disabilities. It wasn't treatment, education or understanding. It wasn't even decoding, pressure cookers or protection mode. Learning about all these things made a huge difference both to my children and to me.

But at the end of the day it all came down to one thing. Hope.

Nothing will ruin our children's lives more than a lack of hope. If the future looks hopeless, what is the point of getting out of bed in the morning? Why even bother with homework? Why find a special interest and people who share it? Why even think about treatments?

Without hope, what is the point...in anything?

This book aimed to give us hope that our child can have a great life. That life may be different from what we expected for our child.

Some of us are lucky and have access to specialist services for our children, such as good schools, doctors and social services. Many of us do not. Having these things is important and worth fighting for, if we are able.

Holding on to hope for our children when help is being denied them and people are judging is a big challenge. It may well be our biggest challenge.

If we have hope for our child, there is a reasonable chance that our child will have hope for him- or herself. This is the only way to tackle the downward spiral of hopelessness.

The best way we can do this is to understand what our child is experiencing and what her behaviour may be trying to communicate to us. The better we get at decoding our child, the better we will be at figuring out strategies to keep her out of protection mode.

Helping to get our child out of protection mode gives him a chance to engage with life, to learn, to participate and to have hope for the future. Free from the shutdown caused by stress hormones, he can celebrate his many strengths and learn to accept his challenges and weaknesses.

She can learn to accept herself as an individual with a hidden disability. She may even be able to use aspects of the hidden disability for previously unimaginable achievements. Many people with hidden disabilities are highly successful innovators, focused and determined with things that truly interest them.

Nothing gives them more hope than finding something that makes them happy. For our child this may be caring for a pet, devising an algorithm or producing beautiful art work.

Lack of hope is a vicious cycle. Without hope, our children will probably not want to do the things that can make them happy. Not doing things that make them happy and have meaning for them will make them feel more hopeless.

Luckily it also works the other way, in what is known as a *virtuous cycle*. The more our children can do things that make them happy and have meaning for them, the more hope they will feel. And the more hope they feel, they more they will want to engage with life and thrive.

Hope breeds hope and success breeds success. This is why even the tiniest success or thread of hope can grow and be a catalyst to transform our child's life.

Conventional pathways through education and work may not be a good fit for our children's disability needs. Their schools and workplaces may be able to offer reasonable adjustments to help them, and we can use the disability laws to fight for this.

At the end of the day, many of our loved ones have to do it *their way*. Every time we support them with this we are giving them more hope.

Hope doesn't mean that everything is going to be OK. We can't know that or even know what 'being OK' even means. Hope is actually more about *trust*. It means trusting that life can unfold for our child in a way that serves him or her and gives meaning and a reason to get out of bed each day.

When we trust life in this way, we can accept that there will be ups and downs, challenges and successes, horrible and helpful people along the way.

Clearly this applies equally to us. As parents of children with hidden disabilities, our lives may be a constant battle: with our children, with other people and with unhelpful organisations. Our relationships and careers may be on the brink and our physical and mental health may be spent. And that's before we even take a look at our finances.

Holding on to hope for ourselves is as important as it is for our child. If we do not have hope for our own future, it will be very hard for our children to look positively at theirs.

This is why I wrote the companion book, *How to Cope When Your Child Has a Hidden Disability: Self-Care for Parents,* which is a book of hope for stressed out parents of children with hidden disabilities. I wrote it because for much of my time I was absolutely not coping, at least on the inside, although to the outside world maybe it seemed like I was.

When I looked for help nothing seemed to be designed for parents like us or 'get' what we are going through day after day, crisis after crisis. Hope came from talking to and learning from parents who really were coping well despite huge adversity at home and were able to share what really might help us.

We don't just owe it to our kids to look after ourselves. We mainly owe it to ourselves.

Nelson Mandela summed up the power of hope beautifully when he wrote that 'Our human compassion binds us the one to the other – not in pity or patronisingly, but as human beings who have learnt how to turn our common suffering into hope for the future.'[1]

NOTES

INTRODUCTION

1 National Center for Education Statistics (NCES) (May 2021) Students with disabilities, https://nces.ed.gov/programs/coe/indicator_cgg.asp. In the school year 2019–2020, 14 per cent of students age 3–21 were registered as disabled. Of these 1 per cent had mobility disabilities and 75 per cent had hidden disabilities. The rest had other conditions such as diabetes.

2 www.spectrumnews.org/opinion/multiple-diagnoses. See also Susan E. Levy *et al.* (2010). Autism spectrum disorder and co-occurring developmental, psychiatric, and medical conditions among children in multiple populations of the United States. *Journal of Developmental and Behavioral Pediatrics*, https://pubmed.ncbi.nlm.nih.gov/20431403

3 ASD – autism spectrum disorder, PDA – pathological demand avoidance, OCD – obsessive compulsive disorder, ADHD – attention deficit hyperactivity disorder, ADD – attention deficit disorder, HFA – high-functioning autism.

CHAPTER 1: WHAT IS A HIDDEN DISABILITY?

1 GOV.UK (n.d.) Definition of disability under the Equality Act 2010, www.gov.uk/definition-of-disability-under-equality-act-2010. Note that this Act does not include Northern Ireland, which is covered by the Disability Discrimination Act 1995 and which uses the same definition of disability.

2 Citizens Advice (2021) What counts as disability, www.citizensadvice.org.uk/law-and-courts/discrimination/protected-characteristics/what-counts-as-disability

3 ADA (n.d.) Information and Technical Assistance on the Americans with Disabilities Act, www.ada.gov/ada_intro.htm

4 GOV.UK (n.d.) Disability rights, www.gov.uk/rights-disabled-person/education-rights

5 For example, see Symptoms – mood changes (2017, 5 March), https://parkinsonsdisease.net/symptoms/mood-changes-depression-anxiety

6 N. Zeliadt (2018, 8 January) Large study ties gut issues in autism to inflammation, www.spectrumnews.org/news/large-study -ties-gut-issues-autism-inflammation

7 E. Casanova (2020) Researchers have identified a relationship between Ehlers-Danlos Syndrome and autism: guest editorial. Autism Research Institute, www.autism.org/researchers-have-identified-a-relationship-between-ehlers-danlos-syndrome-and-autism

8 See, for example, NHS (2019) www.nhs.uk/conditions/autism/what is-autism

9 For an explanation of the importance of assessing disability and mental illness separately, see Norman Sartorius (2009) Disability and mental illness are different entities and should be assessed separately. *World Psychiatry*, www.ncbi.nlm.nih.gov/pmc/articles/PMC2691158

10 L.I. Iezzoni *et al.* (2001, 16 April) Mobility difficulties are not only a problem of old age. *Journal of General Internal Medicine*, www.ncbi.nlm.nih.gov/pmc/articles/PMC1495195

11 National Center for Education Statistics (NCES) (May 2021) Students with disabilities, https://nces.ed.gov/programs/coe/indicator_cgg.asp. In the school year 2019–2020, 14 per cent of students age 3–21 were registered as disabled. Of these 1 per cent had mobility disabilities and 75 per cent had hidden disabilities. The rest had other conditions such as diabetes.

CHAPTER 2: WHAT'S IN A WORD?

1 In England, the *Special Educational Needs and Disability Code of Practice: 0 to 25 Years* (Department for Education and Department of Health 2015) is quite clear on this point – there is no basis in law for a local authority to reject a professional diagnostic report simply because it was privately obtained. See paragraph 9.14.

2 L. James (2015, 16 November) Why I love knowing I have high-functioning autism, www.telegraph.co.uk/health-fitness/body/why-i-love-knowing-i-have -high-functioning-autism

3 A.K. Halladay *et al.* (2015) Sex and gender differences in autism spectrum disorder: summarizing evidence gaps and identifying emerging areas of priority, https://molecularautism.biomedcentral.com/articles/10.1186/s13229-015-0019-y

4 S. Bargiela *et al.* (2016) The experiences of late-diagnosed women with autism spectrum conditions: an investigation of the female autism phenotype. *Journal of Autism and Developmental Disorders 46*, 3281–3294.

5 Understood Team (n.d.) Celebrity spotlight: why will.i.am says ADHD fuels his creativity, www.understood.org/en/learning-thinking-differences/personal-stories/famous-people/celebrity-spotlight -why-william-says-adhd-fuels-his-creativity

6 A. Rourke (2019, 2 September) Greta Thunberg responds to Asperger's critics: 'It's a superpower', www.theguardian.com/environment/2019/sep/02/greta-thunberg-responds-to-aspergers-critics-its-a-superpower

7 D.Z. Hambrick and M. Marquardt (2017, 5 December) Bad news for the highly intelligent, www.scientificamerican.com/article/bad-news-for-the-highly-intelligent

8 D. Chan and L. Sireling (2010) 'I want to be bipolar'...a new phenomenon. *The Psychiatrist*, www.cambridge.org/core/services/aop-cambridge-core/content/view/CD7DCB2BFE1C2BA5118A1084F7307304/S1758320900004649a.pdf/i_want_to_be_bipolara_new_phenomenon.pdf

9 V. Hughes (2010, 6 May) Multiple diagnoses, www.spectrumnews.org/opinion/multiple-diagnoses. See also Y. Leitner (2014) The co-occurrence of autism and attention deficit hyperactivity disorder in children – what do we know? *Frontiers in Human Neuroscience*, www.ncbi.nlm.nih.gov/pmc/articles/PMC4010758

CHAPTER 3: DECODING THE HIDDEN DISABILITY

1 M.M. Seltzer *et al.* (2010) Maternal cortisol levels and behavior problems in adolescents and adults with ASD. *Journal of Autism Developmental Disorders*, https://pubmed.ncbi.nlm.nih.gov/19890706

2 Michelle Myers (2015, 1 October) Autism and the delayed effect, http://asliceofautism.blogspot.com/2015/10/autism-and-delayed-effect.html. Reproduced with kind permission.

3 Michelle Myers (2015, 1 October) Autism and the delayed effect, http://asliceofautism.blogspot.com/2015/10/autism-and-delayed-effect.html. Reproduced with kind permission.

4 Chloe Estelle (2018, 1 May) Dear Mom & Dad, this is why I can't stand you, www.ourtism.com/blog/dear-mom-dad-this-is-why-i-cant-stand-you. Reproduced with kind permission.

5 Max Sparrow (2017, 21 March) Autistic shutdown alters brain function, http://unstrangemind.com/autistic-shutdown-alters-brain-function

6 Danny Raede (2018, 19 July) Defense mode: why people with Asperger's seem stuck & shutdown so often, www.aspergerexperts.com/blogs/entry/25-defense-mode-why-people-with-aspergers-seem-stuck-shutdown-so-often

7 Danny Raede (2020, 27 September) What it feels like to be in defense mode, www.aspergerexperts.com/blogs/entry/110-what-it-feels -like-to-be-in-defense-mode

8 For example, A. Vogel and L. Schwabe (2016) Learning and memory under stress: implications for the classroom. *NPJ Science of Learning*, www.nature.com/articles/npjscilearn201611

9 Danny Raede (2018, 19 July) Defense mode: why people with Asperger's seem stuck & shutdown so often, www.aspergerexperts.com/blogs/entry/25-defense-mode-why-people-with-aspergers-seem-stuck-shutdown-so-often

10 H.E. Marano (2016) Our brain's negative bias, www.psychologytoday.com/gb/articles/200306/our-brains-negative-bias

11 WebMD (2020) What is rejection sensitive dysphoria?, www.webmd.com/add-adhd/rejection-sensitive-dysphoria

CHAPTER 4: HOW PROTECTION MODE AFFECTS BEHAVIOUR

1 Chloe Estelle (2017, 31 October) Chloe Estelle shares some insights on why she had tantrums, www.ourtism.com/blog/chloe-estelle-shares-some-insights-on-why-she-had-tantrums

2 Temple Grandin (2008) *The Way I See It: A Personal Look at Autism and Asperger's*. Arlington, TX: Future Horizons.

3 Asperger Experts, *Surviving & Thriving with Asperger's: Stories & Tools to Help You Relax, Communicate, and Navigate the World*, www.aspergerexperts.com/products/books/how-to-books/satwa/surviving-thriving-with-aspergers-paperback

4 Chloe Estelle (2018, 12 May) Screens are not addictive substances, www.ourtism.com/blog/screens-are-not-addictive-substances

5 P. Gray (2012, 7 January) The many benefits, for kids, of playing video games, www.psychologytoday.com/us/blog/freedom-learn/201201/the-many-benefits-kids-playing-video-games?fbclid=IwAR34YD9LQ8IaTWDugdG9keZS2qXAtx5yssfxGUL6ORWCO4K4xpNGTA6DRzw

6 Asperger Experts, *Surviving & Thriving with Asperger's: Stories & Tools to Help You Relax, Communicate, and Navigate the World*, www.aspergerexperts.com/products/books/how-to-books/satwa/surviving-thriving-with-aspergers-paperback

7 Danny Raede (2018, 19 July) I was a picky eater until age 25... here's what changed, www.aspergerexperts.com/blogs/entry/1-i-was-a-picky-eater-until-age-25-heres-what-changed

8 Danny Raede (2018, 19 July) I was a picky eater until age 25... here's what changed, www.aspergerexperts.com/blogs/entry/1-i-was-a-picky-eater-until-age-25-heres-what-changed

9 Foreword by Anne Rice to *The Metamorphosis, In the Penal Colony, and Other Stories* by Franz Kafka (June 1995). New York: Schocken Books.

10 M. Wolfe-Robinson (2019, 22 July) Autistic children more likely to be involved in bullying – study, www.theguardian.com/society/2019/jul/22/autistic-children-sibling-bullying-study

11 S. Porges (2004) Neuroception: a subconscious system for detecting threats and safety. *Zero to Three 24*, 5, 19–24.

12 Mona Delahooke (2016, 28 September) Oppositional defiance or faulty neuroception?, http://monadelahooke.com/oppositional-defiance -faulty-neuroception

13 Chloe Estelle (2017, 31 October) Chloe Estelle shares some insights on why she had tantrums, www.ourtism.com/blog/chloe-estelle-shares-some-insights-on-why-she-had-tantrums

14 V. Leatham (2006) *Bloodletting: A Memoir of Secrets, Self-Harm, and Survival.* London: Allison & Busby.

15 B. Jancin (2020, 15 September) Girls with ADHD at high risk for self-injury, www.medscape.com/viewarticle/937461

16 M. Hassall and B. Hunter (n.d.) Fight, flight, freeze...or fib?, www.additudemag.com/why-lie-adhd-fight-flight-freeze

CHAPTER 5: HOW PROTECTION MODE AFFECTS MIND AND BODY

1 A. Lowery (2017, 2 August) Tics and stims. Alex Lowery speaks about autism, www.alexlowery.co.uk/tics-and-stims

2 N. Carvill (2016) How to boost executive function in children & why it's important to helping them thrive, www.heysigmund.com/how-to-boost-executive-function-in-children

3 A.A. Milne (1992, reprint) *The Complete Tales of Winnie-the-Pooh.* London: Hamlyn Young Books.

4 Posted anonymously on www.sanvello.com/community/quotes/post/7673334

5 drangie (2018, 9 February) Autism and impulsivity: 'Why did he do that?', www.drangiesplace.com/autism-and-impulsivity -why-did-he-do-that

6 drangie (2018, 9 February) Autism and impulsivity: 'Why did he do that?', www.drangiesplace.com/autism-and-impulsivity -why-did-he-do-that

7 M. Mantzios (2014) Exploring the relationship between worry and impulsivity in military recruits: the role of mindfulness and self-compassion as potential mediators. *Stress & Health*, https://self-compassion.org/wp-content/uploads/2015/03/Mantzios.pdf, p.397.

8 Deepak Chopra and Rudolph Tanzi (2013, 17 May) Balancing impulses, www.deepakchopra.com/articles/balancing-impulses

9 C. Kim (2012, 24 October) The angry Aspie explains it all. Musings of an Aspie, https://musingsofanaspie.com/2012/10/24/the-angry-aspie-explains-it-all

10 C. Kim (2012, 24 October) The angry Aspie explains it all. Musings of an Aspie, https://musingsofanaspie.com/2012/10/24/the-angry-aspie-explains-it-all

CHAPTER 7: OUT OF PROTECTION MODE: PRACTICAL STRATEGIES

1 Danny Raede (2018, 19 July) Defense mode: why people with Asperger's seem stuck & shutdown so often, www.aspergerexperts.com/blogs/entry/25-defense-mode-why -people-with-aspergers-seem-stuck-shutdown-so-often

2 The quote is attributed to the Buddha, although there is some controversy about whether he or one of his contemporaries actually said it. A similar idea is expressed and translated in the Chinese Sutra of 42 Sections.

3 Building self-acceptance for spectrum teens (2019, 17 June) Seen in May 2020 at www.theinvisiblestrings.com/autism-building-self-acceptance-for spectrum-teens and reproduced with the kind permission of Emma Pretzel.

4 www.aspergerexperts.com/plus

5 Steve Jobs (2005, 12 June) Commencement Address, https://news.stanford.edu/2005/06/14/jobs-061505

6 About me (2020) Seen in May 2020 at https://emmapretzel.wordpress.com/about and reproduced with the kind permission of Emma Pretzel.

7 Lee Binz (2008) *Use your annoy-o-meter skillfully*, www.homehighschoolhelp.com/use-your-annoy-o-meter-skillfully

8 L. Honos-Webb (2008) *The Gift of Adult ADD*. Oakland, CA: New Harbinger.

9 E. Selhub (updated February 2021) A doctor explains how to take advantage of the healthy benefits of nature, www.mindbodygreen.com/0-30024/a-doctor-explains-how-to-take-advantage-of-the-healing-powers-of-nature.html

10 Melanie Tonia Evans, Facebook post called Nature Magic, 21 November 2019.

11 Mental Health Foundation (n.d.) How to look after your mental health using exercise, www.mentalhealth.org.uk/publications/how-to-using-exercise

12 L. Waters (2015, 30 June) How meditation could be beneficial in schools, www.independent.co.uk/life-style/health-and-families/features/how-meditation-could-be-beneficial-schools-10355650.html

CHAPTER 8: OUT OF PROTECTION MODE: BUILDING TRUST

1 Asperger Experts (n.d.) *Surviving & Thriving with Asperger's: Stories and Tools to Help You Relax, Communicate, and Navigate the World*. www.aspergerexperts.com/products/books/how-to-books/satwa/surviving-thriving-with-aspergers-paperback

2 J. Bolte-Taylor (2009) *My Stroke of Insight*. London: Hodder & Stoughton.

3 Asperger Experts (n.d.) *Surviving & Thriving with Asperger's: Stories and Tools to Help You Relax, Communicate, and Navigate the World*, www.aspergerexperts.com/products/books/how-to-books/satwa/surviving-thriving-with-aspergers-paperback

4 P. Chödrön (2012) *Living Beautifully with Uncertainty and Change*. Boston, MA: Shambhala, p.12.

5 T.N. Hanh (1991) *Old Path White Clouds: The Life Story of the Buddha*. London: Rider, p.433.

6 Bruce Lee (2000) *Striking Thoughts: Bruce Lee's Wisdom for Daily Living, Part VIII: On Ultimate (Final) Principles*. North Clarendon, VT: Tuttle Publishing, p.121.

7 Hazel Muir (2003, 30 April) Einstein and Newton showed signs of autism, www.newscientist.com/article/dn3676-einstein -and-newton-showed-signs-of-autism

8 Totally Meditation (n.d.) Asperger's and meditation: why it works, https://totallymeditation.com/category/aspergers-syndrome-meditation

9 D. LaRock (n.d.) What it really means to be there and 'hold space' for someone else, https://tinybuddha.com/blog/what-it-really-means-to-be-there-and-hold -space-for-someone-else

CHAPTER 9: TEACHING POSITIVE ATTITUDES

1 Interactive Autism Network (2012) *IAN Research Report: Bullying and Children with ASD*, https://iancommunity.org/cs/ian_research_reports/ian_research_report_bullying

2 Quoted in M. Bergeisen (2010, 22 September) The neuroscience of happiness. *Greater Good Magazine*, https://greatergood.berkeley.edu/article/item/the_neuroscience_of_happiness

3 Joshua Brown and Joel Wong (2017, 6 June) How gratitude changes you and your brain. *Greater Good Magazine*, https://greatergood.berkeley.edu/article/item/how_gratitude_changes_you_and_your_brain

CHAPTER 10: PARENTING TEENS AND YOUNG ADULTS

1 National Autistic Society (2021, 19 February) New shocking data highlights the autism employment gap, www.autism.org.uk/what-we-do/news/new-data-on-the-autism -employment-gap

2 R. Barkley *et al.* (2008) *ADHD in Adults: What the Science Says*. New York: Guilford Press, p.351.

3 Lara Honos-Webb (2008) *The Gift of Adult ADD*. Oakland, CA: New Harbinger Publications, p.31.

CHAPTER 11: PARENTING SIBLINGS

1 D.B. Zager (ed.) (2004) *Autism Spectrum Disorders: Identification, Education, and Treatment* (3rd edn). Philadelphia, PA: Lawrence Erlbaum Associates.

CHAPTER 12: DECIDING ABOUT TREATMENTS

1 Denys Reid Margolin (2021) My story: I lost my son when he was in 3rd grade, but I finally have him back 25 years later, http://mentalwellnessmatters.com/about-me/my-story

2 US Food and Drug Administration (2016, 4 May) Drug research and children, www.fda.gov/drugs/information-consumers-and-patients-drugs/drug-research-and-children

3 House of Commons Committee of Public Accounts (2017) *Mental Health in Prisons*, https://publications.parliament.uk/pa/cm201719/cmselect/cmpubacc/400/400.pdf

CHAPTER 13: DRUG TREATMENTS

1 Mind (2021) Antidepressants, www.mind.org.uk/information-support/drugs-and-treatments/antidepressants/withdrawal-effects-of-antidepressants

2 Rashmi Patel *et al.* (2015) Do antidepressants increase the risk of mania and bipolar disorder in people with depression? A retrospective electronic case register cohort study. *BMJ*, www.ncbi.nlm.nih.gov/pmc/articles/PMC4679886

3 These side effects are listed by the FDA (Federal Drugs Agency) in this report from the NIMH: National Institute of Mental Health (n.d.) Mental health medications, www.nimh.nih.gov/health/topics/mental-health-medications

4 https://www.dbsalliance.org/support/for-friends-family/for-parents/balanced-mind-parent-network

5 National Institute of Mental Health (n.d.) Mental health medications, www.nimh.nih.gov/health/topics/mental-health-medications

6 R. Boorady (n.d.) Understanding ADHD medications. Child Mind Institute, https://childmind.org/article/the-facts-on-adhd-medications

7 I. dela Peña *et al.* (2014) Prefrontal cortical and striatal transcriptional responses to the reinforcing effect of repeated methylphenidate treatment in the spontaneously hypertensive rat, animal model of attention-deficit/hyperactivity disorder (ADHD). *Behavioral and Brain Functions*, https://pubmed.ncbi.nlm.nih.gov/24884696

8 C. Sherman (2020) The truth about ADHD and addiction, www.additudemag.com/the-truth-about-adhd-and-addiction

9 Mind (2021) Antidepressants, www.mind.org.uk/information-support/drugs-and-treatments/antidepressants/how-antidepressants-can-help

10 Ann Pietrangelo (2021) Drugs to treat anxiety disorder, www.healthline.com/health/anxiety-drugs#betablockers

11 National Institute of Mental Health (n.d.) Mental health medications, www.nimh.nih.gov/health/topics/mental-health-medications

12 FDA (2016, 4 May) Drug research and children, www.fda.gov/drugs/drug-information-consumers/drug-research-and-children

CHAPTER 14: NON-DRUG TREATMENTS

1 *Science Daily* (2019, 30 May) Research confirms gut–brain connection in autism, www.sciencedaily.com/releases/2019/05/190530101143.htm

2 M. Campos (2018, 25 June) Probiotics for bipolar disorder mania, www.health.harvard.edu/blog/probiotics-for-bipolar -disorder-mania-2018062514125

3 R.J. Hedaya (2012, 2 February) Vitamin B12: what is a vitamin B12 deficiency?, www.psychologytoday.com/intl/blog/health-matters /201202/vitamin-b12

4 Walsh Research Institute, www.walshinstitute.org

5 J.M. Greenblatt and B. Gottlieb (n.d.) Omega 3S: the ultimate (ADHD) brain food, www.additudemag.com/adhd-omega-3-benefits

6 Top 8 autism therapies – as reported by parents of kids with autism (2012, 11 July), www.myautismteam.com/resources/top-8-autism-therapies-as-reported-by-parents -of-kids-with-autism

7 Susan Vaughan Kratz *et al.* (2017) The use of CranioSacral therapy for autism spectrum disorders: benefits from the viewpoints of parents, clients, and therapists. *Journal of Bodywork and Movement Therapies*, https://pubmed.ncbi.nlm.nih.gov/28167177

8 ADDitude (2021) How ADHD Resembles Retained Primitive Reflexes, and Vice Versa, https://www.additudemag.com/retained-primitive-reflexes-and-adhd-symptoms-treatment

9 Access Potential (n.d.) What we do, https://www.accesspotential.net

10 See article on the Brain and Sensory Foundations website (www.moveplaythrive.com/learn-more/item/retained-primitive-reflexes-in-adhd-and-asd-among-children-in-an-inpatient-psychiatric-setting). Retained primitive reflexes in ADHD and ASD among

children in an inpatient psychiatric setting about research carried out by Khiela Holmes and colleagues at the University of Arkansas.

11 *Attention Please* (2019) Dir.: Andrea Thornton, Richard Topping. AT Film Works.

12 Alan Brauer (1999, 1 February) Biofeedback and anxiety, www.psychiatrictimes.com/view/biofeedback-and-anxiety

Mirjam E.J. Kouijzer *et al.* (2013) Is EEG-biofeedback an effective treatment in autism spectrum disorders? A randomized controlled trial. *Applied Psychphysiology and Biofeedback 38* 1, 17–28, https://pubmed.ncbi.nlm.nih.gov/22903518

Srabani Banerjee and Charlene Argáez (2017, 13 November) Neurofeedback and biofeedback for mood and anxiety disorders: a review of clinical effectiveness and guidelines. Canadian Agency for Drugs and Technologies in Health, www.ncbi.nlm.nih.gov/books/NBK531603

13 L.S. Wenck *et al.* (1996) Evaluating the efficacy of a biofeedback intervention to reduce children's anxiety. *Journal of Clinical Psychology*, https://pubmed.ncbi.nlm.nih.gov/8842885

CHAPTER 15: FINAL THOUGHTS

1 Nelson Mandela (2000, 6 December) Message to the Healing and Reconciliation Service, dedicated to HIV/AIDS sufferers and for the healing of our land. Nelson Mandela 6 Dec 2000. Quoted in *Nelson Mandela by Himself: The Authorised Book of Quotations* (2011) Johannesburg: Pan Macmillan.

GLOSSARY OF ABBREVIATIONS

ADD
Attention Deficit Disorder

ADHD
Attention Deficit Hyperactivity Disorder

ASD
Autism Spectrum Disorder

HFA
High-functioning Autism

OCD
Obsessive Compulsive Disorder

PDA
Pathological Demand Avoidance

COVERS AUTISM, ADHD, BIPOLAR, OCD, UNDIAGNOSED AND MORE

RAISING KIDS WITH HIDDEN DISABILITIES

'Getting It'

NAOMI SIMMONS

Other JKP books

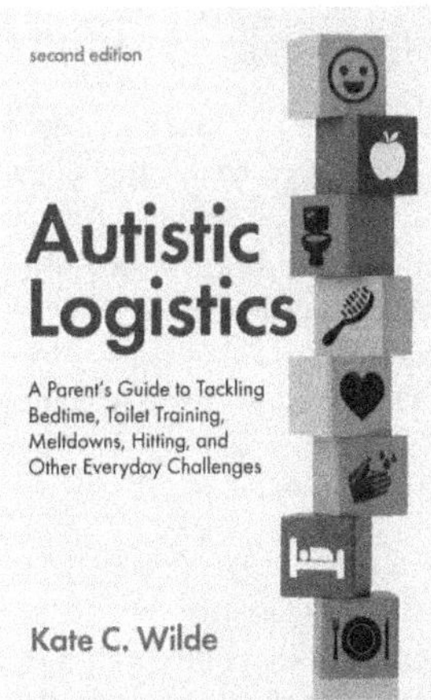

Autistic Logistics, Second Edition

A Parent's Guide to Tackling Bedtime, Toilet Training, Meltdowns, Hitting, and Other Everyday Challenges

Kate Wilde

£14.99 | $19.95 | PB | 336PP |
ISBN 978 1 78775 749 3 | eISBN 978 1 78775 750 9

- **'This book will transform your entire home experience.' – Kristin Selby Gonzalez**
- **'A must-read for parents' – *Autism Eye***
- **'This book will be a game-changer for you and your family.' – Raun K. Kaufman**

Have you ever wished there was a manual for parenting children on the autism spectrum? This book provides just that, offering clear, precise, step-by-step advice on everything you want to know, including:

- how to toilet train your child without pushing or pressuring
- how to get your child to sleep in their own bed and through the night
- what to do when your child misbehaves/lashes out, hits or bites
- how to introduce new foods without a fight.

This updated edition is based on Kate Wilde's decades of experience and the latest autism research. Tackling a wide range of common parenting milestones, the book offers tried-and-tested techniques to help you transform the challenges of home life and create harmony. Catering to all age ranges and points on the spectrum, this book will be invaluable to parents, caregivers, teachers and teaching assistants

Kate Wilde has spent the whole of her life working with children on the autism spectrum. She has a degree in Music and Education from the University of Surrey, UK, and has studied with Dr Rachel Pinney. Kate is the Director for Global Outreach at the Autism Treatment Center of America®, where she has worked for over 20 years, working one on one with over 1500 children from more than 40 different countries. She also works in private practice serving families worldwide.

The Parents' Guide to ADHD Medicines

Professor Peter Hill

£14.99 | $19.95 | PB | 256PP |
ISBN 978 1 78775 568 0 | eISBN 978 1 78775 569 7

- **'Everything you wanted to know but were afraid to ask – this book provides the answers.' – Professor Susan Young**
- **'The absolute "go to" book.' – Valerie A. Ivens**

This reassuring guide explains prescribed ADHD medicines for children in clear, everyday language. Based on questions the author has received from countless families in his work as a consultant psychiatrist, the expert information in this book answers the most pressing questions a parent will have about ADHD medicines: how they work, what they do, what is available and how to talk about them to your children.

This book sheds light on why not all medicines are easily available, the differences between certain medications and their level of effectiveness, all based on scientific evidence. This information will support parents in discussions with medical professionals, explaining the practicalities and demystifying the terminology around medication and treatments. The book also provides insights into the decisions behind prescribing certain medicines and how they should be taken. Armed with this guide, parents – as well as teachers and others working with kids with ADHD – can feel confident and assured when their child is prescribed treatments for ADHD.

Professor Peter Hill is Emeritus Professor in Child and Adolescent Psychiatry and a consultant psychiatrist in independent and clinical advisory practice. He has over 40 years' experience of treating ADHD with medicine.

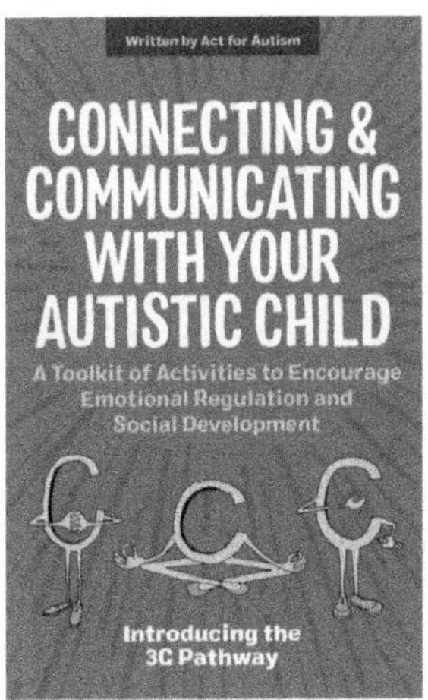

Connecting and Communicating with Your Autistic Child

A Toolkit of Activities to Encourage Emotional Regulation and Social Development

Act for Autism; Tessa Morton and Jane Gurnett

£14.99 | $19.95 | PB | 176PP |
ISBN 978 1 78775 550 5 | eISBN 978 1 78775 551 2

- **'Readable, accessible and relatable.' – Paul Isaacs**

This book teaches drama and immersive theatre-based activities for parents and professionals working with children and young people on the autism spectrum. The exercises follow the author's simple, person-centred '3C pathway' of connecting, calming and communicating, and enable parents to gain an understanding of the challenges an autistic child may face by 'walking in their shoes', while empowering children to become more self-aware and express themselves in healthy ways.

The activities included in the book are tried-and-tested, accessible and easy to implement, such as breathing exercises, mirroring movements and treasure hunts. Using these activities, parents and professionals can gain insight into the sensory and social challenges experienced by those on the spectrum and can work to build a positive and trusting relationship, offering a secure base for children's emotional development.

Tessa Morton has been a coach, mentor and workshop leader for over 30 years. She is a trained drama teacher and BACP-registered CBT counsellor specialising in supporting autistic students, their families and schools. She founded Act for Autism with Jane and together they have created the acclaimed Connections Workshop, the 3C pathway and the award-winning Autistic Voices project.

Jane Gurnett holds an MA in The Advanced Teaching of Shakespeare and a BPhil in Autism (Children). She is an actor, teacher of drama and workshop leader, and has written articles published in *Advances in Autism* (Emerald Publishing) and *Good Autism Practice*. She co-founded Act for Autism and develops workshops and strategies for the organisation.

Act for Autism delivers country-wide training and presents nationally at conferences such as the Autism Show, the National Autistic Society's professionals conference and at universities. In 2020 they won a NAS professionals award for their community projects

A Parent's Guide to Autism Diagnosis

What to Expect and How to Support Your Child

Dr Sophia Mooncey and Adele Devine

£14.99 | $19.95 | PB | 288PP |
ISBN 978 1 78775 424 9 | eISBN 978 1 78775 425 6

- **'Insightful and reassuring.' – Dr Tony Attwood**
- **'Accurate, comprehensive and written with empathy.' – Professor Paul Gringras**

Autism diagnosis can be an overwhelming time for many families. This is an accessible, easy-to-navigate guide for parents, answering the questions they may have before, during and after diagnosis.

Written by a highly experienced author team, this book will support parents from the moment somebody mentions autism, through the diagnosis process and beyond. It provides reliable advice on every stage, with guidance on what to do during the long wait for assessment and diagnosis. Working from a pro-neurodiversity perspective it encourages parents to see beyond the diagnosis and to celebrate each child's unique personality and strengths.

Combining information on medical diagnosis, educational needs and more, the book shares case studies and direct quotes from families to help parents to give their children the best start following an autism diagnosis, and help them to achieve their full potential. There is also a bonus downloadable chapter with information from the key professionals involved in the diagnostic process, so you know who you can turn to for the support and help you need.

Dr Sophia Mooncey is a highly experienced consultant paediatrician working in the NHS for over 30 years and also in the private sector. She has four children and enjoys cooking, tennis, travel and long walks.

Adele Devine is a special needs teacher at a school for young people with severe learning difficulties and autism. In 2010 she co-founded the multi-award-winning SEN Assist autism software with her husband.

Helping Your Child with PDA Live a Happier Life

Alice Running

£12.99 | $19.95 | PB | 128PP |
ISBN 978 1 78775 485 0 | eISBN 978 1 78775 486 7

- **'A must-read for parents/carers.' – Leanne Jaques**

Drawing on the author's personal experience of parenting a child with PDA, this insightful and informative guide offers strategies and tips for all aspects of daily life, including sensory issues, education and negotiation.

Full of advice and support, this book is not intended to provide information on how to change your children. Rather, it is focused on creating the type of environment that will allow children to be authentically themselves, thereby enabling them to flourish and thrive.

Alice Running writes about autism (blogging and as a journalist) to create space for autistic voices. She has had articles published in *The Mighty, Yahoo, Special Needs Jungle, Huffington Post, Yorkshire Evening Post* and *The Big Issue* in the North. She is an autistic woman and has two sons with autism (one with PDA also).